Territorial Designs and International Politics

Territory is back with a vengeance. Although territorial politics never really went away, it was often perceived as a vanishing topic in public discussion and among scholars. The territorial conflicts of the last several years, however, have raised new academic and policy questions, revived old debates, and forced us to rethink many of our common conceptions. Social scientists broadly agree that territory, as well as the boundaries that confine it and group identity that relates to it, are socially constructed. But how and through which mechanisms is the meaning of territory constructed? By whom? For which purposes and by what tools? Which forces influence such "territorial designs"? How do different territorial designs affect state behavior in particular, and the dynamics of international politics in general? This book brings together political scientists and geographers—both disciplines in which scholars have long researched such questions—to create a mutually fertilizing dialogue, which will advance our understanding of territorial designs. The authors tackle core theoretical questions, institutions and ideas of territoriality, borders, space, place, and identity, as well as the methodologies used to study them. They utilize case studies as far apart as the Ottoman Empire, the colonization of Ireland, and current day Middle East; and they interrogate the characteristics of spaces as different as land, air, and water.

The chapters were originally published as a special issue of *Territory, Politics, Governance*.

Boaz Atzili is an Associate Professor at the School of International Service of American University, with a PhD from MIT. He is the author of *Good Fences Bad Neighbors: Border Fixity and International Conflict* (2012) and a forthcoming book on "Triadic Coercion," as well as numerous articles in journals such as *International Security, Security Studies, International Studies Review, and Studies in Conflict and Terrorism*.

Burak Kadercan is an Associate Professor of Strategy and Policy at the U.S. Naval War College. He received his PhD in political science from the University of Chicago. Kadercan's scholarly contributions have appeared in numerous outlets, including *International Security*, *Review of International Studies*, and *International Theory*.

Regions and Cities

Series Editor in Chief
Joan Fitzgerald, *Northeastern University, USA*

Editors
Maryann Feldman, *University of North Carolina, USA*
Gernot Grabher, *HafenCity University Hamburg, Germany*
Ron Martin, *University of Cambridge, UK*
Kieran P. Donaghy, *Cornell University, USA*

In today's globalised, knowledge-driven and networked world, regions and cities have assumed heightened significance as the interconnected nodes of economic, social and cultural production, and as sites of new modes of economic and territorial governance and policy experimentation. This book series brings together incisive and critically engaged international and interdisciplinary research on this resurgence of regions and cities, and should be of interest to geographers, economists, sociologists, political scientists and cultural scholars, as well as to policy-makers involved in regional and urban development.

For more information on the Regional Studies Association visit www.regional-studies.org

There is a **30% discount** available to RSA members on books in the *Regions and Cities* series, and other subject related Taylor and Francis books and e-books including Routledge titles. To order just e-mail Joanna Swieczkowska, Joanna.Swieczkowska@tandf.co.uk, or phone on +44 (0)20 3377 3369 and declare your RSA membership. You can also visit the series page at www.routledge.com/Regions-and-Cities/book-series/RSA and use the discount code: **RSA0901**

Territorial Designs and International Politics

Inside-out and Outside-in

Edited by
Boaz Atzili and Burak Kadercan

Routledge
Taylor & Francis Group

LONDON AND NEW YORK

First published 2018 by Routledge

2 Park Square, Milton Park, Abingdon, Oxfordshire OX14 4RN
52 Vanderbilt Avenue, New York, NY 10017

Routledge is an imprint of the Taylor & Francis Group, an informa business

First issued in paperback 2019

British Library Cataloguing in Publication Data
A catalogue record for this book is available from the British Library

ISBN 13: 978-1-138-57909-5 (hbk)
ISBN 13: 978-0-367-89269-2 (pbk)

Typeset in Times New Roman
by RefineCatch Limited, Bungay, Suffolk

Publisher's Note
The publisher accepts responsibility for any inconsistencies that may have arisen during the conversion of this book from journal articles to book chapters, namely the possible inclusion of journal terminology.

Disclaimer
Every effort has been made to contact copyright holders for their permission to reprint material in this book. The publishers would be grateful to hear from any copyright holder who is not here acknowledged and will undertake to rectify any errors or omissions in future editions of this book.

Contents

Citation Information

The chapters in this book were originally published in *Territory, Politics, Governance*, volume 5, issue 2 (May 2017). When citing this material, please use the original page numbering for each article, as follows:

Chapter 6

Drone Strikes, Ephemeral Sovereignty, and Changing Conceptions of Territory
Katharine Hall Kindervater
Territory, Politics, Governance, volume 5, issue 2 (May 2017) pp. 207–221

Chapter 7

Between Land and Sea: Spaces and Conflict Intensity
Ehud Eiran
Territory, Politics, Governance, volume 5, issue 2 (May 2017) pp. 190–206

For any permission-related enquiries please visit:
http://www.tandfonline.com/page/help/permissions

Notes on Contributors

Boaz Atzili is an Associate Professor at the School of International Service of American University.

Jordan Branch is Assistant Professor of Political Science at Brown University, USA.

Ehud Eiran is Assistant Professor of International Relations at the School of Political Science, University of Haifa, Israel.

Ryan D. Griffiths is Senior Lecturer at the Department of Government and International Relations, University of Sydney, Australia.

Burak Kadercan is an Associate Professor of Strategy and Policy at the U.S. Naval War College.

Gerry Kearns is Professor and Head of Department at the Department of Geography, Maynooth University, Ireland.

Katharine Hall Kindervater is Postdoctoral Fellow at the Department of Geography, Dartmouth College, USA.

Harris Mylonas is Associate Professor of Political Science and International Affairs, Department of Political Science, George Washington University, USA.

Nadav Shelef is Associate Professor at the Department of Political Science, University of Wisconsin, USA.

Territorial designs and international politics: the diverging constitution of space and boundaries

Boaz Atzili and Burak Kadercan

ABSTRACT

Territorial designs and international politics: the diverging constitution of space and boundaries. *Territory, Politics, Governance*. The debate about the role and direction of territory and territoriality – especially with respect to the politically and socially constructed nature of territory – has been evident within political geography and political science, as well as in other disciplines, for some time. Interdisciplinary interaction over the study of territory, however, has so far been less than impressive. Aiming to enhance our understanding of the place of territory in international relations, broadly defined, and to bridge disciplinary divides, this paper introduces the concept of 'territorial designs'. Territorial designs pertain to the delineation of the external boundaries, to the constitution of the society within these boundaries, and to the interaction between delineation and constitution. It is a process by which elites, in interaction with their own society and their external environment, intentionally and systematically constitute and institutionalize territoriality, and hence also territory. Territorial designs framework, as the papers in this volume collectively highlight, sheds a light on four key areas: the strategic logic and interaction behind different territorial systems; the unintended consequences of such designs; the tensions between regional/local territorial arrangements and global ones; and the roles that technology and knowledge play in the emergence of different forms of territoriality.

摘要

领土计画和国际政治: 分歧的空间和边界构成。*Territory, Politics, Governance*. 有关领土和领域性的角色及方向之辩论——特别是关于在政治上与社会上建构的领土本质——在政治地理学与政治科学中相当显着, 对其他学科而言有时亦是如此。但领土研究的跨领域互动至今仍不足。为了促进理解领土在广义定义的国际关系中的地位, 以及缝合领域的分野, 本文引入'领土计画'的概念。领土计画关乎外部边界的刻划, 这些边界内部的社会构成, 以及刻划和构成之间的互动。这是菁英与其身处的社会和外部环境互动下, 刻意并系统性地构成和制度化领域性的过程, 因此也是领土。如同本专集收录的文章共同强调, 领土计画架构为四个关键领域提出洞见: 不同领土系统背后的策略逻辑与互动; 此般规划无预期的后果; 区域／地方和全球的领土安排之间的紧张关系; 以及技术与知识在不同领域性形式的浮现中扮演的角色。

1

RÉSUMÉ

L'esquisse territoriale et la politique: l'établissement divergent de l'espace et des frontières. *Territory, Politics, Governance*. Le débat au sujet du rôle et de l'orientation du territoire et de la territorialité – surtout par rapport au caractère du territoire qui est détermine sur le plan politique et au niveau social – est depuis longtemps évident au sein de la géographie et de la science politiques, ainsi que dans d'autres disciplines. Néanmoins, l'interaction interdisciplinaire sur l'étude du territoire est jusqu'ici loin d'être impressionnante. Dans le but de mieux comprendre la place du territoire dans les relations internationales, au sens large, et de colmater la brèche disciplinaire, ce présent article introduit la notion 'd'esquisse territoriale'. L'esquisse territoriale se rapporte à la délimitation des frontières externes, à l'établissement de la société au sein de ces frontières, et à l'interaction entre la délimitation et l'établissement. C'est un processus par lequel les élites, en entrant en interaction avec leur propre société et leur milieu externe, établissent et institutionnalisent intentionnellement et systématiquement la territorialité, et donc également le territoire. Le cadre des esquisses territoriales, comme le soulignent collectivement les articles parus dans ce numéro, éclaircit quatre domaines prioritaires: la logique stratégique et l'interaction qui étayent divers systèmes territoriaux; les conséquences imprévues de telles esquisses; la tension entre les dispositions régionalo-locales et mondiales; et les rôles que jouent la technologie et la connaissance quant à l'émergence de différentes typologies de territorialité.

RESUMEN

Diseños territoriales y política internacional: la constitución divergente del espacio y las fronteras. *Territory, Politics, Governance*. Desde hace tiempo el debate sobre el papel y la dirección de territorio y territorialidad –especialmente con respecto a la naturaleza de territorio construida política y socialmente– es evidente en la geografía política y la ciencia política, así como en otras disciplines. Sin embargo, hasta ahora la interacción interdisciplinaria sobre el estudio de territorio no ha sido especialmente impresionante. Con el objetivo de comprender mejor el lugar de territorio definido ampliamente en las relaciones internacionales y superar las divisiones que existen entre las disciplinas, en este artículo introducimos el concepto de 'diseños territoriales'. Los diseños territoriales pertenecen a la delineación de las fronteras externas, a la constitución de la sociedad en estas fronteras y a la interacción entre delineación y constitución. Es un proceso en el que las élites, en interacción con su propia sociedad y su entorno externo, constituyen e institucionalizan intencionada y sistemáticamente la territorialidad, y por tanto también el territorio. El marco de los diseños territoriales, tal como se destaca colectivamente en los artículos de este volumen, clarifica cuatro áreas clave: la lógica estratégica y la interacción detrás de los diferentes sistemas territoriales; las consecuencias no intencionadas de tales diseños; las tensiones entre los acuerdos territoriales regionales y locales, y los acuerdos internacionales; y los papeles que desempeñan la tecnología y el conocimiento en el surgimiento de diferentes formas de territorialidad.

Territory is back with a vengeance. Although territorial politics never really went away, it was often perceived that way in public discussion and among scholars (Sassen, 1996, 1998; Strange, 1998; Friedman, 2000, 2007). The territorial conflicts of the last several years, however, have raised new academic and policy questions, revived old debates that were nearly forgotten, and forced us to rethink many of our common conceptions. China's creation of artificial territory in the South

China Sea defies conventional understandings of territorial waters.[1] Russia's annexation of Crimea and its exploits in eastern Ukraine challenge stable international norms of international boundaries. The 'Islamic State' conquests in Syria and Iraq, and its aspirations to re-establish an Islamic Caliphate require reconsideration of the territorial conception of the nation-state, and provocatively suggest an alternative. Scotland's 2014 independence referendum, although unsuccessful this time around, suggests that even long-established strong nation-states such as the UK lack true guarantees of territorial integrity.

The debate about the role and direction of territory and territoriality has been evident within Political Geography and Political Science, as well as in other disciplines, for some time. The articles in this volume aim to enhance our understanding of the place of territory in international relations, broadly defined, and to bridge disciplinary divides, by introducing the concept of 'territorial designs'. We start this introductory article with a broad discussion of the divergent conceptualizations of territory and territoriality in political science and political geography. We then define the concept of 'territorial designs', and explain the ways in which we believe it can address and advance debate on these issues. We propose a framework for understanding territorial designs as the constitution of both boundaries and the space within these boundaries. Lastly, we summarize the main focus and arguments of the articles in this volume.

The abundance and saliency of contemporary international territorial issues counter the expectations that many scholars espoused in the 1980s and 1990s. In his seminal work on the changing nature of international politics, Rosecrance (1986) famously declared that the so-called 'territorial state' that had been the key actor in world politics for three centuries was becoming an archaic entity for one simple reason: territory. The control of territory, Rosecrance argued, had been the territorial state's key source of wealth and military power, but it was losing importance and relevance in the face of globalization, as the 'trading' (and, later, the 'virtual') state rose in its place. Rosecrance was not alone in his assertions about the fading relevance of territory in world politics. The late 1980s and early 1990s witnessed the rise of arguments about the 'end of geography' (Greig, 2002) and the coming of a 'borderless world' (Ohmae, 1999). Mary Kaldor noted that 'new wars' are typically not fought over territory (Kaldor, 1999). As the above examples highlight, however, territory remains not only relevant but also salient in world politics. This argument, though, does not necessarily contradict or undermine the network-based process of globalization and the impact of increasing flow of goods, services, and people across these borders (Agnew, 2009; Kahler & Walter, 2006). 'In reality', as David Newman suggests, 'we have a world where the constant power and reconfiguration of fixed territories, through a system of ordering, takes place at one and the same time as the dynamics of cross-border flows and networks' (Newman, 2010, 775).[2]

Until the end of the Cold War, with few notable exceptions, such as Herz (1957) and Kratochwil (1986), IR scholars paid little attention to territory, mostly taking it for granted. IR literature rediscovered territory as a subject of interest in the early-1990s. Spearheaded by the works of scholars such as Goertz and Diehl (1992), Vasquez (1993), Ruggie (1993), Huth (1996), and Starr (2005), empirical and theoretical inquiries into the relationship between territory and conflict have grown into a very robust research programme.

Two main reasons undergird the increased interest in this line of research in IR. First, both qualitative and quantitative research into the origins of interstate wars revealed that territory is the single most salient issue over which humans go to war (Goertz & Diehl, 1992; Vasquez, 1993; Vasquez & Henehan, 2001; Huth, 1996; Kahler & Walter, 2006; Holsti, 1991). Second, some territorial 'issues' are more readily 'quantifiable' and thus allow scholars inclined to use quantitative methods to more readily operationalize and include territorial indicators in their research models. These include issues that Newman (2006) referred to as 'tangible' features of territory, such as the size and location of political units, or their proximity and contiguity to one another. This makes it possible for scholars who lean towards quantitative methods to operationalize territory, broadly defined, in their research. While quantitative research on territory has made considerable contributions to our understanding of territory's place in world politics, since it takes the 'character' of territory as rather constant (and/or homogeneously distributed), it remains insufficient for a full understanding. Quantitative research of territory in IR too often ignores the politically and socially constructed nature of territory.[3] Yet, current territorial issues such as the China, Ukraine, and Scotland cases noted above reveal that the global territorial order is – and in fact has always been – remarkably heterogeneous.

Parallel to the increased volume of quantitative works about territory, the malleable socially and politically constructed nature of territories has also attracted interest from IR scholars who, while mostly constructivists, also adhere to positivism and hypothesis testing. The notion of 'indivisible territory', which is commonly accepted as a 'variable' that is affected by domestic, cultural, and strategic considerations, has been studied in depth by scholars such as Lustick (1993), Toft (2003), Hassner (2009), and Goddard (2010). Similarly, Shelef (2016) has explored the construction of notions of 'homeland' and how such constructions affect patterns of conflict between states, while Mylonas and Shelef (2014) have explained variation in territorial claims made by stateless nationalist movements. By contrast, scholars such as Zacher (2001), Fazal (2007), and Atzili (2012) emphasized the construction of the territorial order at the interstate level, pointing towards the impacts of the so-called territorial integrity (or border fixity) norm on patterns of interstate and intrastate conflict. Branch (2014) and Larkins (2010), in turn, explored the European and colonial history of territoriality.

Some IR works on territory deserve special attention for engaging with deeper conceptual questions of territory and territoriality. John Herz's *World Politics* article on the origins and demise of the territorial state (1957) emphasized the interaction between ideational and material factors, such as the rise of nationalism and nuclear weapons, respectively, with respect to their influence on the relationship between states and the territories they control. Kratochwil (1986) suggests the contingent and changing nature of boundaries in world history. Ruggie's (1993) interpretation of the evolution of territory and territoriality reflects IR debates about the nature of world politics, especially in the immediate post-Cold War era. As mentioned above, an extended debate arose in the 1990s between those who argued that both the territorial Westphalian state form and territory itself were losing their salience in world politics and others, most prominently realists, who argued that the so-called territorial state remained robust. In this context, Ruggie, following a dominant view in political geography, argued that, from a theoretical and historical perspective, the notions of territory and territoriality were not static. He then used this argument to discredit state-centric accounts in IR, suggesting that world politics was entering a post-territorial phase.

Ruggie's argument ultimately also ascribes to a territorial/a-territorial dichotomy. Put simply, Ruggie's framework assumes – roughly – three phases in world politics: a pre-territorial phase, the age of Westphalian territoriality, and the advent of a post-territorial and network-oriented political landscape.[4] While most political geographers would adhere to Ruggie's position about the non-static nature of territory and territoriality, his dichotomous reading of territoriality – territorial vs. a-territorial political systems – is not necessarily shared with the same fervour. Most notably, Agnew (2009) implies that such a dichotomous approach to territory suggests a misleading and oversimplified vision of different territorial systems – the 'territorial gap'. It implicitly imposes categorical constraints on the ways in which we think about different political organizations' approach to space. The difference may be not between territorial and a-territorial but between different kinds of territorial orders, a position that is shared among the authors in this volume.

In political geography, scholarly interest in the topic of territories and territoriality can be traced from the seminal works of Gottmann (1973) and Sack (1986) to a recent contribution by Stuart Elden, whose *The Birth of Territory* (2013) offers a comprehensive analysis of the ideational evolution of the term territory. These studies deal with the meanings, practices, and processes involved with territories generally. Additionally, political geographers in the late

1980s and 1990s began to focus on the various configurations of territory and international politics. This latter line of academic inquiry is usually associated with both so-called 'critical geopolitics' as well as John Agnew's influential critique of the 'territorial trap' inherent within IR theories.

Critical geopolitics refers to a broad research programme that primarily addresses the ways in which different territorialization mechanisms are employed by core powers and hegemonic states (Ó Tuathail, 1996; Ó Tuathail & Agnew, 1992).[5] Critical geopolitics exposes invisible relationships between diverging spatialization strategies in international politics and forms of domination, often using discourse analysis. This literature typically starts from the assumption that territories are best seen not as 'things', but as platforms through which the hegemonic powers or economic elites either establish or perpetuate their domination over the rest.

From within this critical geopolitics tradition, John Agnew's conceptualization of the so-called territorial trap identifies a multidimensional analytical problem in IR theory. IR scholars tend to treat sovereign spaces as unchanging in nature, to overemphasize the polarity between domestic and international political spaces, and to assume that the so-called territorial state can exist 'prior to and as a container of' society (Agnew, 1994, 59). These assumptions, Agnew argues, obfuscate understandings of how international politics is conducted vis-à-vis territorial practices. Over the course of the last 20 years, critical geopolitics, including Agnew's territorial trap, has become a staple of the political geography literature, especially its segments that deal directly with international politics and their unofficial flagship journal *Geopolitics*.

More recently, the debates in political geography over territory have taken a turn towards the history of ideas and political theory. The most influential work along this line thus far is Elden's (2013) *The Birth of Territory*. For Elden (18), 'the idea of a territory as bounded space under the control of a group of people, with fixed boundaries, exclusive internal sovereignty, and equal external status is historically produced'. Elden is particularly interested in the conceptual origins of territory, which he argues are rarely examined or even questioned. In particular, Elden utilizes a study of texts from Ancient Greece to seventeenth-century Europe to show how the notion of territory developed as a political subject in the Western practice and thought (2013). Following his former work (especially 2009), Elden conceptualizes territory as a political technology and emphasizes the ways in which 'the legal and the technical' (10) interact with respect to the relationship between geography and politics. While Elden's book is hard to situate vis-à-vis mainstream human geography (Minca et al., 2015, 93), it has motivated much debate, attracting both praise and criticism. Elden's 'history of ideas' approach, coupled with its emphasis on political theory, has already impacted political geography by challenging the ways in which many scholars approach the relationship between geography and politics.

In many ways, then, contemporary political scientists and political geographers researching the malleable nature of territories in international politics start from similar premises – territory as a social and political construct – and deal with similar topics ranging from international competition and conflict to cooperation. However, there is little conversation between them.

To be sure, the poverty of the dialogue[6] is not without reason. The research in political geography tends to focus on the 'problematization' of dominant discourses and practices. It rarely deals directly with the 'why' questions that lie at the heart of much political science research on territory. Additionally, there are significant methodological differences across disciplines, with political geographers leaning towards methods such as discourse analysis and political scientists concerned with hypotheses testing. Furthermore, while 'interdisciplinary research' is a popular catch phrase in academia these days, disciplinary 'walls' remain well-guarded and academic outlets for publishing such 'adventurous' inquiries are limited (Kadercan, 2015, 127).

Even so, we argue that much common ground exists across disciplines especially with respect to the 'territorial heterogeneity' of world politics, the relationship between political power and territoriality, and the interaction between identities and territories. The exploration of such common ground can produce valuable insights and perspectives, but creating a shared vocabulary is a prerequisite for such mutual endeavour. This volume seeks to promote an interdisciplinary cross-fertilization by starting to build such a shared vocabulary, using the term 'territorial design' as a cornerstone.

DEFINING TERRITORIAL DESIGN

In order to define 'territorial design', we first need a working definition of territoriality, which in turn demands a discussion of 'territory'. It is well established among students of territory that the term implies more than just a piece of land or physical space (Storey, 2012). Following the work of political geographer Robert Sack (1986), territory is conceived as being shaped by territoriality (Penrose, 2002, 279). Territoriality, in turn, refers to 'a geographic strategy that connects society and space' (Penrose, 2002, 279). More recently, Kadercan (2015) offered the term 'territorial constitutions', which are the set of dominant territorial discourses and practices at the legal, administrative, cultural, and political spheres that configure the association between state, society, and space.

Our definition builds on Kadercan's conceptualization, but we also take two additional steps. The first involves the question of whether territoriality is best studied from a dichotomous perspective that distinguishes between territorial and a-territorial political organizations and systems. We believe, to the contrary, that territory has been and will be an essential component of global politics for the foreseeable future. From a world-historical point of view, we do not adhere to the idea that we are approaching an era during which global politics will divorce itself from territories or borders. Territory has never been a static or fixed phenomenon and/or practice, but it has remained of essential importance for the study of international politics and will likely remain so in the coming decades.

Our second addendum to Kadercan's concept of territory responds to the emerging literature in political geography and its emphasis on the 'history of ideas' (see especially Kearns on this point, 2016, in this volume). Future research will undoubtedly benefit from further engagements with the insights offered in Elden's *The Birth of Territory*, but this volume does not engage in extended conversations with the genealogical approach and the conceptual historiography it offers. Rather, we adopt a perspective that considers territory to be a space of practice.

Our rationale is one of practicality. We intend for our territorial design approach to stimulate inter-disciplinary conversations and thus we endeavour to create frameworks and research questions useful (and palatable) to scholars from different disciplines and divergent disciplinary perspectives. Much political science research on territory and international politics is empirical in nature. The 'theory' is usually interpreted in terms of causal or constitutive mechanisms, which are then utilized to explain and/or describe empirical puzzles. Apart from a few exceptions,[7] IR literature has scarcely paid attention to the conceptual history of the term territory and rarely builds on political theory to understand it. We hope to ease the tension between how we approach territory and how political geographers associated with Elden's approach treat the concept by suggesting a 'looser' understanding of the term than the one used by Elden. We find it both compelling and useful to conceptualize territory and territoriality as simply about the relationship between politics and space. Our hope, of course, is to work towards establishing more robust links and engaging in deeper conversations with the history of ideas approach that Elden advances. To a similar end, Jordan Branch (2016, in this volume) offers a novel framework for juxtaposing the terms technology and that can stimulate discussions across disciplinary borders.[8] Building on the conceptualizations, we then suggest an analytic framework that we refer to as territorial design. We define territorial design as the process by which elites, in interaction with their own society and their competitors, intentionally and systematically constitute and institutionalize territoriality, and hence also territory.

It is critical to note how our concept of territorial design departs from a functionalist interpretation of political and social systems[9] in at least two ways. First, we do not argue that the territorial 'designs' observed in global politics are necessarily direct functions of powerful actors' preferences, opportunities, and constraints; these territorial systems often emerge from the interaction of multiple actors with different capabilities, incentives, and design strategies, and at different levels of analysis, or scales.[10] Second, the designs we may observe at a particular time period or space may not necessarily reflect the preferences of the contemporary elites. In other words, territorial designs can be 'sticky', sustaining themselves long after they outlive their initial usefulness for the elites who initially constituted and institutionalized the territorial order.

The implications of different territorial designs on international politics[11] are numerous, divergent, and important. In order not to stray too much and to be able to conduct a useful dialogue, the authors in this project are concentrating on the relations between territorial designs and foreign policy. They explore questions such as: To what extent do different territorial designs generate different kinds of foreign policies? To what extent does foreign policy affect the way in which different societies or nationalist movements conceive of, and change, their territorial designs? And what could the interaction between scholars of international relations and political geographers contribute to our mutual understanding of such concepts and processes?

TERRITORIAL DESIGN AS A FRAMEWORK FOR RESEARCH

Territory can be conceptualized in three dimensions: the physical features of space (or land), the demarcation processes, and the constitution of demarcated space. First, the physical components of territory comprise the natural (or geographical) attributes of territory as well as economic and demographic resources attached to it. Although these physical components are a core feature of territory, they are fairly straightforward and more commonly discussed in both literature and policy consideration of territory, and hence will not be the focus of this volume.

Second, territorial demarcation involves the process of delineating and compartmentalizing space. Demarcation inherently requires human agency and can range from the Westphalian 'hard' borders to the vaguely demarcated frontiers of traditional empires to the porous and fluid frontiers that characterize nomad societies (Kratochwil, 1986). In the context of demarcation, one also needs to note the differentiation between the ideal representation of each form of demarcation, and its actual implementation. 'Hard' borders on paper might be quite porous in reality (Krasner, 1999). Demarcation processes will determine the modes of transaction across different political units, as well as their proximity and contiguity vis-à-vis each other.

Third and finally, the constitutive properties of territory refer to the particular political and social functions as well as meanings assigned to demarcated space. These flow from the institutionalization of legal, administrative, political, and cultural practices that manage and regulate the relationship between society, state, and space. This constitutive dimension includes questions of citizenship and residence, as well as the particular characterization of relations between the people and 'their' territory (see Mylonas and Shelef, 2017, this volume). It also addresses questions of sovereignty and authority. Like with demarcation, we see a significant variation over time and space between various territorial constitutions. Territories that determine citizenship according to territorial residency (civic criteria), for example, are very different from communities in which citizenship is determined by ethnic delimitation. And both of these constitutions are far removed from the medieval European order, which divided authority between state and church, and included many forms of authority rather than the modern exclusive notion of sovereignty.

Note that while demarcation necessarily influences the constitutive properties of territory, the latter do not automatically follow from the former. Similar demarcation practices do not guarantee that territories 'inside' the borders will be socially and politically constructed in identical ways. The interaction between the processes related to demarcation and constitution of territorial units, we argue, is where the bulk of territorial design – and competition as well as cooperation over territorial design(s) – takes place.

One way to envision the interaction between the demarcation processes and the constitutive properties of the demarcated space is to examine the politics of territorial designs in terms of the level (or scale) that is the primary focus of the design. In other words, one asks at which level (and therefore through the actions of whom) is the design occurring. Figure 1 focuses on the interaction of the level/scale of the territorial design with the demarcation and constitution of territory. Note that the framework we suggest in Figure 1 does not offer a 'typological theory', as the categories developed are not mutually exclusive. Instead, the framework is best seen as a set of lenses that facilitate the examination of a single phenomenon from different perspectives, or multiple cases from a particular perspective, depending upon the subject of inquiry.

To illustrate this point, consider nationalistic territorial designs. Murphy (2013) recently reminded us that nationalism is necessarily a territorial phenomenon. The 'design' component, in this particular instance, would refer to the ways in which modern nation-states aim to organize the space–society–politics relationship (Breuilly, 1994). Such designs could be examined from three different aspects, or three different 'boxes'. First, we can think about nationalistic territorial design as one that naturally lies within the purview of the (national) domestic agency in designing both the whereabouts of the borders (delineation) and the characteristics of the nation (constitution), and thus in Box A. Nations may need to fight with others over the location of borders and internally over the determination of their citizenship and constitution, but, in principle, these are national choices.

Second, consider the classical Westphalian design, with authority demarcated by the interstate relations – wars and treaties – along clearly delineated territorial lines and in a mutually exclusive way, and domestic agency is responsible for the internal constitution of the country. Such interpretation of national design will lend itself to categorization in Box B. This combination of externally set demarcation and internally designed constitution became even clearer in the post-Second World War era with what Atzili (2012) refers to as the border fixity norm that prohibits foreign conquest and annexation of homeland territory. Under such circumstances, the

		How Space Inside Boundaries is constructed (Constitution of territory)	
		Domestic	Interstate/External
How boundaries are constructed (Delineation of Territory)	Domestic	**Box A: Domestic Delineation and Constitution** Examples: Nationalist designs (the nation determines its borders and then its internal constitution); Ottoman design (fluid frontiers, heterogeneous territories)	**Box C: Domestic Delineation and External Constitution** Example: EU (delineation of borders bounded by domestic identities, but the constitution of territory is increasingly subjected to external standards)
	Interstate/External	**Box B: External Delineation and Domestic Constitution** Examples: Westphalian design (fixed borders, internal constitution)	**Box D: External Delineation and Constitution** Example: Colonizing designs (both demarcation and constitution externally imposed)

Figure 1. Constructing territorial design.

interaction between fixed borders and homogeneity of spaces inside borders leads to territorial stability and a low probability of interstate conflict over territory.[12] Alternatively, Atzili's framework can be utilized to examine the consequences of externally imposed fixed borders with heterogeneous territorial designs that are the hallmark of many weak states. In such cases, the lack of coherence between external borders and internal identities might result in civil conflicts and spillover of violence across borders (Miller, 2007).

We use this table as a heuristic to allow us a more fruitful discussion of the interaction of domestic and foreign sources of territorial design. It helps to illuminate the various shapes territorial designs could take, and the relations between the construction of external boundaries and construction of internal space. We are nevertheless cognizant of the fact that reality is much more complicated. The mere act of border demarcation, for example, can be utilized by nationalist movements not only for 'othering' populations but also to borrow identity features from them (Agnew, 2007). Alternatively, interstate relations between states with unassimilated ethnic groups and external powers backing these groups have crucial effects on whether policies of accommodation, exclusion, or assimilation will be pursued (Mylonas, 2012). The table helps us to focus the discussion to the external and internal influences on various forms of designing the delineation and constitution of territory.

Paths to territorial designs

The papers in this volume reveal some important insights for territorial designs and for the study of territoriality, boundaries, and borders. Here, we outline a few of these insights:

#1 – Strategic logic(s) of territorial designs: The social–cultural–political construction of territories takes place in an arena where competing actors try to influence how spaces will be 'imagined' and/or governed. Territorial designs are rarely spontaneous, though the sources, motivations, and incentives that lead to their construction vary greatly. The strategic logic that may underpin different forms of territorial designs might be situated within different 'levels of analysis', in IR parlance, or 'scales' in the terms of political geography. In other words, understanding the motivation and processes of territorial designs might require focus on domestic politics, on international politics, or on the interaction between these two arenas, depending upon the case. Once established, territorial designs set the 'context' into which foreign policy strategies are developed, defining constraints and opportunities.

#2 – Unintended consequences of territorial designs: 'Territorial designs' differ from Koremenos, Lipson, and Snidal's (2001) concept of the 'rational design' of (international) institutions and its functionalist logic. As noted in #1, some designs stem from motivations that have little to do with making the territorial system work better as a whole. Moreover, some territorial designs constituted to address a specific problem at hand might subsequently create other problems and foreign policy dilemmas.

#3 – The tension between micro-designs and global order(s): The global territorial order is defined in terms of the nation-state model and enshrined by the United Nations (UN) at the interstate level. The order has been institutionalized over time, but rival 'micro' territorial orders continue to exist in many parts of the globe. This includes, for example, lands that were governed by imperial designs for a very long time, only to be recently 'dropped' into the Westphalian ideal. It also includes national groups that do not aspire to possess a territorial state of their own or to be 'admitted to the sovereign club'. These incompatible territorial orders are likely to be a source of continuous tension.

#4 – Territorial designs have much to do with 'technology' and 'knowledge': The territorial design framework also recognizes that how territorial systems are constituted as spaces of political practice in a particular context depends largely on the technologies available to the relevant actors and the dominant forms of 'knowledge'. As Branch (2014) masterfully showed in *The*

Cartographic State, technology and knowledge vary tremendously and these variations have remarkable subsequent impacts on how political organizations evolve. Building on this logic, we argue that the availability of a certain technology will affect how political actors think about demarcating and constituting space. Furthermore, this has direct impacts on how actors think about not only their own but also others' foreign policy strategies.

THE ROAD AHEAD

This volume is aimed at both problematizing and operationalizing the 'constitutive properties' of territorial orders, boundaries, and borders. By way of doing so, we hope to encourage dialogue between International Relations and Political Geography on how and why territory is constructed, thus creating a new interdisciplinary space. Juxtaposing competing accounts and perspectives to explain or describe the same phenomena can only contribute to our understanding of the relationship between territory and international politics. If our goal is to advance the knowledge of territory's role in international politics, it is not particularly important for scholars hailing from different perspectives and disciplines to agree on everything. Instead, we believe that it is important that scholars with competing perspectives find a common ground from which to talk with each other. This is certainly preferable to shutting the doors to each other's work. Overall, 'interdisciplinary research' is a popular catchphrase in academia, but, given the entry barriers associated with crossing over to a seemingly alien literature, it is not necessarily a popular enterprise in practice. For such interaction to take place, both political scientists and political geographers need to make a concerted effort to create a shared space for discussion, in other words, make disciplinary boundaries more flexible and permeable. We see at least two ways in which this dialogue can promote our understanding of territory, territoriality, and borders.

First, in political science, territory is often portrayed as a constant, or a 'thing'. It is either ignored or treated or considered – for example, by Realist theories of power politics – as an asset of the state. An approach that goes beyond the physical attributes of territory to ask how and why territories serve different roles in different times and across different spaces would allow for a more nuanced and accurate understanding of international politics. The territorial design approach introduced and elaborated upon here thus highlights the character of territory as a political, social, and cultural construct; as both an independent and dependent variable; and as a process in the context of foreign policy and interstate politics.

Second, just as political scientists can benefit from interacting with political geographers over the role of territory and territoriality in world politics, so can political geographers gain from the interaction. One benefit would be the introduction to geographers of an abundance of existing research in political science-oriented international relations. Looking more closely at the type of questions asked and research being done 'on the other side of the fence' would allow political geographers to extend the scope of their territorial interpretations of international politics. Currently, one of the most challenging barriers to such interdisciplinary interaction is the esoteric jargon that individual disciplines generate. The territorial designs framework we introduce here aims to stimulate the creation of a common vocabulary so as to overcome such barriers. Also, political scientists have taken the material and institutional dynamics of international politics very seriously. Taking such material and institutional insights from political science is likely to be useful for political geographers, especially with respect to the assessment and refinement of their own approaches to territories and boundaries.

With the territorial designs framework, we intend to facilitate debate on the relationship between different territorial arrangements and the interests and strategic behaviour of various political actors. Koremenos et al.'s (2001) 'rational design' perspective argues that political actors use certain arrangements (in their case, international institutions) to further their goals and aim to 'offer a systematic account of the wide range of design features that characterize' (762) Most importantly, the implication of this argument is that these arrangements are not random, but are in fact explicit and negotiated settlements 'that prescribe, proscribe, and/or authorize behavior' (762). Similarly, we argue that territorial arrangements are not random but follow from some element of 'design', which itself can follow from the political cooperation or competition over managing space–society relationship. There are, however, three key differences between our approach and the rational design perspective.

First, our focus on territory as a socially and politically constructed phenomenon allows for more emphasis on ideational dynamics and informal arrangements, in addition to accommodating more explicit and formal ones. Second, we treat territorial designs as 'sticky' in nature. Most spatial arrangements might be taken for granted today, but this does not mean that there was a 'logic' that was dictated by a single set of actors behind such arrangements when they were first constructed, or that this logic remains valid today. Our territorial designs framework distances itself from a 'functionalist' understanding of territorial systems that is subject to an inherent analytical trap. Instead, we suggest that territorial designs are usually products of compromises and negotiations. They are struggles over the very nature of the politics–space–society nexus. Territorial designs thus exist not necessarily because they unilaterally serve the needs and preferences of a particular political actor, but because they represent sticky, 'punctuated equilibria' that reflect the interaction among various domestic and international political and social actors.[13] Third, while Koremenos et al. (2001) focus on how designs help political actors solve their collective problems, we are additionally interested in how space–society–politics nexus can be manipulated to establish authority, or, alternatively, to challenge it. Constructivist IR scholars have contributed much in the last few decades to help us understand the socially constructed nature of intersubjective relationships *between actors*. As a rule, however, constructivists tend to pay much less attention to how 'spaces' are created and re-created inter-subjectively. Furthermore, IR constructivists have focused much of their attention on questions such as 'how cooperation takes place despite anarchy', at least more so than how certain ideas can be utilized, or even 'weaponized', to sustain political authority and dominance.[14] Political geographers, in this context, do point towards the importance of spaces with respect to political interactions between different actors. They also explore the ways in which different territorial orders can create different forms of authority and domination and how powerful actors can affect space–society–politics nexus to substantiate their authority over other actors. An interdisciplinary dialogue can help bridge this gap as well, and address the 'analytical blind spots' that result from institutionalist explanations that undervalue the role of power relations in the construction, management, and evolution of different political systems.

SUMMARY OF THE ARTICLES

The authors in this volume represent both political science and political geography. As such, they hold different perspectives and might not necessarily agree with one another's arguments or lines of reasoning. Yet, the articles share two attributes: their commitment to dialogue across disciplinary lines and an interest in 'territorial design'.

Writing on 'Territory as an Institution: Spatial Ideas, Practices, and Technologies', Jordan Branch (2016) offers a novel analytical framework to bridge the study of territory and institutions, and directly speaks to the origins and consequences of various territorial designs. Branch's framework examines the intersection of three dimensions that collectively constitute territory as an institution: ideas about political space, practices of political authority, and technology. Branch operationalizes technology – a dimension that has usually been left out of the scholarly work examining the historical evolution of institutions – as a material factor whose 'meanings, importance, and impact are shaped by ideas and practices'. His framework aims to advance interdisciplinary conversations over the role of territory in world politics in the context of technological advances, a goal that also lies at the heart of this territorial design project. Branch then applies his institutional definition of territory to a number of topics, including territorial conflict and territorial change in the context of the rise of nationalism and international norms such as border fixity. In particular, Branch examines the interaction and tension between system-wide and domestic-level dynamics as they affect, and are affected by, distinct territorial systems.

Harris Mylonas and Nadav Shelef (2017) offer an epistemological and methodological discussion that focuses on the territorial claims of stateless nationalists, but has much broader implications for territorial designs writ large. In 'Methodological Challenges in the Study of Stateless Nationalist Territorial Claims', they probe the pros and cons of different research designs that investigate change in territorial claims. The authors emphasize three methodological topics. First, they stress the importance of distinguishing between the initial origins and the subsequent change in territorial designs. Second, they highlight the multidimensional nature of the process and suggest that it is particularly useful to study the timing, the direction, and initiating agents of the change. Third, Mylonas and Shelef discuss the importance of paying sufficient attention to the unit of analysis and case selection.

Burak Kadercan (2017) explores the relationship between different territorial designs and interstate as well as intrastate violence from a macro-historical perspective. Kadercan's essay focuses on an empirical puzzle embedded in classical era Ottoman rule (roughly from 1300 until 1700). He asks: how can we explain that the Ottomans were able to rule an expansive terrain – ranging from the Balkans to the Middle East and North Africa – with relative peace and stability while also fighting numerous wars of conquest? Building on the analytical framework presented in this introduction article, the essay pushes forward a 'territorial' interpretation. Kadercan argues that the Ottoman state-building and power-projection mechanisms that collectively also shaped its grand strategy were influenced by the Empire's approach to territory. This approach differs from the European states of the Westphalian system who aimed at 'hardening' their borders and 'homogenizing' space–society–politics association within their domains. By contrast, the early Ottomans pursued a territorial strategy built on 'soft' demarcation mechanisms and territorial heterogeneity vis-à-vis the space–society–politics relationship in the lands they ruled. This particular territorial design, Kadercan proposes, allowed the Ottomans not only to wage near-continuous interstate war, but also to rule their domain with relative peace and stability. Kadercan concludes by commenting on the co-evolution of different territorial designs in the European state system and the Ottoman Empire and the implications of the 'clash' of such designs from the nineteenth century onwards.

Ryan Griffiths (2016) looks at the international aspect of territorial design in his article, 'Admission to the Sovereignty Club: The Past, Present, and Future of the International Recognition Regime.' Conceptualizing international sovereignty norms as club goods, Griffith surveys the evolution of such norms from the pre-Westphalia era to today's system. He discusses the tensions between these norms and various territorial designs – including those of aspiring states like Somaliland, Kurdistan, and Catalonia – and notes how the 'terms of admission' to the club clash with the domestic designs of such actors. In highlighting the mutually constitutive nature of the club (sovereignty norms) and its members (the states), the author further emphasizes the role of the interplay between Liberal norms and norm of sovereignty in determining territorial design.

While Griffiths' article explores the implications of a crowding humanity in a fixed-space realm, the next article suggests that this space might not be as fixed as first assumed. In his article, entitled 'Between Land and Sea: Spaces and Conflict Intensity', Ehud Eiran (2017) explores the interaction of international norms and domestic political actors in two different territorial domains of the Israeli–Lebanese border. Partly because the territories involved are either empty or sparsely populated, this article is concerned mainly with the construction of boundaries or the delineation of territory. Eiran uses the 'natural experiment' provided by the countries' territorial disputes of land and sea boundaries to explore the impact of international norms in different territorial domains. The article emphasizes two of the main points discussed above: the strategic logic of territorial design, and the tension between micro-designs and global orders. Specifically, the authors show how international norms that depict sovereignty over land as binary and absolute and sovereignty over water as partial make the former a more attractive domain for violent conflict, despite the higher material value of the latter.

Katherine Hall Kindervater's (2016) 'Drone Strikes, Ephemeral Sovereignty, and Changing Conception of Territory' examines the role of a relatively new military tool and its impacts on the practice of territoriality and sovereignty. Through the prism of a critical approach, Kindervater examines relationship between law and the projection of power to scrutinize the ways in which the US has 'stretched' legal justifications for extra-territorial drone strikes in Yemen and Pakistan. She explains how such strikes create moments where state sovereignty is being 'folded', if only temporarily, a phenomenon she associates with the concept of 'ephemeral sovereignty'. In particular, Kindervater argues that the use of drones is reshaping the territorial order, explaining that drones and their temporary 'justification' are being 'weaponized' as tools that can pierce through borders and render territorial sovereignty contingent (see also, Elden, 2009). As a result, the spatiality or territory of sovereign power is reconfigured at both the system level and with respect to the perpetrator (in this case, the US) and the target state (here, Yemen or Pakistan). She suggests that in the age of drones, state power is no longer tied to the fixed territory of the state, but has become global and mobile. In line with other essays in this volume, Kindervater starts from the 'malleable, dynamic, multiplicitous character of territory' and, from a critical perspective, draws attention to the unintended causes and origins of different territorial designs. She also pays attention to the tension between domestic and 'external' construction of territorial systems, especially in the context of the interaction between power projection, foreign policy, and the law.

Finally, Gerry Kearns' (2016) 'The Territory of Colonialism' also offers a critical reading of the theory and practice of territory and territoriality from both conceptual and historical perspectives. Kearns is a political geographer and his article in this volume aims to explicitly bridge the gap between discourse studies and empirical work. For Kearns, the separation between the two lines of inquiry is 'not as necessary as might appear', for 'any particular discursive formation' that is associated with territories is bound to have 'material as well as textual circumstances'. Kearns' article examines the case of colonization of Ireland by the English in the early-modern era. He suggests that colonialism, which itself necessarily involves territorial strategies, took place not only outside Europe/West but also inside the 'West', most notably in Ireland. Building on historical materialism for methodology, Kearns argues that the notion of territorial sovereignty can be traced to its feudal and colonial roots, which are exemplified by England's strategy to remake the Irish lands roughly from the late-twelfth century to the sixteenth. The English rulers tampered with the politics–society–space relationship to establish and perpetuate their rule over the Irish people by combining 'material' aspects of power (such as use or threat of use of force, control over distribution of food and other vital resources) and the legal regulations relating to territory. Interpreted from the lenses of the territorial design framework, the English colonial rule involved territorial strategies where an external political actor aimed to 'break' an existing territorial design and impose a new one that better suited its aspirations. Kearns concludes by suggesting that understanding the origins of the notion of territorial sovereignty requires exploring the alternative forms of territoriality, or alternative territorial designs. Political actors constructed and utilized such designs across time and space, which then help us further explore the ways in which the interaction between power, space, and society has evolved from a historical perspective.

The conceptualization of 'territorial designs' in this introductory article neither opens nor concludes the debate. Rather, it and all of the articles in this volume aim to integrate separate discourses and research agendas through a constructive interdisciplinary dialogue. Beyond that, we also hope to focus this discussion in a way that will promote a better understanding of the constitution of territories and of the boundaries that surround them.

ACKNOWLEDGEMENTS

The Authors thank Jordan Branch, Ashan Butt, Ehud Eiran, Carolyn Gallaher, Ryan Griffith, Anne Kantel, Garry Kearns, Katherine Kindervater, Harris Mylonas, Aviad Rubin, Nadav Shelef, Ariel Zellman, the anonymous reviewers, and the journal editors for very helpful comments. They also thank Laura Bosco and Karen Sounders for research assistantship.

DISCLOSURE STATEMENT

No potential conflict of interest was reported by the authors.

NOTES

1. The creation of such new space is not the first in history (e.g., the Netherlands in the seventeenth century). The creation of such a space in order to expand the territorial waters of a country, though, is most likely a novelty.
2. See also Agnew (2009).
3. 'Territory' consists not only of the material physicals space, but also of its demarcation and constitution, both of the socially constructed (Kadercan, 2015).
4. For a similar way of thinking, see Herz (1957).
5. Both critical geopolitics and the majority of studies emanating from political geography that deal with international politics share important epistemological and methodological similarities with critical IR scholars. For a thorough discussion, see Kadercan (2015).
6. This 'poverty' is not limited to interdisciplinary synergies but also applies to intra-disciplinary interactions, if to a lesser degree.
7. These studies themselves usually remain well outside of what we can call mainstream IR (e.g., see Larkins, 2010)
8. We refrain from directly engaging Elden's work at present for two additional reasons. First, Elden does not sufficiently engage the 'material articulations of power that [territory] reflected and shaped' (Minca et al., 2015, 95); however, such articulations are important for 'territorial design'. Second, while Elden's book 'most certainly is Eurocentric' (Minca et al., 2015, 96), we intend to construct a framework that can speak to and benefit from the study of non-European cases as well as intra-European cases where more 'nuanced' practices and discourses of territoriality were in practice (see especially Kearns and Kadercan in this volume) when compared with the 'Western' European experience that lies at the heart of Elden's study.
9. For Koremenos et al. (2001), rational design does exactly that, going for a decidedly functionalist interpretation of how international institutions are created and function.
10. See, for example, Atzili and Kantel (2015).
11. We use this term here because of its commonality, despite the fact that it is not a good fit for this project, as 'international' already refers to a particular territorial design.
12. For some of the mechanism through which such dynamic could work, see Darden and Mylonas (2016) and Gibler (2014)
13. Mylonas and Shelef (2014) propose such an argument in the context of the study of stateless nationalist movements. Atzili and Kantel (2015) apply it to the study of shifting West German territorial concepts of their state.
14. Other IR scholars, such as feminists and post-colonialists, do use such interpretation.

REFERENCES

Agnew, J. A. (1994). The territorial trap: The geographical assumptions of international relations theory. *Review of International Political Economy*, 1(1), 53–80.

Agnew, J. A. (2007). No borders no nations: Making Greece in Macedonia. *Annals of the Association of American Geographers, 97*(2), 398–422.

Agnew, J.A. (2009). *Globalization and sovereignty*. Lanham, MD: Rowman and Littlefiled.

Atzili, B. (2012). *Good fences, bad neighbors: Border fixity and international conflict*. The Chicago, IL: University of Chicago Press.

Atzili, B., & Kantel, A. (2015). Accepting the unacceptable: Lessons from west Germany's changing border politics. *International Studies Review, 17*, 588–616.

Branch, J. (2014). *The cartographic state: Maps, territory and the origins of sovereignty*. Cambridge: Cambridge University Press.

Branch, J. (2016). Territory as an institution: Spatial ideas, practices and technologies. *Territory, Politics, Governance*. doi:10.1080/21622671.2016.1265464

Breuilly, J. (1994). *Nationalism and the state*. Chicago, IL: University of Chicago Press.

Darden, K., & Mylonas, H. (2016). Threats to territorial integrity, national mass schooling, and linguistic commonality. *Comparative Political Studies, 49*(11), 1446–1479.

Eiran, E. (2017). Between land and sea: Spaces and conflict intensity. *Territory, Politics, Governance*. doi:10.1080/21622671.2016.1265466

Elden, S. (2009). *Terror and territory: The spatial extent of sovereignty*. Minnesota, MN: University of Minnesota Press.

Elden, S. (2013). *The birth of territory*. Chicago, IL: University of Chicago Press.

Fazal, T. M. (2007). *State death: The politics and geography of conquest, occupation, and annexation*. Princeton, NJ: Princeton University Press.

Friedman, T. L. (2000). *The lexus and the olive tree: Understanding globalization*. New York, NY: Picador.

Friedman, T. L. (2007). *The world is flat: A brief history of the twenty-first century*. New York, NY: Picador.

Gibler, D. M. (2014). Contiguous states, stable borders, and the peace between democracies. *International Studies Quarterly, 58*(1), 126–129.

Goddard, S. E. (2010). *Indivisible territory and the politics of legitimacy: Jerusalem and northern Ireland*. Cambridge: Cambridge University Press.

Goertz, G., & Diehl, P. F. (1992). *Territorial changes and international conflict*. New York, NY: Routledge.

Gottmann, J. (1973). *The significance of territory*. Charlottesville: University Press of Virginia.

Greig, M. J. (2002). The end of geography? Globalization, communications, and culture in the international system. *Journal of Conflict Resolution, 46*(2), 225–243.

Griffiths, R. D. (2016). Admission to the sovereignty club: The past, present, and future of the international recognition regime. *Territory, Politics, Governance*. doi:10.1080/21622671.2016.1265463

Hassner, R. E. (2009). *War on sacred grounds*. Ithaca, NY: Cornell University Press.

Herz, J. H. (1957). Rise and demise of the territorial state. *World Politics, 9*(4), 473–493.

Holsti, K. J. (1991). *Peace and war: Armed conflicts and international order, 1648-1989*. Cambridge: Cambridge University Press.

Huth, P. K. (1996). *Standing your ground: Territorial disputes and international conflict*. Ann Arbor, MI: University of Michigan Press.

Kadercan, B. (2015). Triangulating territory: A case for pragmatic interaction between political science, political geography, and critical IR. *International Theory, 7*(1), 125–161.

Kadercan, B. (2017). Territorial design and grand strategy in the Ottoman Empire. *Territory, Politics, Governance*. doi:10.1080/21622671.2016.1265465

Kahler, M., & Walter, B. F. (2006). *Territoriality and conflict in an era of globalization*. Cambridge: Cambridge University Press.

Kaldor, M. (1999). *Old and new wars: Organized violence in a global era*. Stanford, CA: Stanford University Press.

Kearns, G. (2016). The territory of colonialism. *Territory, Politics, Governance*. doi:10.1080/21622671.2016.1266961

Kindervater, K. H. (2016). Drone strikes, ephemeral sovereignty, and changing conceptions of territory. *Territory, Politics, Governance*. doi:10.1080/21622671.2016.1260493

Koremenos, B., Lipson, C., & Snidal, D. (2001). The rational design of international institutions. *International Organization, 55*(4), 761–799.

Krasner, S. D. (1999). *Sovereignty: Organized hypocrisy*. Princeton, NJ: Princeton University Press.

Kratochwil, F. (1986). Of systems, boundaries, and territoriality: An inquiry into the formation of the state system. *World Politics, 39*(1), 27–52.

Larkins, J. (2010). *From hierarchy to anarchy: Territory and politics before Westphalia*. New York, NY: Palgrave Macmillan.

Lustick, I. (1993). *Unsettled states, disputed lands: Britain and Ireland, France and Algeria, Israel and the West Bank-Gaza*. Ithaca, NY: Cornell University Press.

Miller, B. (2007). *States, nations, and the great powers: The sources of regional war and Peace*. Cambridge: Cambridge University Press.

Minca, C., Crampton, J. W., Bryan, J., Fall, J. F., Murphy, A. B., Paasi, A., & Elden, S. (2015). Reading Stuart Elden's the birth of territory. *Political Geography, 46*, 93–101.

Murphy, A. B. (2013). Territory's continuing allure. *Annals of the Association of American Geographers, 103*(5), 1212–1226.

Mylonas, H. (2012). *The politics of nation building: Making Co-nationals, refugees, and minorities*. Cambridge: Cambridge University Press.

Mylonas, H., & Shelef, N. G. (2014). Which land is our land? Domestic politics and change in the territorial claims of stateless nationalist movements. *Security Studies, 23*, 754–786.

Mylonas, H., & Shelef, N. (2017). Methodological challenges in the study of stateless nationalist territorial claims. *Territory, Politics, Governance*. doi:10.1080/21622671.2017.1284020

Newman, D. (2006). The lines that continue to separate us: Borders in our 'borderless' world. *Progress in Human Geography, 30*(2), 143–161.

Newman, D. (2010). Territory, compartments and borders: Avoiding the trap of the territorial trap. *Geopolitics, 15*, 773–778.

Ohmae, K. (1999). *Borderless world: Power and strategy in the interlinked economy* (Revised ed.). New York, NY: Harper Collins.

Ó Tuathail, G. (1996). *Critical geopolitics: The politics of writing global space*. Minneapolis, MN: University of Minnesota Press.

Ó Tuathail, G., & Agnew, J. (1992). Geopolitics and discourse: Practical geopolitical reasoning in American foreign policy. *Political Geography, 11*(2), 190–204.

Penrose, J. (2002). Nations, states and homelands: Territory and territoriality in nationalist thought. *Nations and Nationalism, 8*(3), 277–297.

Rosecrance, R. N. (1986). *The rise of the trading state: Commerce and conquest in the modern world*. New York, NY: Basic Books.

Ruggie, J. G. (1993). Territoriality and beyond: Problematizing modernity in international relations. *International Organization, 47*(1), 139–174.

Sack, R. D. (1986). *Human territoriality: Its theory and history*. Cambridge: Cambridge University Press.

Sassen, S. (1996). *Losing control? Sovereignty in an age of globalization*. New York, NY: Columbia University Press.

Sassen, S. (1998). *Globalization and its discontents*. New York, NY: New Press.

Shelef, N. G. (2016). Unequal ground: Homelands and conflict. *International Organization, 70*(1), 33–63.

Starr, H. (2005). Territory, proximity, and spatiality: The geography of international conflict. *International Studies Review, 7*(3), 387–406.

Storey, D. (2012). *Territories*. Milton Park: Routledge.

Strange, S. (1998). *States and markets* (2nd ed.). London: Continuum.

Toft, M. D. (2003). *The geography of ethnic violence: Identity, interests, and the indivisibility of territory*. Princeton, NJ: Princeton University Press.

Vasquez, J. A. (1993). *The war puzzle*. Cambridge: Cambridge University Press.

Vasquez, J. A., & Henehan, M. T. (2001). Territorial disputes and the probability of War, 1816-1992. *Journal of Peace Research, 38*(2), 123–138.

Zacher, M. W. (2001). The territorial integrity norm: International boundaries and the Use of force. *International Organization, 55*(2), 215–250.

Territory as an institution: spatial ideas, practices and technologies

Jordan Branch

ABSTRACT

Territory as an institution: spatial ideas, practices and technologies. *Territory, Politics, Governance*. Territory is unquestionably central to many topics in international relations: political identity, foreign policy orientations, and political conflict at multiple levels, from disputes over land to civil and interstate wars. But what, exactly, is 'territory' in these contexts? This paper argues that territory can be usefully conceptualized as the intersection of a set of ideas, practices and technologies: namely ideas about political space, practices of political authority and rule, and technologies relating to information and infrastructure. Together, these three interrelated fields constitute the institution of territory. Thinking about territory through this particular institutional lens allows insights from a variety of fields – including institutionalist analysis in political science, the history of political thought, science and technology studies, and political geography – to be applied. This makes possible new approaches to issues such as the character and severity of territorial conflicts and the origins and persistence of the territorial state.

摘要

领土作为制度：空间概念，实践与技术。*Territory, Politics, Governance*。领土无疑是国际关系学科内众多主提之核心：政治认同，外交政策导向，以及多重层级的政治冲突，从土地争议到内战和国际战争。但"领土"在这些脉络中究竟为何？本文主张，领土能够有效地概念化为一组概念，实践与技术：亦即有关政治空间的概念，政治权威与统治的实践，以及有关信息和基础建设的技术。这些三个相互连结的领域，共同构成了领土的制度。透过此一特别的制度视角思考领土，可从各种应用领域中获得洞见—包含政治科学中的制度学派分析，政治思想的历史，科学与科技研究，以及政治地理学。这让研究诸如领土冲突的特征与剧烈程度，以及领土国家的起源与续存等议题的新方法成为可能。

RÉSUMÉ

Le territoire comme institution: des idées, des pratiques et des technologies spatiales. *Territory, Politics, Governance*. Sans aucun doute le territoire est l'un des piliers des relations internationales: l'identité politique, l'orientation de la politique étrangère et le conflit politique à de multiples niveaux, des litiges à propos des droits fonciers jusqu'aux guerres à la fois civiles et interétatiques. Mais, qu'est-ce que c'est un 'territoire' dans de tels contextes? Cet article affirme que l'on peut utilement conceptualiser la notion de territoire comme le croisement d'un ensemble d'idées, de pratiques et de technologies: à savoir, des idées à propos de l'espace politique, des pratiques du pouvoir politique, et des technologies relatives à l'information et à l'infrastructure. Considérés dans leur ensemble ces trois domaines interconnectés constituent l'institution appelée le territoire. Penser au territoire dans cette optique permet des aperçus à partir d'une série de domaines – y compris l'analyse institutionnaliste dans la science politique, l'histoire de la pensée politique, des études scientifiques et technologiques, et la géographie politique. Cela facilite de nouvelles façons d'aborder des questions telles les caractéristiques et la gravité des conflits territoriaux, et les origines et la continuité de l'état territorial.

RESUMEN

Territorio como una institución: ideas, prácticas y tecnologías espaciales. *Territory, Politics, Governance*. El territorio es sin lugar a dudas esencial en muchas cuestiones de las relaciones internacionales: identidad política, orientaciones de política exterior y conflicto político en muchos niveles, desde conflictos territoriales a guerras civiles e interestatales. ¿Pero qué exactamente significa 'territorio' en estos contextos? En este artículo se argumenta que el concepto de territorio puede conceptualizarse de modo conveniente como la intersección de un grupo de ideas, prácticas y tecnologías: es decir, las ideas sobre el espacio político, las prácticas de la autoridad política y el gobierno, y las tecnologías relacionadas con la información y la infraestructura. Juntos, estos tres campos interrelacionados constituyen la institución de territorio. Considerar el territorio a través de este prisma institucional específico nos aporta perspectivas que pueden aplicarse desde toda una variedad de campos, por ejemplo: los análisis institucionales en ciencias políticas, la historia del pensamiento político, los estudios científicos y tecnológicos y la geografía política. Esto permite nuevos planteamientos para cuestiones tales como el carácter y la gravedad de los conflictos territoriales y los orígenes y la persistencia del estado territorial.

Territory is a fundamental issue in many fields, including those that explicitly examine the conceptualization and theorization of territory (e.g., political geography) and others that use territory as a basic framework without extensive interrogation (e.g., international relations). There have been many calls to engage such discussions with each other, both from political geographers (Elden, 2013, p. 3) and from international relations scholars (Kadercan, 2015). One way to move this project forward is to explore different ways of conceptualizing territory itself. Not because there are no existing definitions – there are many – nor because existing definitions are insufficient – many are sophisticated and well-suited for their authors' theoretical purposes. Missing, however, is a conceptualization that can build on multiple disciplines and speak to diverse research programs, including both those that have interrogated territory critically and those that have not. This article, therefore, proposes and explores one definition: territory as an institution.

Conceptualizing territory as an institution allows us to combine particular arguments from institutional analysis in political science with existing theorizations and empirical studies of territory. In order to draw on diverse strands of research, here I define the institution of territory in a particular way: as a linked set of spatial ideas, practices, and technologies that, together, constitute territory. We can then use this concept to analyse how territory as an institution operates in international politics, how it has developed and changed over time, and what the impact of future changes in territory might be. This conceptualization allows us to bring together topics, methodologies, and assumptions on both sides of the disciplinary divide between political geography and 'mainstream' international relations (Kadercan, 2015). Conceptualizing territory as an institution builds on the 'territorial designs' approach (Atzili and Kadercan, 2017), which highlights the domestic and international processes by which actors constitute territory – both intentionally and unintentionally.

The rest of this article proceeds as follows. First, I propose to define institutions in general as collections of interconnected ideas, practices, and technologies. Second, I apply this definition to territory, highlighting how the distinction among territorial ideas, practices, and technologies incorporates elements of existing theorizations – particularly from political geography – but is better able to engage with other research programs. Third, I sketch out some of the benefits of this conceptualization of territory for how we think about territorial conflict in international relations and how we analyse the origins and transformation of territoriality. The conclusion then suggests further avenues for research.

INSTITUTIONS AS IDEAS, PRACTICES, AND TECHNOLOGIES

Political science has incorporated institutional analysis for several decades, although to a lesser extent in international relations than in other subfields. Different approaches to institutions, moreover, have defined the concept in diverse ways. Historical institutionalism, for example, emphasizes formal and informal rules that structure how political actors interact (e.g., Thelen & Steinmo, 1992), and sociological institutionalism focuses more on 'shared scripts' than on formal rules and regulations. While my definition of institutions diverges somewhat from how many examples of historical institutionalism define the concept, I build on key arguments from the historical institutionalist approach: arguments about how institutions are created, how they evolve, and how they determine outcomes. This reflects recent calls to bring historical institutionalism into international relations (Fioretos, 2011) and follows from the emphasis within the territorial designs approach on the processes of constituting and institutionalizing territory (Atzili and Kadercan, 2017).

Institutions can be conceptualized as the combination of a set of fundamental ideas, political practices, and material technologies. This does not include every idea held by actors or all technologies in use, but rather the subsets that relate to a particular field of political interaction. I will discuss each component in turn, highlighting the ways in which this conceptualization builds on existing approaches to institutions – particularly in key examples from international relations scholarship – but also brings together the three elements to form a novel, and useful, framework. In short, many existing conceptualizations incorporate ideas, some include practices (in a variety of forms), but few if any consider technology as a distinct institutional component. As will be explored below, this addition proves useful for making institutional analysis speak to a wider range of international relations theories and research programs.

Fundamental *ideas* – such as the nature of political rule and authority – give actors their identities and their notions of what they can or should do in light of their particular capabilities and relationships. Existing applications of historical institutionalism to international relations incorporate ideas as an element of institutions. Campbell (2004), for example, includes 'systems of meaning' alongside 'formal and informal rules' in his definition. Likewise, Holsti (2004, p. 20) defines institutions as 'ideas, practices, and norms', thus including ideas about how the world works, beliefs that serve as justifications for practices, and norms shaping what actors believe they should do.

Following recent applications of the logic of practice to international relations, *practices* are understood as 'socially meaningful patterns of action' (Adler & Pouliot, 2011, p. 6). By analytically separating out the ideational element of formal and informal rules (into the 'ideas' category), the practices that remain can be understood in this slightly narrower way. Yet there is a close relationship between these practices and related ideas: 'practices ... simultaneously embody, act out, and possibly reify background knowledge and discourse in and on the material world' (Adler & Pouliot, 2011, p. 6). Practices are both part of the process of interaction and part of the outcome produced by those interactions. Existing international relations definitions of institutions, again, incorporate some elements of this notion of practices, although not always in the same language. Campbell (2004) includes 'monitoring and enforcement mechanisms' in his definition, with those mechanisms being practices performed by actors involved in institutional creation, maintenance, and change. Holsti (2004) specifically includes 'patterned practices' as a key element defining institutions in the international system, presenting as an example the exchange of ambassadors among sovereign states.

Technologies, finally, are important because material capabilities, constraints, and incentives make certain types of actions likely or unlikely, possible or impossible. In addition, as is pointed out by an extensive literature from Science and Technology Studies, technologies are inevitably embedded in social and political relations (Sismondo, 2010). In the case of political institutions, there is a set of infrastructural, communication, and disciplinary technologies that define the institutional framework of political interaction. This is narrower than simply including all 'material constraints', because technologies are, by definition, manipulated, created, and purposively applied material tools – and that purposive application separates them from baseline material factors such as geography. The purposive nature of technological application, however, does not mean that these tools always serve only one purpose or have only one outcome; unintended consequences are common.

Many definitions of technology include not only material artefacts but also the ideas, practices, and beliefs that put those artefacts to use, that give meaning to those objects, and that thus shape their effects on political or social outcomes. That is undoubtedly a useful means of broadening the concept of technology, since it builds on the connection between social and technical systems. For analytical purposes, however, it is useful to distinguish between material technologies (i.e., systems of artefacts) and the related practices and ideas: the practices that rely on or construct those technologies and the ideas that give them meaning and are sometimes made possible by the technologies. In my concept of institutions, then, I incorporate those non-material 'technological' practices and ideas into the other two component features, distinct from material artefacts. This analytical distinction allows the concept to speak to a wider array of existing research programmes: that is, for theories that have defined technologies in terms of material artefacts, this concept of institutions allows their variables to be incorporated and, simultaneously, draws attention to the practices and ideas that define and implement the technologies and their effects. The analytical distinction in the definition, in short, might allow an incorporation of the non-material aspects of technology into a broader range of scholarship.

The integration of technology as its own element in defining institutions is a significant departure from the ways that institutions have been defined. As will be discussed below in terms of conceptualizing territory as an institution, however, technological factors have sometimes been incorporated into descriptions of particular institutions but without any clear theoretical or conceptual apparatus. Making that inclusion explicit, therefore, allows us to better consider the technological aspects of interaction.

The combination of these three factors constitutes a particular institution: a set of related ideas, practices, and technologies that are purposively put to work by actors and that simultaneously provide part of the structural frame within which actors operate. The three factors are connected not only by their co-constitution of institutions; each factor also interacts with the other two directly. Technologies render certain ideas imaginable, and ideas give meaning to technologies. Ideas constitute some of the essential practices that make up institutions, and practices legitimate – or undermine – particular ideas. Finally, the existence of certain practices can create demand for particular technologies or technological developments, while technologies provide part of the conditions of possibility for practices. None of the three is hierarchically primary, even though change may sometimes appear in one before the others.

This conceptualization of institutions – particularly the incorporation of material technologies as a distinct component – is a departure from the way in which institutions have been defined in scholarship from historical institutionalism. Yet, as Fioretos (2011, pp. 371–372) points out, historical institutionalism is fundamentally about the role of temporality and sequence in the processes of institutional creation, stasis, and change, rather than being defined by a particular definition of institutions. As will be demonstrated below, this article's three-part definition of institutions can be used to examine those very processes of institutional change that historical institutionalist scholarship has outlined. Moreover, the inclusion of technology is essential for bringing those insights into international relations: technological factors are embedded in a wide range of international relations theories and approaches, even if they are not always directly addressed.[1] Thus, combining a new conceptualization of institutions with theories of change from historical institutionalism will speak to diverse research programmes in international relations.

TERRITORY AS AN INSTITUTION

Although nearly any field of interaction in international politics can be defined in these institutional terms, not all institutions are equally important or consequential. As Holsti (2004, p. 25) notes, there are both foundational institutions and procedural institutions in international politics, and one of the most important foundational institutions is territory. Conceptualizing territory as an institution is not meant to replace existing definitions; instead it allows us to highlight certain aspects of how we define territory, helps us think about issues like territorial change or territorial politics, and enables the application of arguments across disciplinary boundaries.

While many international relations studies of territory or territorial issues do not explicitly define territory (beyond a basic operationalization as a spatial area on the earth's surface), political geography has seen extensive discussion of the concept. Many of the existing definitions from geographers share a few central characteristics, tending to agree that territory as we know it is a relatively modern – and thus not universal – phenomenon that serves as part of a political strategy of control. (I am building here on examples that speak particularly to my institutional approach.)

Discussion often begins with influential early definitions, from Gottman (1973) and Sack (1986), for example. Sack (1986, p. 5) defines territoriality as 'a primary geographical expression of social power' and 'a powerful geographic strategy to control people by controlling area'. Territory is strategic and political: examples of territoriality involve 'the attempt by an individual or group to affect, influence, or control people, phenomena, and relationships, by delimiting and asserting control over a geographic area' (Sack, 1986, p. 19). Finally, 'territoriality is always socially or humanly constructed in a way that physical distance is not' (Sack, 1986, p. 30).

Among numerous discussions of territory and territoriality that have followed, the work of Stuart Elden (particularly 2010, 2013) has been broadly influential. According to Elden, 'the term *territory* became the way used to describe a particular and historically limited set of practices and ideas about the relation between place and power' (2013, pp. 6–7). Thus, the key question becomes, 'what is the relation between place and power?' (2013, p. 10). Territorial strategies of control depend on material, ideational, and institutional tools and techniques (Elden, 2010, p. 804). Elden, in other words, incorporates technological elements, albeit in a different fashion from what I am proposing as the material technological aspect of institutions (more on this distinction below).

Other discussions from geographers reflect similar concerns. For example, Painter notes that 'territory can best be understood as the effect of networked relations' (2010, p. 1093). This relates to my argument that territory is an institution, resulting from the relationships among particular ideas, practices, and technologies. Painter argues that the relevant practices that produce territory are 'socio-technical', thus bringing technology into the concept as well. While Painter does not explicitly highlight the role of ideas, he does note that earlier theorists have incorporated ideational elements (such as Michel Lussault's emphasis on 'systems of ideas' [Painter, 2010, p. 1102]). In short, political geographers have conceptualized territory as a complex political strategy involving ideas, practices, and techniques. It is on this foundation that I build my definition of territory as an institution, below.

In international relations, on the other hand, territory is a central factor in numerous research programmes, but it is discussed very differently (especially in what could be labelled 'mainstream' international relations as it is practiced in the U.S.). Territory itself is rarely, if ever, examined conceptually or even defined explicitly. Studies of 'territorial disputes', for example, define the object of analysis simply in terms of conflicting claims over a clearly demarcated piece of land or conflict over where a boundary should fall (e.g., Huth, 1996). This has allowed these studies to generate important findings on the sources of military conflict, but it prevents them from engaging with what makes boundaries so consequential or why territory – understood in this way as a bounded space – is such a prevalent source of international conflict. Likewise, Krasner's (1999, 2001) examination of state sovereignty as 'organized hypocrisy' distinguishes among four different types of sovereignty. Yet, the territory in which these various types of sovereignty are exercised – or violated – is treated as a given, as the default background to political interaction.

These are productive research agendas that have yielded important findings, but the absence of direct interrogation of territory as a concept has made it difficult to bring them into conversation with the explicitly theoretical and conceptual work from political geography (Kadercan, 2015). In light of Elden's (2013) discussion of territory as a relationship between place and power, here I frame territory as an institution which shapes that relationship. The question then becomes: What are the ideas, practices, and technologies that constitute the relationship between place and power?[2]

First, what are the fundamental *ideas* that create the particularly territorial relationship between place and power? Elden (2013) finds the 'birth' of territory in ideas appearing from the early 1600s on, defining jurisdiction as permanently attached to a spatial area. That notion built on new ideas about space in general:

> the notion of space that emerges in the scientific revolution is defined by *extension*. Territory can be understood as the political counterpart to this notion of calculating space, and can therefore be thought of as the *extension of the state's power*. (Elden, 2013, p. 322, emphasis in the original)

In the relatively limited treatments of territory from international relations, ideas such as the exclusivity of rule play a key role (e.g., Holsti, 2004). Put most simply, therefore, the institution of territory incorporates ideas from the notion of space as an extension and the exclusivity of rule within those spaces.

Territorial *practices* include a number of both domestic and international practices, including those involved in how territories are defined and acted upon. Most fundamental are borders and bordering practices (e.g., Andreas, 2000; Gavrilis, 2008; Newman & Paasi, 1998). For one, modern state borders involve a series of sequential practices: identification or allocation, delimitation, and demarcation. Thus, for example, Kadercan (2015) posits 'the demarcation process' as one of the three dimensions of territory. Yet, as border studies scholars have pointed out, the practice of bordering continues long after the 'official' end with demarcation, as the way in which control is effected at the boundary takes on different forms and evolves over time.

In addition to definitional practices like bordering, there are numerous practices involved in how political actors use territory, respond to territory, and are shaped by territorial concerns. Holsti (2004), for example, lists territorial practices such as conquest, partition, sale, exchange, and so on, noting that some of these practices (such as the sale of territory or its exchange through dynastic marriage) have gone from being common in previous eras to being effectively barred in the twentieth century. Again, the inclusion of bordering and other practices allows us to incorporate domestic and international practices into the analysis of territory as an institution. These practices connect with territorial ideas: practices involve the implementation of those ideas into action and simultaneously shape and are shaped by those ideas.

The *technologies* of territory as an institution are the material tools used to make territory real. This includes the tools needed (or perceived to be needed) to implement territorial practices, as well as tools that are demanded, or given new meanings and uses, by territorial ideas. Existing concepts of territory often incorporate technology, even technological artefacts, but rarely in this explicit way. Particular technologies are sometimes discussed under the rubric of practices, or as outcomes, but not as their own distinct category. For example, one of Kadercan's (2015) three dimensions of territory is 'geography', which he argues is not a given but is altered by technologies (such as transportation or communication technologies). Besides technologies that shape the constraints of geography, other technological systems incorporated into the institution of territory include disciplinary and surveillance technologies and the tools of resource extraction.

For a specific example, consider mapping, a technology closely integrated into the institution of territory. The material artefacts involved in mapping – both the maps themselves and the tools involved in producing them, such as surveying, measurement, printing, and distribution tools – give a particular structure to territory (Harley, 2001; Pickles, 2004; Wood, 2010). The definition and operationalization of territory as spatial expanses separated by lines depends on the ability to negotiate, measure, and draw those lines, on maps and on the ground. The technological tools available thus make certain practices possible, but they also can help to constitute particular ideas, such as the notion, visualized in a standard political map, that the entire land surface of the globe should be divided among exclusive state claims. Cartographic tools, of course, are produced and used through processes whose conditions of possibility are shaped by ideas and practices – maps themselves do not provide deterministic constraints or incentives. Thus, although Holsti (2004, pp. 79–80) includes a discussion of mapping when describing territoriality, his theory of institutions as ideas, norms, and practices leaves it unclear where mapping should fit. It is, in part, a practice, but it is also closely integrated with ideas, and there are constraints imposed by the capabilities of the material artefacts that are distinct from practices or ideas and norms. Holsti's analysis of mapping is thus almost entirely in terms of these techniques as *enabling* certain aspects of territoriality, which is certainly part of the story but which then leaves out the *mutually constitutive* interaction between artefacts, their uses, and the ideas that drive those uses.

The inclusion of technologies as a distinct component of the institution of territory builds on, but takes a different approach from, Elden's argument that territory *itself* serves as a 'political technology', a set of material tools and legal and institutional techniques (2010, 2013, pp. 16–17). Elden's argument does not discount the role of material artifacts; instead it simply emphasizes the broader context of technology as technique. Yet, I have a particular goal in mind in separating out the material artefact side of technology (as 'technologies') from the techniques that are made possible by and make use of those artefacts (as 'practices'). This distinction makes it easier to connect with mainstream international relations scholarship and thus offer a means of facilitating a deeper cross-disciplinary conversation. Quantitative studies in international relations that take on technology, for example, are very much focused on technology as systems of artefacts with particular effects on political outcomes.[3] My definition speaks directly to this kind of approach, while also bringing in the broader context of those material technologies (in practices and ideas) in a way that builds on the work of political geographers and others. So, technology is a material factor, but one whose meanings, importance, and impact are shaped by ideas and practices.

In sum, the institution of territory is constituted by a collection of interrelated ideas, practices, and technologies. Key ideas include the ideal of mutually exclusive, linearly bounded authority and norms such as territorial integrity and non-violation of borders. The practices of territory involve the set of patterned actions surrounding borders and the implementation and maintenance of control over a delimited space. Finally, the relevant technologies include infrastructure, transportation, and communication technologies that make possible those practices.

The three elements not only constitute the institution of territory, they also connect to each other in complex ways. For example, bordering practices are made possible by mapping and the infrastructural ability to enforce those delimitations, but the changing evolution of border practices has also created demand for new or different technologies for representing and enforcing those borders. Likewise with ideas: evolution in norms may result from changes in practices, or it could itself force a change in those practices when an exogenously driven normative change occurs.

APPLYING THE INSTITUTIONAL DEFINITION OF TERRITORY

This institutional conceptualization provides a new lens through which to examine topics relating to territory and territoriality. By incorporating ideas, practices, and technologies but keeping them analytically distinct, we are able to build upon a variety of theorizations that have focused primarily on only one of the three. Additionally, the mutual implication of territorial design processes at different levels can be directly examined with this conceptualization (Atzili and Kadercan, 2017). For example, system-wide changes in ideas or technologies may interact with different domestic practices in terms of the implementation of territorial control, bordering, and so on. In other words, this three-part institutional concept of territory offers a new means of addressing the 'territorial trap' identified by Agnew (1994): the way in which international relations scholarship has assumed the bounded, exclusive form of spatial political control of the modern state as the only possible framework, constraining the way in which international relations then approaches major questions. Distinguishing among the three component parts of the institution of territory helps to emphasize the variety of potential ideas, practices, and technologies involved in spatial political claims and control where territory merely represents one specific combination. Below, I explore the application of this concept in two domains: (1) territorial conflict in international relations; and (2) historical and contemporary change in territory and territoriality.

Territorial Conflict

The study of territorial conflict in international relations is an expansive research agenda, building on the observation that disputes over territory have played a role in the vast majority of armed conflicts in the modern era. Influential early works relied on a cross-national quantitative approach, focusing on why some disputes over territory result in military conflict and why others do not (e.g., Goertz & Diehl, 1992; Huth, 1996). Territory is rarely defined explicitly and is instead treated as a spatial expanse, often measured in terms of surface area, within which reside particular resources, populations, strategic advantages, or symbolic attachments. States then dispute control over these spatial expanses, in some cases using military force. This conceptualization also appears in detailed case studies. Fravel (2008), for example, examines the territorial disputes of China and considers how the Chinese state has dealt with different types of disputes in different ways. The territories under dispute are measured in terms of square kilometers and compared in terms of their salience.

Yet, different territories might exhibit different collections of ideas (such as ideas about homelands), practices (defence, settlement, and so on), and technologies (the degree to which the territories are mapped or linked by infrastructure). Separating out the examination of territory in this way might help distinguish between different aspects of territory and how, separately or together, they relate to conflict. For example, China has responded differently to disputes over islands than to contested land boundaries (Fravel, 2008); is this related to the different ideas, practices, or technologies involved in constituting these different forms of territorial claim?

More generally, are there certain ideas that are linked to conflict? If so, is that only in the presence or absence of certain practices or technologies? The notion of 'homeland' territory, for example, plays a central role in some territorial disputes (e.g., Toft, 2003), and the definition of what is or is not a homeland is a product of particular ideas, instantiated then in specific practices. Likewise with technologies like mapping, as Hassner (2006/2007, p. 125) points out: mapping a disputed boundary can make the conflict more intractable. This line of questioning can enable us to consider the interactions between different dynamics of territorial conflict by breaking down territory's different aspects rather than just listing its particular economic, strategic, or symbolic elements.

Territorial Change

In addition to rethinking specific empirical topics that take territory as a causal factor, the study of territory itself – particularly historical and contemporary changes in territory – can be re-examined using the three-part institutional definition. By taking an institutional approach, different modes of change in the institution of territory can be considered, including the often overlooked ways in which technologies create and maintain territorial institutions. Moreover, historical institutionalism provides a variety of concepts of gradual institutional change, concepts that may be usefully applied to the transformation of territorial ideas, practices, and technologies. These include 'displacement' or the removal of existing rules and the introduction of new ones; 'layering' or the introduction of new rules on top of or alongside existing ones; 'drift' or the changed impact of existing rules due to shifts in the environment; and 'conversion' or the changed enactment of existing rules due to their strategic redeployment (Fioretos, Falleti, & Sheingate, 2015, p. 13; building on Mahoney & Thelen, 2010). All of these include both purposive institutional creation and the possibility of unintended institutional consequences and the persistence of particular institutions beyond their 'functional' purpose (Atzili and Kadercan, 2017).

For any institutional change, one or more of the component elements may exhibit a particular type of evolution, but not all of them have to do so simultaneously. New technological capabilities may be layered on top of old ones, leading to an eventual transformation in the overall institutional framework. Or political practices may be subject to institutional drift over time, with what is ostensibly the same practice taking on a fundamentally new meaning as the technologies and ideas relating to it change.

Unless we break down territory and consider all its components, we may end up explaining the origins of one feature of territoriality without explaining the entirety. Thus, for example, many explanations that rely on strategic logic to explain the shift to territorial statehood, or even to territorial politics in general, explain only the basic notion of claiming some control over a place or space, without accounting for the particularities of modern territoriality. For instance, Johnson and Toft (2013/14) put forward a provocative argument for an evolutionary explanation of political territoriality. Territorial behaviours are common among animals, suggesting 'evolutionary "convergence" on a tried and tested strategic solution to a common environmental challenge' (p. 9). Thus, territorial behaviours are 'soft-wired' into humans, making territoriality a strategy that will be applied, not in a single fixed form, but in a way that is 'responsive to prevailing conditions' (p. 11).

Biological explanations for human territoriality have been critiqued by many scholars (e.g., Elden, 2010, p. 802; Kadercan, 2015, p. 129), but, with the institutional definition of territory, we can examine those explanations from a new angle. Biological theories explain only one part of the institution of territory rather than the specific form (ideas, practices, and technologies) that constitutes territory today. Johnson and Toft, for example, note that the literature from biology on animal territoriality 'has shifted from a focus on "territories" to "home ranges," which emphasize frequently used space rather than exclusive areas that are "fenced off" to others' (2014/15, p. 18). Yet that 'fencing off' is one of the central practices of modern territoriality, a feature that distinguishes this form of spatial political claim from others, such as overlapping frontiers or nomadic movement (Ruggie, 1993). Thus this is more of an explanation for general spatial claims than for the boundary-focused ideas and practices of territoriality – and it is the combination of the specific ideas, practices, and technologies of territory that give it power and influence over behaviours and outcomes.

Other explanations for the origins of the territorial aspect of statehood can also benefit from being reframed through the institutional approach. In particular, distinguishing among the three elements not only can help us rethink the way in which each element may change independently but also can highlight the connections among them. For example, a number of studies have emphasized particular technologies such as mapping in the origins of statehood (e.g., Biggs, 1999; Branch, 2014; Neocleous, 2003; Steinberg, 2005; Strandsbjerg, 2008). In the historical shift to modern mapping, which began in the sixteenth century, new techniques and mapping systems were put to use but without immediately displacing older representational practices. Mapping was more than a material tool, however, because it served as a means of representing, and thus understanding, the nature of political rule. Thus, political ideas and practices gradually changed in ways that fit with the new representations – and in turn continued to alter those representations – culminating in the implementation of linear demarcated boundaries between territories. Each element of the institution of territory can change independently, and each has particular dynamics that then affect the overall course of institutional change.

By the late eighteenth century, the foundational ideas, practices, and technologies of territoriality had come together as a basic framework. The institutional approach to territory then allows us to re-examine some of the subsequent transformations in territoriality: the growth of nationalism in the nineteenth century, the consolidation of territorial integrity as a fundamental norm in the mid-twentieth century, and the possibility of change or rescaling of territory today.

Nineteenth-century nationalism altered international politics, including the role of territory (Mayall, 1990). Which of the ideas, practices, and technologies of territory did nationalism change? In terms of ideas, the normative justifications for territorial claims and the norms about what goals territory was meant to serve changed fundamentally. Territories went from being the property of rulers, used for resource extraction, strategic benefits, or symbolic prestige, to being homelands, tied fundamentally to the imagined communities of nationhood. Yet other ideas did not change: territory as a measured, demarcated spatial expanse persisted in spite of the dramatic transformation of the normative framework. As Holsti (2004) points out, many of the procedural practices of territory thus changed during this era, as the practices of exchanging or selling pieces of land between states became less normatively acceptable in an international system in which national territory was held sacred. But bordering practices changed less in their actual content than in their importance – securing borders and preventing territorial 'violations' were not practices that were invented in the era of nationalism; they simply became much more consequential. And regarding technologies, nationalism did little to change the overall trajectory of gradual evolution in mapping, infrastructure, and control technologies, nor did it affect the strengthening of surveillance and direct territorial control.

In the twentieth century, one of the most dramatic changes to the international system's territorial structure was the consolidation of the 'territorial integrity norm' (Zacher, 2001). This normative framework delegitimizes conquest and forcible boundary movements and favours maintaining status quo boundaries. This obviously involves ideational change at the level of the creation and dissemination of a new norm, but it has also involved change in practices (Holsti, 2004). Again, however, these changes in certain norms and practices happen alongside the persistence of others. Borders, for example, can no longer be moved as easily, but the practices surrounding what a border is and how it should be enforced remained unchanged by the post-1945 focus on territorial integrity. Similar to the growth of nationalism in the nineteenth century, there was significant change in normative ideas but little change in the constitutive ideas of territory.

Change transpired in practices about how often and easily boundaries can be moved, but not in how borders are enforced. And the technological aspects of the institution of territory continued to evolve without dramatic transformation.

By the end of the twentieth century, more significant changes to the territorial structure of the international system began to appear. Unlike the preceding changes relating to nationalism or territorial integrity, this de-territorialization or re-scaling of territoriality could involve changes to fundamental ideas and practices and could build upon and reinforce revolutionary – rather than evolutionary – changes in technologies. The literature on globalization and the challenge to (state) territoriality is vast; here I will simply note the way that the institutional definition of territory might give us a new lens for thinking about these changes, particularly as they relate to earlier shifts.

For example, Sassen's (2006) explanation of political structures as assemblages of territory, authority, and rights can be expanded by interrogating the territorial element as an institution. How do the changing ideas, practices, and technologies of territory intersect with the possible transformations in authority and rights? Territoriality is being 'unbundled' in institutional innovations such as the European Union (e.g., Ruggie, 1993). Certain ideas of territory are being altered, in particular, the exclusivity of ideal-typical sovereign statehood, but others remain unchanged: the delineation of authority by spatial jurisdictions is still the main principle at work, even though the scale of different domains has been altered. That is, certain authorities remain at the domestic level but others have been scaled up to be EU-wide, yet all of them remain defined by the territorial delimitation of jurisdiction. Practices have followed suit: for example, the at-the-boundary practices involved in bordering have disappeared between some EU members, but they have remained in place at the EU's external boundaries. (This institutional persistence of bordering as a practice has made it easy to re-impose some controls between EU member states in the face of the migration crisis.) And the technologies of state territoriality are not fundamentally changed by this rescaling *within* ideas and practices.

Yet boundaries – composed of particular ideas, practices, and technologies – may be undergoing other changes that do constitute a transformation of a key element of territoriality. On the one hand, the idea of a boundary has been extraordinarily resistant to change. Even in circumstances where borders are operationalized in much more complex ways, the ideal-typical notion of a clean line separating exclusive authority claims continues to dominate. The 'map image' of the bordered state remains nearly hegemonic, perhaps because of the persistent socialization through standard depictions in classrooms and other settings (Agnew, 2008, p. 185; Migdal, 2004, p. 12).

Yet the practices of bordering have come to vary widely. They have always diverged from the ideal of clear and absolute control within lines, but they may be doing so in new ways today. As Agnew (2008, p. 184) notes, boundaries are practiced throughout the territory and beyond: 'Rather than taking place only at borders on a map, bordering practices are much more widely diffused geographically', to airports, workplaces, and so on. Thus there is a tension between the ideal of a border existing only at the linear boundary and the actual implementation of bordering in practices throughout – and often beyond – the state's territory. Some borders, for example, are clearly more porous to economic flows, although the level of surveillance may be increasing even on the more open borders.

Finally, after several centuries of gradual improvement, the technologies of bordering have recently begun to alter dramatically. For most of the nineteenth and twentieth centuries, bordering technologies evolved but did not change in fundamental goals or orientations. Boundaries were negotiated, delimited, and mapped using sophisticated surveying techniques and were demarcated with physical markers such as ditches or stones. Defence and surveillance technologies gradually evolved, as military and other technological capabilities made easier the observation and defence of boundaries.

In recent decades, however, more dramatic transformations have appeared. For example, mapping as a collection of technologies and practices has been fundamentally reshaped by digitization

(Crampton, 2010), with potentially dramatic implications for boundaries. Boundary delimitations increasingly rely on geographic information systems (GIS) and other digital mapping tools, which provide a number of new capabilities for territorial negotiations in terms of measurement, visualization, and accuracy (Wood, 2000). At the 1999 negotiations for the Dayton Peace Accords, for example, new three-dimensional 'flyover' visualization systems provided much-needed support for efforts to draw a new boundary between the two new Bosnian territories (Johnson, 1999). The ability to display and manipulate multiple layers of spatial information, in extraordinary detail, may enable more complex bargains to be struck, with the potential to draw something other than a linear boundary between two exclusive territorial claims. In other words, while paper mapping technologies were a key constitutive element in the emergence and persistence of linearly defined territory, the very different spatial depictions and relations made possible by digital tools may create the conditions of possibility for new forms of spatial authority.

The possible restructuring of the existing institution of territory through technological change goes beyond mapping, of course, as any number of rapidly developing technical systems could be incorporated into – and thus alter – existing ideas, practices, and technologies of territory. Drones and other unmanned surveillance and weapons systems, for example, are creating new spatial relationships of political control and authority, both in warzones and on peaceful but securitized boundaries. In other words, a technology like drones does not simply operate *within* existing territories, it also creates new types of territorial and spatial relations (Williams, 2015, p. 101). In short, how states or other political organizations 'see' their territory is reshaped by changes to the technological component of the political institution of territory (Scott, 1998).

CONCLUSION

Conceptualizing territory as an institution, made up of an interconnected set of ideas, practices, and technologies, offers a new lens through which to examine key processes and outcomes relating to territory. In particular, it may help to promote cross-disciplinary dialogue among approaches that, typically, have not used the same frameworks and thus have been unable to converse. Theoretical development in political geography and other fields could benefit from incorporating empirical findings from international relations. Likewise, ongoing research programmes in international relations on topics such as territorial conflict could be strengthened by engaging with political geography and its more sophisticated conceptual and theoretical examination of territory itself. By analytically distinguishing among the ideas, practices, and technologies of territory, these literatures may be able to operationalize different aspects of territory more directly, rather than treating territory itself as a spatial container defined by surface area and encompassing particular demographic, strategic, economic, or symbolic resources or interests.

Moving forward, this institutional concept can usefully engage with existing and ongoing discussions of particular aspects of territory and territoriality, such as borders and bordering, surveillance and discipline, and militarized conflict. For each topic, the institutional definition provides new leverage through the application of models of institutional change such as layering, drift, or conversion. This would be an important addition to today's multidisciplinary discussion of territory and its transformation and rescaling.

ACKNOWLEDGEMENTS

The author wishes to thank Boaz Atzili, Burak Kadercan, and the editors and anonymous reviewers for helpful comments and suggestions.

NOTES

1. This includes obvious cases like offensive versus defensive technologies in security studies (e.g., Lieber, 2000), as well as examples like Wendt's (1999, p. 111) incorporation of technology as one of the three 'brute material forces' at the foundation of his 'rump materialist' theory.

2. Again, theorists have addressed these elements separately, but not in this particular framework. For example, Elden's *The birth of territory* sets out primarily to examine the origins of the *idea* of territory, less so its practices (as noted by Minca et al., 2015).

3. See, for example, the recent special issue of the *Journal of Peace Research* on 'Communication, Technology, and Political Conflict' (Vol. 52(3), 2015).

REFERENCES

Adler, E., & Pouliot, V. (Eds.). (2011). *International practices*. Cambridge: Cambridge University Press.

Agnew, J. (1994). The territorial trap: The geographical assumptions of international relations theory. *Review of International Political Economy, 1*(1), 53–80.

Agnew, J. (2008). Borders on the mind: Re-framing border thinking. *Ethics & Global Politics, 1*(4), 175–191.

Andreas, P. (2000). *Border games: Policing the U.S.-Mexico divide*. Ithaca, NY: Cornell University Press.

Atzili, B., & Kadercan, B. (2017). Territorial designs and international politics: The diverging constitution of space and boundaries. *Territory, Politics, Governance*. doi:10.1080/21622671.2016.1266962

Biggs, M. (1999). Putting the State on the map: Cartography, territory, and European State formation. *Comparative Studies in Society and History, 41*(2), 374–405.

Branch, J. (2014). *The cartographic State: Maps, territory, and the origins of sovereignty*. Cambridge: Cambridge University Press.

Campbell, J. L. (2004). *Institutional change and globalization*. Princeton, NJ: Princeton University Press.

Crampton, J. W. (2010). *Mapping: A critical introduction to cartography and GIS*. Malden, MA: Wiley-Blackwell.

Elden, S. (2010). Land, terrain, territory. *Progress in Human Geography, 34*(6), 799–817.

Elden, S. (2013). *The birth of territory*. Chicago, IL: University of Chicago Press.

Fioretos, O. (2011). Historical institutionalism in international relations. *International Organization, 65*(2), 367–399.

Fioretos, O., Falleti, T. G., & Sheingate, A. (2015). Historical institutionalism in political science. In O. Fioretos, T. G. Falleti, & A. Sheingate (Eds.), *The Oxford handbook of historical institutionalism* (pp. 3–28). Oxford: Oxford University Press.

Fravel, M. T. (2008). *Strong borders, secure nation: Cooperation and conflict in China's territorial disputes*. Princeton, NJ: Princeton University Press.

Gavrilis, G. (2008). *The dynamics of interstate boundaries*. Cambridge: Cambridge University Press.

Goertz, G., & Diehl, P. F. (1992). *Territorial changes and international conflict*. London: Routledge.

Gottman, J. (1973). *The significance of territory*. Charlottesville: University Press of Virginia.

Harley, J. B. (2001). *The new nature of maps: Essays in the history of cartography*. Baltimore, MD: Johns Hopkins University Press.

Hassner, R. E. (2006/2007). The path to intractability: Time and the entrenchment of territorial disputes. *International Security, 31*(3), 107–138.

Holsti, K. J. (2004). *Taming the sovereigns: Institutional change in international politics*. Cambridge: Cambridge University Press.

Huth, P. K. (1996). *Standing your ground: Territorial disputes and international conflict*. Ann Arbor: University of Michigan Press.

Johnson, D. D. P., & Toft, M. D. (2013/14). Grounds for war: The evolution of territorial conflict. *International Security, 38*(3), 7–38.

Johnson, R. G. (1999). *Negotiating the Dayton Peace accords through digital maps*. USIP Virtual Diplomacy Report, 25 February 1999.

Kadercan, B. (2015). Triangulating territory: A case for pragmatic interaction between political science, political geography, and critical IR. *International Theory*, 7(1), 125–161.

Krasner, S. D. (1999). *Sovereignty: Organized hypocrisy*. Princeton, NJ: Princeton University Press.

Krasner, S. D. (2001). Rethinking the sovereign state model. *Review of International Studies*, 27, 17–42.

Lieber, K. A. (2000). Grasping the technological peace: The Offense-defense balance and international security. *International Security*, 25(1), 71–104.

Mahoney, J., & Thelen, K. (2010). A theory of gradual institutional change. In J. Mahoney, & K. Thelen (Eds.), *Explaining institutional change: Ambiguity, agency, and power* (pp. 1–37). Cambridge: Cambridge University Press.

Mayall, J. (1990). *Nationalism and international society*. Cambridge: Cambridge University Press.

Migdal, J. S. (2004). Mental maps and virtual checkpoints: Struggles to construct and maintain State and social boundaries. In J. S. Migdal (Eds.), *Boundaries and belonging: States and societies in the struggle to shape identities and local practices* (pp. 3–23). Cambridge: Cambridge University Press.

Minca, C., Crampton, J. W., Bryan, J., Fall, J. J., Murphy, A. B., Paasi, A., Elden, S. (2015). Reading Stuart Elden's the birth of territory. *Political Geography*, 46, 93–101.

Neocleous, M. (2003). Off the map: On violence and cartography. *European Journal of Social Theory*, 6(4), 409–425.

Newman, D., & Paasi, A. (1998). Fences and neighbors in the postmodern world: Boundary narratives in political geography. *Progress in Human Geography*, 22(2), 186–207.

Painter, J. (2010). Rethinking territory. *Antipode*, 42(5), 1090–1118.

Pickles, J. (2004). *A history of spaces: Cartographic reason, mapping, and the geo-coded world*. New York, NY: Routledge.

Ruggie, J. G. (1993). Territoriality and beyond: Problematizing modernity in international relations. *International Organization*, 47(1), 139–174.

Sack, R. D. (1986). *Human territoriality: Its theory and history*. Cambridge: Cambridge University Press.

Sassen, S. (2006). *Territory, authority, rights*. Princeton, NJ: Princeton University Press.

Scott, J. C. (1998). *Seeing like a State: How certain schemes to improve the human condition have failed*. New Haven, CT: Yale University Press.

Sismondo, S. (2010). *An introduction to science and technology studies, second edition*. Malden, MA: Blackwell.

Steinberg, P. E. (2005). Insularity, sovereignty, and statehood: The representation of islands on portolan charts and the construction of the territorial state. *Geografiska Annaler*, 87, 253–265.

Strandsbjerg, J. (2008). The cartographic production of territorial space: Mapping and State formation in Early Modern Denmark. *Geopolitics*, 13(2), 335–358.

Thelen, K., & Steinmo, S. (1992). Historical institutionalism in comparative politics. In S. Steinmo, K. Thelen, & F. Longstreth (Eds.), *Structuring politics: Historical institutionalism in comparative analysis* (pp. 1–32). Cambridge: Cambridge University Press.

Toft, M. D. (2003). *The geography of ethnic violence: Identity, interests, and the indivisibility of territory*. Princeton, NJ: Princeton University Press.

Wendt, A. (1999). *Social theory of international politics*. Cambridge: Cambridge University Press.

Williams, J. (2015). Distant intimacy: Space, drones, and just war. *Ethics & International Affairs*, 29(1), 93–110.

Wood, D. (2010). *Rethinking the power of maps*. New York, NY: The Guilford Press.

Wood, W. B. (2000). GIS as a tool for territorial negotiation. *IBRU Boundary and Security Bulletin*, Autumn, 8(3), 72–79.

Zacher, M. W. (2001). The territorial integrity norm: International boundaries and the use of force. *International Organization*, 55(2), 215–250.

Methodological challenges in the study of stateless nationalist territorial claims

Harris Mylonas and Nadav Shelef

ABSTRACT

Methodological challenges in the study of stateless nationalist territorial claims. *Territory, Politics, Governance*. The territory claimed by stateless nationalist movements can change over time. Following a review of prominent explanations, this article addresses some of the more general methodological challenges involved in studying change in the territorial claims of stateless nationalist movements. It draws attention to the analytical distinction between the origin of territorial claims and their consequent changes. Building on this distinction, it also demonstrates the advantages of using a multidimensional understanding of change in territorial claims focusing on its timing, direction, and process. Then it turns to a discussion highlighting the tradeoffs in the choice of the unit of analysis as well as common problems in case selection, i.e., unjustifiable asynchronous comparisons and anachronism. The article concludes by laying out a roadmap for future research in this area.

摘要

研究无国家国族主义者的领土宣称的方法论挑战。*Territory, Politics, Governance*. 无国家国族主义运动所宣称的领土随着时间而改变。在回顾重要的解释之后，本文将应对研究无国家国族主义运动的领土宣称变迁中涉及的若干更为一般性的方法论挑战。本文关注领土宣称及其所导致的变迁之间的分析性区别。本文根据此一区别，同时证实多面向理解领土宣称的变迁，并聚焦其时间、方向与过程的优势。本文接着转向强调选择分析单位中的权衡以及案例选择中的共同问题之讨论，例如无法合理化的非同期比较与时代错误。本文于结论中，为本领域的未来研究开展了蓝图。

RÉSUMÉ

Problemes methodologiques dans l'etude de revendications territoriales nationalistes sans Etat. *Territory, Politics, Governance*. Le territoire revendiqué par des mouvements nationalistes sans État peut évoluer au fil du temps. À la suite d'un examen d'éminentes explications, le présent article se penche sur certains des problèmes méthodologiques les plus généraux que comporte l'étude de l'évolution des revendications territoriales de mouvements nationalistes. Il attire l'attention du lecteur sur la distinction analytique entre l'origine des revendications territoriales et les changements qui en découlent. En s'appuyant sur cette distinction, il démontre en outre les avantages de l'emploi d'une approche multidimensionnelle pour le changement dans les revendications territoriales, en ce concentrant sur le calendrier, l'orientation, et le processus. Il passe ensuite à une discussion soulignant les compromis dans le choix de l'unité d'analyse, ainsi que les problèmes communs dans le choix des cas, p.ex. comparaisons asynchrones injustifiables et anachronisme. Le présent article se termine en dressant une feuille de route pour de futures recherches dans ce domaine.

RESUMEN

Cambios metodologicos en el estudio de las reclamaciones territoriales por parte de movimientos nacionales apatridas. *Territory, Politics, Governance*. El territorio reclamado por los movimientos nacionales apátridas puede cambiar con el tiempo. Tras una revisión de explicaciones destacadas, en este artículo abordamos algunos de los problemas metodológicos más generales que implica el estudio de los cambios en las reclamaciones territoriales por parte de movimientos nacionales apátridas. Ponemos de relieve la distinción analítica entre el origen de las reclamaciones territoriales y sus consiguientes cambios. A partir de esta distinción, también demostramos las ventajas de utilizar un concepto multidimensional del cambio en las reclamaciones territoriales centrándonos en su momento, dirección y proceso. Luego iniciamos un debate en el que se resaltan las concesiones al elegir la unidad de análisis, así como los problemas habituales en la selección de casos, es decir, comparaciones asincrónicas y anacronismos injustificables. Concluimos este artículo trazando las líneas generales de futuros estudios en este campo.

INTRODUCTION

The control of a national territory is the sine qua non of nationalist movements. Yet, despite the importance of territory for nationalists, the territorial scope of the nation–state desired by stateless nationalist movements can change over time. For example, some Tibetan nationalists initially omitted the Kham region from the state they sought in the interwar period, yet after the 1950s, they widely included it in their territorial claims (McGranahan, 2010, pp. 39–45). The main branch of the Zionist movement changed what it considered to be the 'Land of Israel' in the period before it achieved independence (Shelef, 2007). In joint work, we have also shown that the areas mapped by both the Palestinian Fatah and the Macedonian Revolutionary Organization (MRO) likewise changed over time (Mylonas & Shelef, 2014).

This article explores some of the methodological challenges involved in the empirical study of 'the strategic logic of territorial designs'[1] of stateless nationalist movements. Doing so helps address some of the issues involved in bridging the gap Atzili and Kadercan (2017) identify between political geographers and political scientists interested in studying the role of territory in conflict. A contemporary political geographer might conceive of the stateless nationalist movements we study as counterhegemonic movements opposing dominating hegemonic powers (Ó Tuathail, 1996; Ó Tuathail & Agnew, 1992). Rather than focus on the conflict between the stateless nationalist movement and the state they challenge, we pay direct and explicit attention to the politics of territorial design by the stateless nationalist movements themselves. Doing so allows us to highlight the tradeoffs involved in various research strategies employed to ascertain the impact of those politics vis-à-vis other potential factors that could shape the resulting territorial vision of, in our case, stateless nationalist movements.

It is possible to extrapolate at least six plausible explanations for how changes in the scope of the territory claimed by stateless nationalist movements come about from the literature on nationalism, state-building, and territorial conflict. These literatures have highlighted factors such as domestic political contestation (Goddard, 2010; Mylonas & Shelef, 2014; Shelef, 2010), the external imposition of a new border (Anderson, 1991, pp. 52–53; Carter & Goemans, 2011; Goemans, 2006; Roeder, 2007), adaptation to changes in the ethnic composition of territory following significant demographic shifts (see, e.g., Greenfeld, 1992; Kaufmann, 1998; Saideman & Ayers, 2008; Smith, 1987; Toft, 2005), concessions made to the demands of external patrons (Mylonas, 2012), changes in the relative capacity of a stateless nationalist movement relative to the state it is challenging, and changes in the material value of the land in response to the discovery of valuable resources (Kelle, 2016). Elsewhere we provide a detailed discussion of each of these alternatives (Mylonas & Shelef, 2014; Shelef, 2010) and the tradeoffs between them. Table 1 summarizes these alternative explanations.

Our earlier work leverages the different expectations of these arguments with respect to the expected time, the process, and the direction of changes in territorial claims in order to disentangle the relative plausibility of these mechanisms for stateless movements in Israel, Palestine, and the Balkan Peninsula (Mylonas & Shelef, 2014; Shelef, 2010). We found that explanations rooted in domestic politics consistently provided the best explanation for how and why these movements changed the scope of the area they sought as their national state.

Table 1. A multidimensional dependent variable.

		Dimensions of the dependent variable		
	Mechanism	**Timing**	**Direction**	**Process**
1.	Response to domestic political challenges	Responding to a local political problem that requires modulation of the territorial claim	The new scope of the desired nation–state will conform to the political needs of the movement	Movement solving political problem
2.	Coordination on real new borders	Closely following the drawing of new international borders	The new scope of the desired nation–state will conform to new international border	All movements
3.	Adapting to ethnic geography	Closely following change in the geographic distribution of coethnics	Land newly populated with coethnics will be added. Land newly depopulated of co-ethnics will be excluded	All movements with the same definition of national membership
4.	Concession to external patron	Closely following change in a movement's patron or a patron's foreign policy	The new scope of the desired nation–state will conform to the patron's policy	All clients of the international patron
5.	Change in relative capacity	Closely following new information about the movement's relative strength vis-à-vis the state that is being challenged	As relative capacity increases, the desired scope of the nation–state will increase. As relative capacity decreases, the desired scope of the nation–state will decrease	Movement whose relative capacity changed
6.	New information about the land's value	Closely following new information about the material value of land	The desired scope of the nation–state should expand to include newly valued land	All movements

Here, we draw on this work to explore not the relative purchase of different explanations, per se, but the wider methodological challenges involved in studying stateless nationalist territorial claims. The study of territory and governance, as well as that of nationalist movements, is frequently characterized by the presence of competing explanations for a particular phenomenon of interest because the pace of theoretical development and hypothesis generation often outstrips the ability to evaluate these hypotheses and because the complexity of human interaction rarely provides unambiguous evidence that allows for the complete elimination of alternatives.

In what follows, we build on our earlier work and discuss solutions to the methodological problems scholars face when tackling such questions. In particular, we discuss the importance of parsing the dependent variable in order to maintain the advantages of using a multidimensional dependent variable while still facilitating empirical research. We also address the choices of unit of analysis and case selection.

CONCEPTUALIZATION OF THE DEPENDENT VARIABLE

Parsing the dependent variable: origins versus change

Any study of territorial claims has to cope with the legacy of the past, especially, as in the cases used by Mylonas and Shelef (2014), where imperial legacies play an important role in structuring the actors involved and their politics (Hajdarpašić, 2008; Hartmuth, 2008; Inalcik, 1996; Todorova, 1996; Yilmaz & Yosmaoglu, 2008). A variety of hypotheses related to territorial claims can be drawn from this literature. For example, it might be that nationalist movements base the extent of their territorial claims on prior imperial territorial divisions (Carter & Goemans, 2011). Roeder's (2007) segment state argument holds that subnational administrative borders often become interstate borders because these institutionally and politically semi-autonomous administrative units significantly lower the start-up costs for the nationalist elites that aspire to independence. In a complementary argument, Goemans (2006) shows that pre-existing borders, because they are widely known, can serve as focal points for the definition of the homeland. A similar argument about the role of prior administrative boundaries has also been made specifically in the Ottoman region (Jelavich & Jelavich, 1977). Indeed, most national rebellions in the Ottoman Empire sought control of specific Ottoman administrative centers. It may also be that the plans of imperial powers, such as Britain in Palestine and Russia or Austria-Hungary in the Balkans, shape the claims of stateless nationalist movements if these ideas are used in the constitution of the scope of their claims. However, such explanations are often challenged by the existence of multiple and competing imperial plans.

Another version of the legacy argument refers to territorial claims based on real or imagined borders of the nation's territory in the past and holds that future definitions of the homeland will be shaped by those past claims. Usually, this refers to a period back in time when the 'revived nation' had a specific set of borders that they are simply re-claiming. Clearly, such a hypothesis would be relevant only for national movements that have – or can devise – such a heritage.

While there is a lot of additional work to be done exploring the impact of historical legacies on territorial claims, Mylonas and Shelef (2014) opt for sidestepping the issue entirely. We distinguished between the *origins* of a territorial claim and consequent *changes* in the desired borders of the state articulated by stateless nationalist movements. This allowed us to focus on a smaller set of explanations since many of the time-invariant hypotheses that are clearly important for understanding the original scope of a movement's desired national state, such as legacies of prior administrative boundaries and real or imagined historical autonomy, could be bracketed. The empirical challenge, of course, is daunting since shifts in territorial claims are often masked because nationalist movements fear that revealing such information could undermine the movement's legitimacy. We discuss this issue in our conclusion.

A multidimensional understanding

Scholars often collapse multiple dimensions of their dependent variable into a dichotomous one. In other words, even when the conceptualization of a variable is rich it often gets reduced into a narrow proxy at the operationalization stage. Although there may be good reasons for choosing to do so, collapsing a multidimensional concept into a dichotomous choice comes at the cost of losing potentially valuable information and variation (Collier & Adcock, 1999). Similar choices plague explorations of change, both in general and in the particular context of change in the territorial claims of stateless nationalist movements.

Building on the pragmatic approach advocated by Collier and Adcock, we opt for maintaining the multidimensional character of change. We do so because the variation along the different dimensions provides analytical leverage for explaining why change takes place. Coding change in dichotomous terms (as either having taken place or not) might be useful in ascertaining whether or not change has taken place (especially in large-N contexts), but it is less helpful for explaining *why* it occurred.

We focus on three critical dimensions of change: its timing, direction, and process. Each potential explanation of change contains discrete, observable predictions for the timing, process, and direction of change in the territorial claims of stateless nationalist movements that were compared with the historical record (see Table 1). Any explanation that could account for all three components would be preferable to explanations that could explain either just the presence of change or fewer components because it sets a higher threshold for hypotheses testing. Moreover, this approach opens up the possibility that some hypotheses may be better at explaining certain parts of the variation of a multidimensional dependent variable than others.

For us, timing refers to when each explanation expects the process of change to begin and its completion (the point where the new view of the territory desired is dominant). Scholars in recent years have noted the importance of paying attention to issues of temporality in causal analyses. Grzymala-Busse (2011) usefully unpacks temporality into duration, tempo, acceleration, and timing. Indeed, nearly all the (usually implicit) explanations for how change in the territory desired by stateless nationalist movements takes place contain expectations about each of these aspects of temporality, especially the duration, tempo, and timing of change. Building on Grzymala-Busse's (2011) suggestions, disentangling the relative plausibility of alternative explanations of change requires making these (again, often implicit) expectations explicit and testing them against the historical record. As Grzymala-Busse's (2011, p. 1272) notes, 'specific causal mechanisms are more likely given certain temporal configurations, making some hypothesized causal mechanisms more plausible than others.'

Making the temporal expectations of alternative explanations explicit also has two implications for the kinds of research design and approach that we use to assess whether and how change in territorial aspirations takes place. First, as Grzymala-Busse (2011) exhorts us, the temporal dynamics of causal mechanisms need to be made explicit and measured in order to be analytically useful. Second, the analysis needs to encompass a sufficiently long historical *durée* in order to capture a potentially slow moving process that may govern the pattern of the variation under study. In other words, the period of observation used in the disaggregation of alternative mechanisms has to allow sufficient time to pass if we want to rule out, or rule in, particular explanations of change (see also, Mylonas, 2015, pp. 752–755; Pierson, 2000, pp. 150–151).

Beyond temporality as an important dimension of our dependent variable, we highlight direction and process. Our use of 'direction' refers to whether the territorial claim made by the stateless nationalist movement expands or contracts, and to what particular borderline. By 'process' we mean the expectation of an explanation about *who* undergoes change and whether the change is carried through consistently.

The utility of maintaining a multidimensional dependent variable for the process of hypothesis testing can be illustrated in the case of the transformation of Fatah's desired scope for its coveted nation–state and its acceptance of the partition of Mandatory Palestine. This change is commonly attributed to the results of the 1967 and 1973 wars. According to this explanation, these wars provided new information about the relative weakness of the Palestinians' Arab allies. Which, in turn, led to a re-evaluation of their relative capacity and a reluctant acceptance of Israel's existence (see, e.g., Al-Shuaibi, 1980; Ashrawi, 1995; Iyad, 1980).

This explanation reasonably accounts for the direction of the change in Fatah's claims, but does not fare as well in accounting for the timing and process. In terms of the timing of change, this explanation cannot account for why the change took place only after the 1973 war and not after the 1967 war, since the latter was a much more decisive victory for Israel, and a correspondingly less ambiguous source of information about Israeli strength. However, Fatah did not shift its territorial goals in response to the information provided by the 1967 war. Rather, in its wake, it doubled down on the claim of Palestine in its entirety and, in 1968, rebuffed a proposal to create a Palestinian state in part of the territory even as an intermediate step. This was not just a bureaucratic rejection; the prospect of shrinking their territorial goals was castigated as a betrayal of the nation and its legitimate aspirations. The rejection of the idea that they might shift their territorial goals even slid to violence when Fatah attempted to blow up the home of an advocate of this change (Sayigh, 1997, pp. 51, 82–83, 173, 223, 341).

The existence of such proposals does suggest that the information provided by the 1967 war may have played a role in the development of the 'strategy of phases' with which to gain their national territory by individuals in Fatah's leadership, at the time. But this did not imply a shift in their conception of the appropriate territorial borders of the nation–state that they sought (Jiryis, 1977, p. 5; Sayigh, 1997, p. 335). The proponents of the 'phased approach' openly portrayed it as a tactical, short-term modulation of their position for instrumental reasons and not a transformation of their ultimate goals (Sayigh, 1997, p. 155). In other words, even if the experience of fighting with a more powerful state provided meaningful information to the leaders of this particular stateless nationalist movement, this information, on its own, cannot account for the years between 1974 and 1988 when Fatah changed its strategy for Palestinian liberation but not the scope of the territory it sought to liberate.

The variation that existed within Fatah's leadership about accepting even the phased approach is also inconsistent with explanations of change that point to a single exogenous shock. Fatah's leadership was deeply divided on this question despite experiencing the same reality. The same is true of the Palestinian national movement more broadly. Even if Fatah eventually endorsed the 'phased approach' significant segments of the Palestinian political spectrum continued to reject even this tactical step as a betrayal of core principles. The variation in the way different nationalist movements of the same stateless nation reacted to new information suggests that such information, in and of itself, is not sufficient to bring about a change in the territorial claims of stateless nationalist movements.

The multidimensionality of the dependent variable also allows us to evaluate the plausibility of arguments that would envision a coordination on the actual borders drawn in the region. Although the eventual acceptance of the scope of the national territory as comprising the West Bank and Gaza Strip is consistent with the process of coordination on the actual border between Israel and Palestine, the timing of the transformation is less consistent with the expectations of this explanation. This is the case if only because Fatah did not coordinate on the border when it was a real international border between 1949 and 1967, but only in the 1967–1988 period, when the border between the West Bank and Israel was increasingly emptied of tangible meaning.

Unit of analysis

At what level of analysis should an exploration of changes in nationalist claims take place? Traditionally, scholarship on nationalism is pitched at the level of the state. Such an analysis would lead us to explore changes in the territorial claims by French, German, Russian, etc. nationalisms. Unfortunately, this level of analysis too easily falls into the trap of methodological nationalism and assumes either that there is no variation in territorial claims within a nation or that any variation that does exist does not contribute to how territorial claims change.

Alternatively, it would be reasonable to pitch an analysis of territorial claims at the level of the individual. Such an analysis might ask individuals about the area that they claim for the nation and, using repeated surveys over time, or perhaps survey experiments, could explore the purchase of different mechanisms of change. Unfortunately, to the best of our knowledge such data are unavailable. Indeed, questions about the scope of territorial claims are almost never asked in major national surveys. This could be because the importance of answering this question has been systematically overlooked, because it is politically sensitive and therefore difficult to ask in many contexts, or because a too-easy acceptance of methodological nationalism fostered the assumption that the answer is obvious.

As a result, we opted for selecting an intermediate level of analysis: the nationalist movement. This level of analysis has a couple of clear advantages. First, it is nationalist movements that draw desired national borders and act politically to realize these territorial claims. As a result, they generate materials that can be used as data in a study of how these claims change. Second, pitching the analysis at the level of the nationalist movement allows for the possibility that different nationalist movements claiming to speak for the same nation could differ in the scope of their territorial claims and that the competition among domestic political movements could shape how those claims change. In so doing, this level of analysis builds on the recent attention paid to endogenous processes of institutional transformation more broadly (see, e.g., Lustick, 1993; Mahoney & Thelen, 2010; Shelef, 2010).

Using the 'state' or the 'nation' as a unit of analysis would have obscured the political dynamics we identified in our work because these are impossible to observe at these higher levels of analysis. The link between the level of analysis and the political mechanism we identified imposes important scope conditions on the mechanism itself. Where there is no domestic competition other mechanisms are more likely to operate.

Selecting nationalist movements as the unit of analysis still requires a decision about what counts as a nationalist movement. The answer to this question is key in order to decide which movements ought to be included in our universe of cases. This decision is obviously connected with common methodological problems such as selection bias. We based our approach on an operationalization put forward by Andreas Wimmer and Yuval Feinstein, which limits nationalist movements to those organizations with formally defined memberships (thus excluding clientelist networks and informal factions), institutionalized leadership roles (as opposed to personal followings), and a claim to represent the national community as a whole (Wimmer & Feinstein, 2010).

The question of which nationalist movements are relevant in a particular context is both analytically difficult and politically fraught, especially in such quintessentially contested cases. In our prior work, we limited our inquiry to movements that make claims to a piece of land *as a homeland* and are residing in that territory. Under this definition, for example, movements that claimed part or whole of the region of Macedonia as part of the Greek or Bulgarian or Albanian homeland, or that claim Palestine as part of Israel or Southern Syria were excluded. In the analytical framework we proposed, the main difference between a Greek-Macedonian nationalist and a Slav-Macedonian nationalist was that the former claimed the land as part of the Greek homeland, while the latter claimed it as *the* homeland. This distinction, however, does not imply any normative claim about the relative legitimacy of the movements making any of these claims.

We recognize that this distinction is not watertight. For example, in the case of the struggle for Macedonia, claims for 'Macedonia to the Macedonians' were often made by elites that at different points in time had self-identified as Bulgarians or Serbs. It is likely that there is a great deal of variation among nationalist movements in this regard. Such differences would matter if, for example, the mechanism of change in the definition of the homeland varied systematically among movements that differed on this dimension. We cannot rule this possibility out in this context. Future research could examine whether or not this is the case empirically.

But change is a relative quality. Thus, we differentiate between change in the territorial claims of a nationalist movement and changes in its organizational structure. It is not uncommon for nationalist movements to pose as continuations of older ones, Sometimes even using the same name. In our work we do not perceive these separate movements as one. Instead, we understand this situation as organizational discontinuity. For instance, when a nationalist movement is fully captured by another organization or state then we no longer consider the group as a continuation since it has no independent agency. Thus, the movement that has been captured is seen as distinct from the movement prior to the capture. For example, in our study of the changes in the territorial claims made by the MRO, we stop coding these changes when the MRO began acting as Bulgaria's proxy.[2]

CASE SELECTION

Asynchronous comparisons

The tendency to test hypotheses on cases that are contemporaneous is justifiable for a variety of reasons (including the ability to control for world time effects such as international norms, technological innovations, and so forth, and their impact). However, asynchronous comparisons can also be illuminating. To begin with, different cases may go through the same experience at different points in time. These differences can be meaningful. As Grzymala-Busse (2011, p. 1288) also noted in her discussion of timing as an important aspect of temporality, *when* events take place might influence the ways in which causal processes operate. For instance, if we are studying 'national revivals' one movement may have experienced what Hroch (1985) calls the national agitation stage in the nineteenth-century, while another in the twentieth. Thus, asynchronous comparisons are justified if the research question and the research design require certain initial conditions to pertain before a causal effect can materialize. On top of this, showing that an argument operates in a similar fashion in two distinct periods in different contexts comes with many of the virtues of a most different systems design that John Stuart Mill – and his followers – would applaud (Gerring, 2007, p. 139).

Both these applied to our study of Fatah and the MRO. In an important sense, the decision to examine stateless nationalist movements makes asynchronous comparison likely. Both our cases are in the same 'stage' of nationalist development (without implying a linear or necessary development), in that both are nationalist movements that, in the period under observation, had not achieved their main goals. Moreover, the asynchronous comparison allows us to leverage the differences between the cases: the fact that the two movements unfolded in different historical moments – one prior to World War I and the other following World War II – increases our confidence that the relationship we identified between short-term rhetorical modulations and substantive change in territorial aspirations transcends geographic contexts and geopolitical circumstances.

Cross-regional comparisons

Comparing nationalist movements from different geopolitical contexts is challenging but theoretically rewarding. To begin with, discussing Fatah – a movement operating in the Middle East – and the MRO – a movement which emerged in the Ottoman Balkans – forced us to develop concepts that could travel between the two contexts and thus could also travel beyond these two movements. In other words, our concepts had to be truly comparative.

Beyond the benefits related to conceptualization, cross-regional comparisons enhance our ability to conduct hypothesis testing as well. For instance, variables that matter a great deal in one context, such as religion-based national identity in the Balkans, may be less relevant in other contexts where national identity is more based on racial or linguistic differences. This type of variation could allow us to evaluate whether (and how) such distinctions matter for the process we are interested in understanding. Similarly, by conducting cross-regional comparisons we can also indirectly test several arguments that emphasize the important of regional orders or neighbourhood effects. In the sense that if we can identify an argument that can account for the variation in two completely different geopolitical contexts, then we could argue that these other variables, although relevant in other ways, do not account for the observed variation we are interested in.

Finally, cross-regional comparisons force us to think about world time and diffusion processes. For instance, Herbst (2014) has argued that Sub-Saharan African populations did not have the same understanding about the relationship between identity and territory as in the European cases described by Tilly (1975, 1992). Studying a topic in such a fashion allows one to avoid euro-centric or western-centric explanations and thus build more solid accounts.

Anachronism

Naturally, asynchronous comparisons do not come without caveats. Anachronism, i.e., the practice of attributing certain actions to concepts and/or phenomena that were not politically salient or even understood by the actors under study, leads to mischaracterizations and to functionalist arguments (Mylonas, 2015). As Lawrence (2013, p. 7) argued, 'Hindsight can thus produce biased explanations. Knowledge of the outcome can lead one to erroneously believe that preferences for the outcome caused it to happen, even when the existence of such preferences has to be assumed.' Anyone who has studied the origins of one or more nationalist movements (stateless or not) has experienced the practice of anachronism. Often, actions are assumed to be the product of national feelings and loyalty to the nation even before a coherent definition was in place. For example, we might assume that the territorial claims of nationalist movements date back centuries or even millennia. However, as scholars of political geography have pointed out (Winichakul, 1994; Branch, 2014), Cartesian conceptualizations of territory in which sovereignty is sought and in which there are sharp borders between polities, are the products of technological and cartographical developments that took place at a particular historical period. The meaning of territorial claims before and after these developments may be so different that any comparison between them would be misleading.[3]

Tradeoffs of small-N and large-N research

There are clear tradeoffs between addressing the question of how stateless nationalist movements change their territorial claims using case studies or large-N analyses. The principal advantage of the small-N approach is that it allows a deep dive into the mechanisms at play. Tracing the process of change with sufficient resolution to compare the observable expectations of different mechanisms about the timing, direction, and process of change to the empirical record requires a significant investment of the kind that is difficult to replicate for any scholar (or even team of scholars) across the entire universe of cases.

This level of historical specificity, however, comes at the cost both testing the generalizability of any conclusions drawn and in limits on the ability to draw inferences about the conditions under which particular mechanisms of change operate empirically. For example, while the patterns of similarity and differences between the MRO and Fatah are sufficient to make us confident that political dynamics are likely to play an important role in changes in the territorial claims of stateless nationalist movements more broadly (see Mylonas & Shelef, 2014), there is no way to know whether or not this is the case without examining the wider universe of cases. Similarly, while maintaining the multidimensionality of the change insulates that argument from many of the problems associated with selecting on the dependent variable (Collier & Mahoney, 1996), it does so imperfectly. Ideally, a large-N analysis of the mechanisms of change would include the many cases in which 'domestic' political competition exists, but in which no change takes place.

Finally, it may also be the case that there is something unobserved about the particular cases that are examined in any small-N context that makes the conclusion that a particular mechanism operates more likely. We have no way of knowing, in other words, whether we would have found support for other mechanisms had we examined other cases. Large-N research is better suited, therefore, to answer questions about the relative distribution of mechanisms across cases and for exploring the broader conditions under which some mechanisms are more or less likely to drive change in the claims of stateless nationalist movements.

Steps in this direction have already been taken. Shelef (2016), for example, systematically codes for the presence of homeland claims across all new international borders since 1945. Such data could be leveraged in order to replicate the multidimensional dependent variable that, we believe, is needed to adequately assess mechanisms of change. At the same time, good proxies for the alternative explanations also need to be developed.

CONCLUSION

The study of stateless nationalist movements in relation to territorial design faces a number of methodological challenges. In this article, we focused on some of the research strategies and choices involved in studying precisely how the 'delineation of territory' aspect of territorial design (Atzili & Kardecan, forthcoming) takes place. In particular, we highlighted the importance of conceptualizing the dependent variable in ways that facilitate empirical research and testing. Our work contributes to building a shared vocabulary between political geography and political science that can advance our common effort to unpack the relationship between politics and space. We also addressed the critical role of choosing the appropriate unit of analysis and selecting cases from a clearly delineated universe of cases.

The empirical challenges faced by scholars interested in these questions, however, do not end there. For instance, among the most daunting problems a researcher faces is finding the necessarily empirical evidence. In our previous work, we focused primarily on the public articulation of territorial claims by the movement and its leaders. This source of data, while it has a long tradition in the study of nationalism (Billig, 1995; Greenfeld, 1992; Lustick, 1993; Shelef, 2010), does have important limitations, especially if we consider movements as strategic actors in conflict. In the case of territorial claims in particular, the actors involved often have an incentive to obscure their political decisions out of the fear that revealing such information would undermine their movement's legitimacy or to deploy changes in territorial claims as cheap talk. While future work would ideally also deploy sources of data about the territorial claims of nationalist movements that are less sensitive to these limitations, including internal correspondence, pedagogical materials, and the like, in many historical contexts, such data are often difficult to come by or simply no longer exist.

As the title of our article makes clear, we focus on territorial claims made by *stateless* nationalist movements. By definition, such movements (especially in the contemporary era) fight against the territorial integrity norm. The tension between self-determination and territorial integrity thus provides another example of the tension between micro-designs and global orders identified by Atzili and Kadercan. But the historical record is full of cases of nationalist movements that continue to press territorial claims after gaining independence. We often call these irredentist, revisionist, or expansionist states.

More importantly, it is important to note that the territorial claims of irredentist states also change. For example, in 1877 the Italian nationalist Matteo Renato Imbriani coined the term 'terra irredenta' (unredeemed land) to refer to those parts of the Italian homeland that were not included in the Italian state. The Duke of Litta-Visconti-Arese (1917) explained that this area included 'Trentino, Eastern Friuli, Trieste with Istria, Fiume and Dalmatia'. Italy today includes Trentino and the city of Trieste, but not these other areas of the Italian homeland. While claims to the remainder of 'unredeemed Italy' persist at the margins of Italian politics, few Italian nationalists currently argue that Italy ought to extend its sovereignty over the parts of Croatia and Slovenia that were once seen as inherently Italian. Such changes in the understanding of the territory that ought to be 'ours' are crucial for understanding how deeply contested territories – in the Italian-Yugoslav case there were widespread fears that the conflict over Trieste and Istria would lead to World War III – become peaceful (Gross, 1978).

Our focus on *stateless* nationalist movements is due to our theoretical expectation that the mechanisms of change that shape the territorial claims of nationalist movements after they achieve independence may differ from those that shape those claims while they are stateless. For instance, once a nationalist movement achieves statehood it gains greater access to certain types of resources and additional tools that could be used to effect territorial change, thus rendering relative capacity arguments potentially more plausible. On the other hand, international norms with regard to territorial integrity bind states more than stateless nationalist movements. In light of this, coordination on existing boundaries may become a more potent explanation for changes in the scope of territorial claims by nationalist movements that have achieved statehood. Pursuing these questions in a wider range of contexts constitutes another fruitful extension of this research agenda.

ACKNOWLEDGMENTS

We would like to thank the anonymous reviewers, Barnett Koven, Kai Wang, and the editors of this Special Issue for their useful comments.

DISCLOSURE STATEMENT

No potential conflict of interest was reported by the authors.

NOTES

1. We employ a term Atzili and Kadercan proposed in this issue.
2. For more on the MRO, see Perry (1988). There are, of course, other potential reasons for organizational discontinuity, see, for example, Taylor (1989).
3. For a discussion of the problem of anachronism manifested in the realm of understandings of nationhood, see Mylonas (2015).

REFERENCES

Al-Shuaibi, I. (1980). The development of Palestinian entity-consciousness: Part 3. *Journal of Palestine Studies, 9* (Spring), 99–124.
Anderson, B. (1991). *Imagined communities: Reflections on the origin and spread of nationalism.* New York: Verso.
Ashrawi, H. (1995). *This side of Peace.* New York: Simon and Schuster.
Atzili, B., & Kadercan, B. (2017). "Territorial designs and international politics: The diverging constitution of space and boundaries." *Territory, Politics, Governance,* doi:10.1080/21622671.2016.1266962
Billig, M. (1995). *Banal nationalism.* London: Sage.

Branch, J. (2014). *The cartographic state: Maps, territory and the origins of sovereignty*. Cambridge: Cambridge University Press.

Carter, D. B., & Goemans, H. E. (2011). The making of the territorial order: New borders and the emergence of interstate conflict. *International Organization, 65*(April), 275–309.

Collier, D., & Adcock, R. (1999). Democracy and dichotomies: A pragmatic approach to choices about concepts. *Annual Review of Political Science, 2*, 537–565.

Collier, D., & Mahoney, J. (1996). Insights and pitfalls: Selections bias in qualitative research. *World Politics, 49*, 56–91.

Duke of Litta-Visconti-Arese. (1917). Unredeemed Italy. *The North American Review, 206*(October), 561–574.

Gerring, J. (2007). *Case study research: Principles and practices*. New York: Cambridge University Press.

Goddard, S. E. (2010). *Indivisible territory and the politics of legitimacy: Jerusalem and Northern Ireland*. Cambridge: Cambridge University Press.

Goemans, H. (2006). Bounded communities: Territoriality, territorial attachment, and conflict. In M. Kahler & B. F. Walter (Eds.), *Territoriality and conflict in an era of globalization* (pp. 25–61). Cambridge: Cambridge University Press.

Greenfeld, L. (1992). *Nationalism: Five roads to modernity*. Cambridge, MA: Harvard University Press.

Gross, F. (1978). *Ethnics in a borderland: An inquiry into the nature of ethnicity and reduction of ethnic tensions in a one-time genocide area*. Westport, CT: Greenwood Press.

Grzymala-Busse, A. (2011). Time will tell? Temporality and the analysis of causal mechanisms and processes. *Comparative Political Studies, 44*(9), 1267–1297.

Hajdarpašić, Edin. (2008). Out of the ruins of the ottoman empire: Reflections on the ottoman legacy in south-eastern Europe. *Middle Eastern Studies, 44*(5), 715–734.

Hartmuth, M. (2008). De/constructing a 'legacy in stone': Of interpretative and historiographical problems concerning the Ottoman cultural heritage in the Balkans. *Middle Eastern Studies, 44*(5), 695–713.

Herbst, J. (2014). *States and power in Africa: Comparative lessons in authority and control*. Princeton, NJ: Princeton University Press.

Hroch, M. (1985). *Social preconditions of national revival in Europe: A comparative analysis of the social composition of patriotic groups among the smaller European nations*. New York: Columbia University Press.

Inalcik, H. (1996). The meaning of legacy: The Ottoman case. In C. Brown (Ed.), *Imperial legacy: The Ottoman footprint in the Balkans and the Middle East* (pp. 17–29). New York, NY: Columbia University Press.

Iyad, A. (Salah Khalaf). (1980). *My home, my land: A narrative of the Palestinian struggle*. New York: Times Books.

Jelavich, C., & Jelavich, B. (1977). *The establishment of the Balkan National States, 1804–1920*. Seattle, WA: The University of Washington Press.

Jiryis, S. (1977). On political settlement in the Middle East: The Palestinian dimension. *Journal of Palestine Studies, 7*(Autumn), 3–25.

Kaufmann, C. (1998). When all else fails: Ethnic population transfers and partitions in the twentieth century. *International Security, 23*(Autumn), 120–156.

Kelle, F. L. (2016). To claim or not to claim? How territorial value shapes demands for self-determination. *Comparative Political Studies*, doi:0010414016666837

Lawrence, A. (2013). *Imperial rule and the politics of nationalism: Anti-colonial protest in the French empire*. New York: Cambridge University Press.

Lustick, I. S. (1993). *Unsettled states, disputed lands: Britain and Ireland, France and Algeria, Israel and the West Bank-Gaza*. Ithaca, NY: Cornell University Press.

Mahoney, J., & Thelen, K. (2010). A theory of gradual institutional change. In J. Mahoney & K. Thelen (Eds.), *Explaining institutional change: Ambiguity, agency, and power* (pp. 1–37). Cambridge: Cambridge University Press.

McGranahan, C. (2010). *Arrested histories: Tibet, the CIA, and memories of a forgotten War*. Durham, NC: Duke University Press.

Mylonas, H. (2012). *The politics of nation-building: Making Co-nationals, refugees, and minorities*. New York: Cambridge University Press.

Mylonas, H. (2015). Methodological problems in the study of nation-building: Behaviorism and historicist solutions in political science. *Social Science Quarterly*, *96*(3), 740–758.

Mylonas, H., & Shelef, N. G. (2014). Which land is our land? Explaining change in the desired state borders by stateless nationalist movements. *Security Studies*, *23*(4), 754–786.

Ó Tuathail, G. (1996). *Critical geopolitics: The politics of writing global space*. Minneapolis: University of Minnesota Press.

Ó Tuathail, G., & Agnew, J. (1992) Geopolitics and discourse: Practical geopolitical reasoning in American foreign policy. *Political Geography*, *11*(2), 190–204.

Perry, D. M. (1988). *The politics of terror: The Macedonian liberation movements, 1893–1903*. Durham, NC: Duke University Press.

Pierson, P. (2000). Increasing returns, path dependence, and the study of politics. *American Political Science Review*, *94*(June), 251–267.

Roeder, P. G. (2007). *Where nation-states come from: Institutional change in the age of nationalism*. Princeton, NJ: Princeton University Press.

Saideman, S. M., & Ayers, R. W. (2008). *For kin or country: Xenophobia, nationalism, and war*. New York: Columbia University Press.

Sayigh, Y. (1997). *Armed struggle and the search for state: The Palestinian National Movement, 1949–1993*. Oxford: Clarendon Press.

Shelef, N. G. (2007). Testing the logic of unilateral withdrawal: Lessons from the history of the labor zionist movement. *Middle East Journal*, *61*(3) (Summer), 460–475.

Shelef, N. G. (2010). *Evolving nationalism: Homeland, identity, and religion in Israel, 1925–2005*. Ithaca, NY: Cornell University Press.

Shelef, N. G. (2016). Unequal ground: Homelands and conflict. *International Organization*, *70*(1) (Winter), 33–63.

Smith, A. (1987). *The ethnic origins of nations*. New York, NY: Blackwell.

Taylor, V. (1989). Social movement continuity: The women's movement in abeyance. *American Sociological Review*, *54*(5), 761–775.

Tilly, C. (1992). *Coercion, capital, and European states, AD 990–1992*. Malden, MA: Blackwell publishers.

Tilly, C. (Ed.) (1975). *The formation of national states in Western Europe* (Vol. 8). Princeton, NJ: Princeton University Press.

Todorova, M. (1996). The ottoman legacy in the balkans. In C. Brown (Eds.), *Imperial legacy: The Ottoman footprint in the Balkans and the Middle East* (pp. 45–77). New York, NY: Columbia University Press.

Toft, M. D. (2005). *The geography of ethnic violence: Identity, interests, and the indivisibility of territory*. Princeton, NJ: Princeton University Press.

Winichakul, T. (1994). *Siam mapped: A history of the geo-body of a nation*. Honolulu, HI: University of Hawaii Press.

Wimmer, A., & Feinstein, Y. (2010). The rise of the nation-state across the world, 1816–2001. *American Sociological Review*, *75*, 764–790.

Yilmaz, Ş., & Yosmaoglu, İ. K. (2008). Fighting the spectres of the past: Dilemmas of Ottoman legacy in the Balkans and the Middle East. *Middle Eastern Studies*, *44*(5), 677–693.

Admission to the sovereignty club: the past, present, and future of the international recognition regime

Ryan D. Griffiths

ABSTRACT

Admission to the sovereignty club: the past, present, and future of the international recognition regime. *Territory, Politics, Governance.* The rules and practices of sovereign recognition are basic elements of the territorial design of the international system, but our understanding of these processes is under-theorized. This paper first conceptualizes sovereignty as a club good – excludable and non-rival – and specifies the threat that secession poses to existing states. It then examines the ways in which the club of sovereign states has limited membership in the past, including: (1) the pre-1816 European order in which liberal norms were absent and states colluded to deny independence to aspiring nations; (2) the age of de facto statehood from 1816 to 1918 in which self-determination came to be perceived as a negative right; and (3) the post-1945 era in which an evolving constitutive order has attempted to define which nations are eligible for independence. The paper then explores three potential futures of the international recognition regime, including an exclusive emphasis on sovereign consent, the consolidation of a remedial right to secede and the implementation of a primary right to choose independence. Throughout the discussion it is shown how each regime has balanced the competing demands of the sovereign and liberal traditions, and the strengths and weaknesses of each for international order are highlighted.

摘要

获准进入主权俱乐部: 国际承认体制的过去, 现在与未来。*Territory, Politics, Governance.* 主权承认的原则与实践, 是国际系统的领土设计的基本元素, 但我们对此般过程的理解却未受到充分理论化。本文首先将主权概念化为俱乐部财—具排他性且非竞争性—并具体说明退出该系统对现存国家带来的威胁。本文接着检视主权国家俱乐部在过去限制会员的方式, 包含: (1) 1816年欧洲秩序确立之前, 缺乏自由主义常规, 而各国之间共谋以拒绝追求民族独立者; (2) 1816年至1918年间, 民族自决被认为是消极权利的实际建国年代; 以及 (3) 1945年后的年代, 演化中的构成秩序, 企图决定那些民族得以独立。本文接着探讨国际承认体制的三种可能未来, 包含排他性地强调主权合意, 巩固分裂做为最后的补救权利, 以及实施选择独立做为主权利。透过上述讨论, 本文显示每个体制如何平衡主权及自由传统之间相互竞争的要求, 并凸显每个体制对国际秩序的长处与短处。

RÉSUMÉ

L'adhésion au club de souveraineté: le passé, le présent, et le futur du régime international de reconnaissance. *Territory, Politics, Governance*. Les règles et les pratiques de la reconnaissance de la souveraineté sont des socles de la conception territoriale du système international. Néanmoins, la compréhension de ces processus reste peu théorisée. Dans un premier temps, ce présent article conceptualise la souveraineté comme une manne pour les clubs – excluable et libre de rivalité – et précise la menace que pose la sécession aux états existants. Il s'ensuit un examen des façons dont le club des états souverains a limité l'adhésion dans le passé, y compris : (1) l'ordre européen avant 1816 où les normes libérales n'étaient pas évidentes et où les états complotaient les uns avec les autres afin de refuser l'indépendance aux pays candidats; (2) l'époque de devenir un État de facto entre 1816 et 1918 où l'auto-détermination était considérée un droit négatif; et (3) la période après 1945 où un ordre constitutif en pleine évolution cherchait à définir quels pays remplissait les conditions pour obtenir l'indépendance. Il s'ensuit un examen de trois scénarios éventuels pour le futur du régime de reconnaissance internationale, y compris l'accent exclusivement mis sur le consentement de décret souverain, la consolidation d'un droit de redressement à la sécession et la mise en oeuvre d'un droit primaire de choisir l'indépendance. Tout au long de la discussion on montre comment chaque régime a pesé les demandes concurrentielles des traditions souveraine et libérale, et on souligne leurs forces et leurs faiblesses quant à l'ordre international.

RESUMEN

Entrada en el club de la soberanía: pasado, presente y futuro del régimen de reconocimiento internacional. *Territory, Politics, Governance*. Las normas y prácticas para el reconocimiento soberano constituyen elementos básicos del diseño territorial del sistema internacional, pero nuestros conocimientos sobre estos procesos se han teorizado insuficientemente. En este artículo primero conceptualizo la soberanía como el bien de un club –excluible y sin rival– y especifico la amenaza que la secesión supone para los Estados existentes. Luego analizo el modo en que el club de los Estados soberanos tenía antes miembros limitados, incluyendo: (1) la orden europea antes de 1816 en la que las normas liberales no existían y los Estados se confabulaban para negar la independencia a las naciones aspirantes; (2) la edad de condición de Estado de facto de 1816 a 1918 en la que la autodeterminación llegó para ser considerada un derecho negativo; y (3) la era después de 1945 en la que una orden constituyente en evolución ha intentado definir qué naciones cumplen los requisitos para llegar a la independencia. Luego analizo tres posibles futuros del régimen de reconocimiento internacional, incluyendo un énfasis exclusivo sobre el consentimiento soberano, la consolidación de un derecho correctivo para separarse y la aplicación de un derecho primario para elegir la independencia. Durante todo el debate, se muestra el modo en que cada régimen ha equilibrado las demandas competitivas de las tradiciones soberanas y liberales, y se destacan las ventajas e inconvenientes de cada una para el orden internacional.

INTRODUCTION

What are the rules guiding the recognition of new sovereign states? How and why have those rules changed historically, and how might they change in the future? These are important questions about the territorial design of the international system. The answers to these questions would help explain why some aspiring nations are granted independence when others are not, how the rules of sovereign recognition are formed, and why there are historical patterns in statehood and the number of sovereign states. They also place current efforts at gaining independence in context, suggesting how secessionist movements in places such as Kurdistan, Catalonia, and Somaliland would have fared in the past and how they may fare in the future.

My analysis of these questions proceeds in several stages. I first conceptualize the sovereign state system as a club good (excludable and non-rival) where the constituent members (sovereign states) develop admission criteria to limit membership and prevent crowding. I then argue that the admission criteria at any point in time are the product of a tension between two competing normative traditions in international life – sovereignty and liberalism – and the interpretation and application of derivative norms like border fixity and self-determination.[1] In the remainder of the essay I describe several recognition regimes that have existed historically and may exist in the future, and I explore the consequences of each. I contend that the recognition regime will remain a central feature of international politics, and that potential future configurations emphasizing admission by consent, remedial rights, or primary rights, will turn to a large extent on the normative contest between sovereignty and liberalism.

My argument thus contributes to this special issue by advancing a theory for the origins of what Kadercan (2015) calls 'territorial constitutions'. The normative, legal, and political factors that determine how state boundaries are produced and how territory is delineated are largely constructed at the international level, at least in the modern period. I identify the normative traditions and arguments as well as the strategic concerns of states that shape these constructions. In doing so, I provide an answer to the question posed by Atzili and Kadercan (2017, p. 10) in the lead article of this edition: who is responsible for territorial design and at what level (domestic/interstate) are they located? The answer is the international recognition regime (see Agne et al., 2013; Banai, 2014).

THE SOVEREIGNTY CLUB

I argue that the set of sovereign states is a club. In making this argument I refer to the formally sovereign, territorially defined state. There may have been other forms of political organization in the past, and new forms may arise in the future, but the dominant form of political organization for some time now has been the sovereign state (Krasner, 1999; Osiander, 2001; Spruyt, 1994). Furthermore, I am referring to states that are recognized as sovereign by the international community and I thus exclude dependencies and other forms of semi-autonomy that fall short of full independence, as well as secessionist regions that remain unrecognized. In my view, these are all potential applicants to the sovereignty club.

The sovereign state system satisfies the definition of a club good: it is excludable and non-rival (see Figure 1). The most salient feature of a club good, and that which delineates it from a public good, is excludability; members can set up rules for admittance into the club (Buchanan, 1965). The reason members would choose to exclude is that the good in question is only non-rival up to a point. In that sense, a club good sits between the two extremes of private (excludable and rival) and public (non-excludable and non-rival) goods: 'For a pure public good the addition of one more member to the club never detracts from benefits of club membership ... [for] a pure private good, say an apple, crowding begins to take place on the first unit' (Mueller, 1989, p. 131). Thus, a club good is one in which members have the ability and incentive to limit membership beyond a certain threshold.

The sovereign state system has all the features of a club good. It is a good insofar as it provides a legal identity to its members with which they can enjoy a surprisingly large set of benefits, including voting rights in major international organization, access to financial aid, and the ability to use international post and conduct commerce with foreign banks (Fazal & Griffiths, 2014; Griffiths, 2016a).

	Excludable	**Non-Excludable**
Rival	Private Good	Common Good
Non-Rival	Club Good	Public Good

Figure 1. Types of goods.

In addition, the sovereign state system is non-rival, but only up to a point. Although crowding does not necessarily begin with each additional state, and the state system could arguably increase in number and remain efficient, the current members have posited a number of explanations for why membership should be limited. One concern is that additional states will dilute the vote share and political influence of existing members in key organizations like the United Nations. A different issue pertains to viability: are microstates truly viable, or will they constitute a drain on international resources? Such efficiency arguments are openly discussed and are evident in the international legal discourse on secession (Halperin, Scheffer, & Small, 1992). But by far the biggest concern is the issue of uncontrolled fragmentation. What nations are eligible? How are they defined? And how can existing states support secessionist efforts when doing so may set a precedent and lead to their own territorial dismemberment? Just as aspiring nations have incentive to join the club, existing members have incentive to control admission.

My argument contributes to an old debate regarding state emergence (Agne et al., 2013; Buzan & Little, 2000; Coggins, 2014; Erman, 2013; Fabry, 2010). Do states exist ontologically prior to international order and simply declare that they are sovereign? Or do states come into being by virtue of the collective and constitutive judgment of the international community? These contrasting views are known as the declaratory and constitutive theories of statehood. Although states in earlier periods may have simply declared their existence without too much concern over mutual recognition, it is hard to deny its importance in modern times. As aspiring states like Kurdistan and Somaliland know all too well, declaring yourself a state and even functioning like a state does not make you a state unless the international community approves. In the absence of that approval, aspiring nationalists are relegated to a status where the benefits of formal statehood are denied them, and where a neighbouring sovereign has legal ownership over them (Fazal & Griffiths, 2014).

In procedural terms, the defining feature of joining the sovereignty club is obtaining a full seat in the United Nations General Assembly. More than just a marker of legitimacy, this provides the state with a legal identity that is useful for a range of economic and diplomatic reasons. The UN membership process requires that the Security Council must approve applications before they are submitted to the General Assembly. Thus, the Security Council acts as the gatekeepers to the club, especially the five permanent veto-holding members: France, Russia, China, the United Kingdom, and the United States.

Overall, the members of the sovereignty club have incentive to exclude and the ability to do so. As I discuss below, the politics of sovereign recognition is intricate, and it consists of an evolving body of international legal norms, rules, and principles – that is, the recognition regime – that determine when an applicant nation has the right to withdraw from an existing state and join the club of sovereign states.

SOVEREIGNTY, LIBERALISM, AND THE CLASH OF NORMS

How does the sovereignty club develop rules for controlling admission? Such rules are not conjured whole cloth without recourse to history and existing practices. Rather, the exclusion mechanism, or recognition regime, that exists at any point in time is the product of international diplomacy and the development and evolution of international norms. As Sandholtz and Stiles (2008) argue, international norms typically originate in one of two traditions: sovereignty norms that emphasize the right of states, and liberal norms that stress the right of individuals. Norms are continuously evolving phenomena, and the character and strength of a given norm at any moment is determined through persuasion, in relation to power, and via the dialectic between sovereign and liberal rights. It is in the normative contest between these two traditions that, for example, norms emphasizing human rights (e.g., humanitarian intervention, anti-genocide, and the responsibility to protect, R2P) conflict with the right of sovereign states to manage their own affairs.

Much of international relations over the last few centuries are made sensible from this normative vantage point. In the sovereign tradition, rights accrue to the state or, in older times, the person who embodied the state (Osiander, 2001; Spruyt, 1994). This tradition is quite old, dating to at least the seventeenth century in Europe. In the liberal tradition, rights accrue to the individual. More of an upstart, this tradition can point to intellectual forefathers such as John Locke, but its force in international life was not really felt until the American and French revolutions (Fabry, 2010; Manela, 2007). Importantly, these traditions, and the specific norms they encompass, evolve in relation to one another and come into conflict at various friction points (Jackson, 1990; Osterud, 1997; Sandholtz & Stiles, 2008). For example, the 2011 intervention in Libya is viewed by many as a victory for R2P over the sovereign right of states to resolve domestic disputes. However, that sort of liberal intervention has remained out of reach in Syria partly because great powers like China and Russia have defended Syria's sovereign right to manage its internal affairs.

This is a useful framework for studying the dynamics of the sovereignty club and the possible solutions for controlling admission. Arguments against the recognition of a break-away state are usually made by defending the sovereignty of the larger state from which it wants to exit, citing the right of states to manage their internal affairs and/or preserve their territorial boundaries. Arguments for recognition are more varied, but they are usually grounded in the liberal tradition, emphasizing the right of individuals to determine their political fate and/or be free from persecution. Importantly, the power of individual states plays an important role in these dynamics (Krasner, 2013). The actions and interests of strong states influence the normative tension, just as their behaviour is shaped by it. This normative tension is quite fluid and, as I show below, the interpretation of the related norms has changed over time.

THE EVOLVING RECOGNITION REGIME

Viewed from a wide angle, one can trace the international recognition regime through several periods, with each representing a particular solution for limiting admission to the sovereignty club. The first encompassed the European-based system during the eighteenth century, if not earlier, and existed until the American and French revolutions. The sovereign tradition was dominant during this time and, as a result, states followed a practice that I call recognition by consent. Foreign leaders – usually monarchs – were expected to support other leaders and deny recognition to break-away regions unless they received the blessing of their sovereign. As the American revolutionaries learned, recognition was difficult to achieve in the absence of British consent. Only the

French were willing to break the taboo, largely for strategic reasons, and they were criticized for it (Fabry, 2010). The problem for the Americans is that the ideals they invoked in their declaration of independence were somewhat novel (Armitage, 2007). They were liberal in orientation – indeed, they were radical – and they were not grounded in a commonly accepted system of thought regarding the right of individuals to statehood.

This changed after the Napoleonic wars with the advent of the norm of self-determination. Broadly speaking, self-determination upholds the right of a nation to control its political destiny. When nations possess their own state – the state and the nation are congruent – then the interest of the nation is identical to that of the state. It is for this reason that observers will sometimes refer to the sovereign right of a state to self-determination.[2] But such congruencies are rare given the multinational character of most states and the malleability of national identity.[3] Indeed, Gellner famously asserted that there are many more nations than states and, in fact, most nations are stateless (1983, pp. 43–44). It is when minority or stateless nations call on the right of self-determination that it conflicts with the sovereign right of the larger state. Ultimately, self-determination is liberal in orientation, covering the right of individuals to organize and identify as co-nationals, but its interpretation has changed with time (Beran, 1998; Buchanan, 2003; Mayall, 1990; Wellman, 2005).

During the period running from the Concert of Europe through the First World War, self-determination came to be regarded as a negative right. The international community was obliged to not interfere, leaving the aspiring nation to pursue its independence on its own. However, should the nation prevail over its sovereign and establish de facto statehood as a self-determined fact, the international community was expected to recognize its sovereignty and admit it into the sovereignty club. This approach to recognition was led by the United Kingdom and the United States, who operated from a position of principle – leaders such as Lord Castlereigh, George Canning, and John Quincy Adams held this view of self-determination – and one of strategy – their primary opponents were the conservative European monarchies who sought to maintain the traditional international order. Following Fabry, I refer to this as the practice of de facto recognition. Beginning with the secessions in Latin America, break-away nations were generally granted recognition once they could establish statehood as a self-determined fact (Fabry, 2010, p. 10; Jackson, 1990).

The convulsions of the world wars produced normative change in two important ways. First, the Wilsonian Moment at the end of the First World War led to 'a shift in the understanding of self-determination from a negative to positive international right' (Fabry, 2010, p. 12; Manela, 2007). If the negative right meant that nations were entitled to become free by their own effort and without external intervention, the positive right obliged the international community to assist national aspirations. Under the first interpretation, third parties were obliged to do nothing and only grant recognition once the break-away region had established a de facto state. Under the second interpretation, third parties were obliged to take a more active role and assist such efforts even when they had not prevailed over their sovereign, and perhaps had little chance of ever doing so. That shift in interpretation dramatically altered the exclusion mechanism for the sovereignty club. If the earlier approach could be summed up as 'wait and see the outcome', the latter became a question of 'who counts?' As I discuss below, answering that question requires an additional set of criteria.

The second important normative change was sovereign in orientation. The destruction of the world wars gave rise to a prohibition on conquest and emphasis on treating sovereign borders as inviolable. Atzili calls this the border fixity norm, saying, 'conquest and annexation of one's neighbor's land, commonplace in the history of the state system, is no longer on the "menu of choice" for post-World War II leaders and states' (Atzili, 2012, p. 1). Others have referred to the same prohibition as the norm of territorial integrity, but Atzili's more specific name rightly notes what is arguably the most salient feature of the norm: the preservation of sovereign borders (Zacher,

2001). According to Fazal, the norm resulted in a near disappearance of formal territorial conquest after 1945 (Fazal, 2007). If, however, the norm was created to prevent external aggression, it has been remarkably effective at blocking internal fragmentation (Fazal & Griffiths, 2014; Griffiths, 2016a). Treating the existing territorial grid as sacrosanct presents an obstacle to conquerors and secessionists alike.

This double normative movement produced a recognition regime defined largely by the sharp tension between sovereignty and liberalism, one that has characterized the international system since 1945. On one hand, there is a value placed on sovereign boundaries as a means to maintain territorial stability. On the other hand, there is an emphasis on helping minority nations to achieve self-determination. The solution for adjudicating these competing demands was to develop criteria for which nations should count, a difficult and evolving task. Fabry refers to this as constitutive recognition because it requires that the relevant international actors agree on what criteria should be used to determine who counts (2010). In the time of de facto recognition that decision was easier because it was effectively pinned to the outcome of the contest between the secessionists and their government. However, in a constitutive regime where such contests are unnecessary and even discouraged, the community of states has to take a more active role in determining who should have a right to the fullest expression of self-determination: an independent state.

Since 1945 the question of who counts has been answered in several ways. First, nations that have the consent of their sovereign are eligible for independence (e.g., Slovakia and Montenegro). This is not a controversial move insofar as it requires little from third parties – the decision has been worked out domestically – and it is no different in form from earlier periods. The second way to independence was far more dramatic, involving the expansion and application of self-determination to colonized peoples. Born from noble intentions, decolonization was a complicated and controversial process for the simple reason that it is quite difficult, and perhaps impossible, to sort the colonized nations from the rest. The fortunate were simply those who were seen to command first-order administrative units of saltwater empires, a distinction that elided minority nations in large continental states like Russia, China, and the United States, and the numerous colonized peoples of Africa and Asia who were disadvantaged by the colonial administrative map. Jackson estimates that the legal emphasis on administrative boundaries, known as *uti possidetis* (as you possess), reduced the number of acceptable independence claims in Africa from 400–500 to 40–50 (1993, p. 122), and gave birth to a set of states with diverse, multiethnic populations that hardly fit the ideal of the nation-state. Despite what some may think, there is no bright line separating the nations that classified for decolonization, such as Uganda, from those who did not, like Buganda, Tibet, Chechnya, or Lakotah. The sorting mechanism has its critics (Bartos, 1997; Fabry, 2010; Jackson, 1990; 1993; Ratner, 1996; Shaw, 1996).

A third entry point into the sovereignty club is for members of dissolved states, a solution that was created during the Yugoslav and Soviet breakups. Like decolonization, this was in part a legal solution meant to create a conceptual distinction between cases of dissolution and other forms of secession. According to Bartos, 'the [Badinter] Commission preferred to view the Yugoslavian situation as one of dissolution, refusing to set a precedent for the secession of national groups within existing States' (1997, p. 75). Of course, the Serb government saw things differently, as did other secessionist regions that were simultaneously denied independence from those same 'dissolving' states, such as Chechnya and South Ossetia. The distinction between secession and dissolution is at best a matter of degree – the ethical merits of the distinction are debated in the legal discourse (Bartos, 1997; Radan, 2002) – and it is a fine example of the difficulty in limiting membership to the sovereignty club.

Finally, the example of Kosovo hints at a potentially new route to independence, one based on human rights. After fighting a bloody secessionist civil war against Serbia in the 1990s, Kosovo was placed under United Nations administration. After consultation with western powers, Kosovo declared independence in 2008 and has been recognized by some 108 countries (Meetser, 2012).

Kosovar success in securing that level of recognition is considered by some to be evidence for an emerging remedial right to secession in the face of human rights abuses by the state. Notably, the United States endorsed Kosovar independence but shied away from calling it a remedial right. Although it highlighted the ethnic cleansing and human rights abuses, the United States called Kosovo a special case that 'cannot be seen as a precedent for any other situation in the world today' (Condoleeza Rice, Secretary of State, February 18, 2008). Other powerful states like China and Russia have taken a more pessimistic view and refused to recognize Kosovar independence on the grounds that it would violate Serb sovereignty. Kosovo's current precarious status of semi-sovereignty exists precisely because the international community cannot agree completely on who should count. The normative crosswinds of international life have rendered Kosovo's future uncertain.

Conjectures on the future of the recognition regime

The tension between sovereign and liberal norms provides a useful framework for considering future designs of the recognition regime. Here I identify three reasonable possibilities, but others could be imagined. All of them are feasible when the relative balance between sovereign and liberal norms shifts one way or the other.

One possibility is the strengthening of a remedial right to secession. For some this was the future foretold in the Kosovo decision. Remedial rights theory, also called Just Cause theory, posits that groups have a right to secede because other rights have been violated (Buchanan, 2003; Norman, 1998). In its most common form, a minority nation gains the right when the larger state has failed to uphold the social contract by not providing an acceptable level of order and security. The appeal of the right rises in relation to the predatory (or perhaps genocidal) nature of the state. This future seemed tantalizingly within reach in the late 1990s with the establishment of the R2P, a similar normative argument that falls short of endorsing secession, and a decade later with the legal decision on Kosovo. However, the defence of sovereignty remains a formidable barrier to the establishment of a remedial right, especially with advocates like China and Russia, permanent members of the United Nations Security Council who can veto membership applications to the UN. Moreover, security experts worry about the potential for moral hazard that arises with a remedial right – it is possible that actors may try to provoke the state into a fight as a way to activate the right (Kuperman, 2008).

A second possibility is the consolidation of a primary right to secession. Choice theory, or Primary Rights theory, stresses the right of human beings or groups of human beings to secede from the larger state according to a democratic process (Beran, 1998; Wellman, 2005). There is some variation in terms of how groups are delimited, how minorities within minorities are dealt with, and how referenda should be held, but the overall approach is quite liberal in orientation. However, despite the historical trend toward more democracies over the last century, the implementation of a right to choose independence is difficult given that it would create fragmentary pressures within states, even hale states that are meeting the social contract. The 2014 Scottish referendum on independence was in some respects an example of choice theory in action, but, of course, the British government was in full support. As the Catalan nationalists know, Choice theory is far harder to put into practice when governmental consent is absent. Such a development seems unlikely in the near future, but it could arise with added liberalization and democratization of international space. Like the first possibility – the entrenchment of a remedial right – this future constitutes a modification and extension of the current constitutive recognition regime.

Set against these possibilities is a move in the opposite direction toward the fortification of sovereignty. A likely possibility here is added support for the border fixity norm and a roll back of the application of self-determination, especially its current interpretation as a positive right. This would be a return to recognition by consent, a conservative exclusion mechanism that would resemble the eighteenth century in some respects. The key difference would be the retention of the modern border fixity norm and its prohibition on conquest. Such a system would reinforce the existing territorial grid and promote territorial stability, but it would come at the expense of liberal rights. I have argued elsewhere that this shift away from liberalism toward sovereignty is a real possibility given the rise of relatively pro-sovereign states like China, India, and Indonesia (Griffiths, 2016b). Less grounded in the liberal tradition, these fissiparous states almost always insist that the consent of the home state is a prerequisite for granting recognition to breakaway regions. China is particularly important here given its potential to project power and influence.

In comparison with these three possibilities is the prospect of returning to a regime based on de facto recognition. Such a return is hard to imagine given the absence of supporters. Most liberal thinkers accustomed to humanitarian intervention will reject the argument that third parties should remain neutral while civil wars rage, and supporters of sovereignty would surely deny the principle that internal nations can gain recognition by prevailing over the state. The age of de facto statehood was thus a unique moment in international life, following the articulation of a negative right to self-determination, but prior to the advancement of a positive right and the sovereign emphasis on border fixity.

Comparative statics of different recognition regimes

There are advantages and disadvantages to the design of any recognition regime, and I will not attempt to claim that one is superior to the others. I will, however, summarize the regimes covered above and highlight some of their consequences. In doing so I proceed from the assumption that the legal/normative framework of any regime shapes the behaviour of the key actors, in this case the state governments and minority nations. There will be exceptions to be sure, and powerful actors will often do what they want, but in the aggregate these frameworks do matter. After all, leaders in contemporary secessionist movements are well aware of the rules of the game. The government of Nagorno-Karabakh has a wealth of legal scholars and political advisors at home, in Armenia, and throughout the larger Armenian diaspora who have expertise in these matters. During the 1990s, Bougainville's leadership networked with their counterparts in East Timor, discussing different strategies for courting international favour. There is even a private dimension to the contemporary regime, where consulting firms like Independent Diplomat assist aspirants like Kosovo and Somaliland, among others, to navigate the rules and norms that determine recognition.

Figure 2 displays the five regime types that have been discussed. These include recognition by consent, de facto recognition, and constitutive recognition in the form that has existed since 1945, and in the form it could take if a remedial right or primary right to independence became entrenched. Each regime type is the product of the relative balance between sovereign and liberal norms and their particular interpretations. Whereas the sovereign tradition is clearly dominant in a

	Consent	De Facto	Post-1945	Constitutive Post-1945 + Remedial Right	Post-1945 + Primary Right
Sovereign or Liberal Dominant?	sovereign	mixed	mixed	liberal	liberal
General Effects?	minority exclusion	oppression, revolution	international discord	international discord, cooptation, provocation	international discord, cooptation, fragmentation
Fitness of New States?	indeterminate	strong	strong / weak	strong / weak	strong / moderately weak

Figure 2. Different recognition regimes.

consent-based system, the remedial and primary rights regimes represent periods of relative liberal dominance. Meanwhile, the de facto and contemporary post-1945 regimes represent more balanced configurations.

What are the general effects of territorial design in each of these regimes? In a consent-based regime, the primary danger is minority exclusion. If the international community honours the home state veto, and there is no positive right to self-determination, then each state would control the fate of their internal nations. Some governments will no doubt treat their minority nations with fairness, but the pressure to do so is less than in other regimes, and the costs of exclusion are low (Mylonas, 2013). In contrast, a de facto regime implies an altogether different strategic environment. Here, governments have to take care and prevent the rise of secessionist groups strong enough to challenge the state, defeat it, and thereby garner international recognition. Meanwhile, dissatisfied groups have strong incentives to challenge the state when they anticipate success. In comparison to a consent-based regime, we should expect to see greater patterns of oppression and revolution.

Constitutive regimes ought to produce different general effects. First, the inculcation of a positive right to self-determination creates pressure for consensus that is hard to attain in a diverse international environment, and interstate discord can result. This is one of the reasons why Fabry argues that the de facto regime is superior: it requires less consensus and therefore makes for clearer recognition criteria (Fabry, 2010, p. 220). However, the assertion of a positive right to self-determination means that minority nations can appeal to the international community for support, without having to first prevail over their sovereign. This possibility to bypass the state suggests interesting dynamics should a remedial or primary right become entrenched. In both cases, states would have incentive to co-opt potential secessionists as a way to prevent conflicts that can generate remedial claims, or dampen support for referenda that can result in fragmentation. In other respects these regime types differ. The downside to a remedial right is the potential for moral hazard: secessionists have an incentive to provoke the state into behaving badly (Kuperman, 2008). The downside to a primary right is the possibility of excessive fragmentation if referenda are easy to hold.

It is interesting to speculate on the institutional and socioeconomic fitness of the states that may emerge in each regime. Fabry argues that a weakness of the current constitutive regime is that it sometimes admits weak and unfit states that meet the criteria for admission and denies other nations like Somaliland that are actually functional states (Fabry, 2010, p. 220). In contrast, the de facto regime has the advantage that while states may be born from blood, they will tend to be strong since the unfit will usually be defeated by their government. Fabry's argument could be extended to cover the remaining constitutive regimes. A remedial right could lead to the creation of states whose primary virtue, with respect to obtaining recognition, is that they were the site of conflict, human rights abuses, or perhaps genocide. Such developments often occur precisely where state structures are weak. Primary rights are less of an issue in that regard since conflict is not the catalyst, and, at a minimum, the region has to have the institutional capacity to hold a plebiscite on independence. Whether a consent-based regime is likely to produce strong or weak states is indeterminate since it is unclear what factors generate patterns of consent and how those factors correlate with the strength of break-away regions.

CONCLUSION

The recognition regime will remain a cornerstone of international politics as long as it takes place in a closed system. There is no additional land to expand into, not since the global enclosure movement of the late nineteenth century brought all land outside of Antarctica into the system. The combination of a growing and increasingly interconnected human population in a fixed amount of space only intensifies the problem of crowding and the need to control admission to sovereign statehood. Research into earlier state systems suggests that low-density environments where frontier zones and open land were realities of diplomatic life tended to possess few, if any, constitutive processes to regulate membership (Butcher & Griffiths, 2015). States could often simply declare themselves because crowding was not a problem and the rules to regulate crowding were undeveloped. I submit that the ontological question of which is prior – states or the system (Coggins, 2014; Erman, 2013) – can be answered by bringing in the theory of clubs. States are prior to systems, but once systems thicken and crowding becomes an issue and order develops, the club members need to determine who can be a state.[4] To paraphrase Tilly, the state made the system and the system made the state (1975, p. 42).

Unless a new political form develops, or new land it created off-world or from the sea, the future design of the recognition regime will be determined by the normative conflict between sovereignty and liberalism. Should the pendulum swing in the direction of greater liberal rights, we may see the coalescence of remedial and/or primary rights criteria. Conversely, a swing toward sovereignty may produce a consent-based regime. For aspiring nations these considerations amount to more than just an intellectual exercise. Both Somaliland and Kurdistan would likely be sovereign were we living in a period of de facto statehood, and they would both have strong claims if the sovereignty club recognized a remedial right. Catalan nationalists have demanded an independence referendum and Spain has denied them. If the international community came to support a primary right to independence, Catalonia would have a clear path to statehood. Sovereignty, however, would remain elusive for all three nations in a consent-based system.

ACKNOWLEDGEMENTS

I am obliged to Boaz Atzili and Burak Kadercan for assembling an excellent research group, and I thank them and Jordan Branch, Ahsan Butt, Ehud Eiran, Gerry Kearns, Katharine Kindervater, Aliza Luft, Ian Lustick, Harris Mylonas, Nadav Shelef, Ches Thurber, and Ariel Zellman for their useful feedback.

DISCLOSURE STATEMENT

No potential conflict of interest was reported by the author.

FUNDING

I thank the Department of Government and International Relations at the University of Sydney for funding my research.

NOTES

1. When discussing norms I adopt the following definition: norms are 'standards of appropriate behaviour for actors with a given identity' (Finnemore & Sikkink, 1998).
2. There is no automatic tension between sovereignty and self-determination. The tension arises when stateless nations seek independence and their state denies them.
3. My argument proceeds from the premise that national identity is constructed. The often fuzzy and overlapping contours of nations shift over time in relation to state boundaries and the efforts of governments, among other factors.
4. See Kim and Wolford (2014) on the relationship between interaction capacity and international order.

REFERENCES

Agne, H., Bartelson, J., Erman, E., Lindemann, T., Herborth, B., Kessler, O., ... Krasner, S. D. (2013). Symposium 'the politics of international recognition'. *International Theory*, 5(1), 94–107.

Armitage, D. (2007). *The declaration of independence*. Cambridge, MA: Harvard University Press.

Atzili, B. (2012). *Good fences, bad neighbors: Border fixity and international conflict*. Chicago, IL: University of Chicago Press.

Atzili, B., & Kadercan, B. (2017). Territorial designs and international politics: The diverging constitution of space and boundaries. *Territory, Politics, Governance*. Forthcoming.

Banai, A. (2014). The territorial rights of legitimate states: A pluralist interpretation. *International Theory*, 6(1), 140–157.

Bartos, T. (1997). Uti possidetis. Quo vadis? *Australian Year Book of International Law*, 18, 37–96.

Beran, H. (1998). A democratic theory of political self-determination for a new world order. In Percy Lehning (Ed.), *Theories of secession* (pp. 32–59). New York, NY: Routledge.

Buchanan, A. (2003). The making and unmaking of boundaries: What liberalism has to say. In Allen Buchanan & Margaret Moore (Eds.), *States, nations, and borders* (pp. 231–261). Cambridge: Cambridge University Press.

Butcher, C., & Griffiths, R. (2014). Alternative International Systems? System Structure and Violent Conflict in 19th Century West Africa, Southeast Asia, and South Asia. *Review of International Studies*, 41(4), 715–737.

Buchanan, J. M. (1965). An economic theory of clubs. *Economica*, 32(125), 1–14.

Buzan, B., & Little, R. (2000). *International systems in world history: Remaking the study of international relations*. Oxford: Oxford University Press.

Coggins, B. L. (2014). *Power politics and state formation in the twentieth century: The dynamics of recognition*. Cambridge: Cambridge University Press.

Erman, E. (2013). The recognitive practices of declaring and constituting statehood. *International Theory*, 5(1), 129–150.

Fabry, M. (2010). *Recognizing states: International society and the establishment of new states since 1776*. Oxford: Oxford University Press.

Fazal, T. (2007). *State death: The politics and geography of conquest, occupation, and annexation*. Princeton, NJ: Princeton University Press.

Fazal, T., & Griffiths, R. (2014). Membership has its privileges: The changing benefits of statehood. *International Studies Review*, 16(1), 79–106.

Finnemore, M., & Sikkink, K. (1998). International norm dynamics and political change. *International Organization*, 52(4), 887–917.

Gellner, E. (1983). *Nations and nationalism*. Ithaca, NY: Cornell University Press.

Griffiths, R. D. (2016a). *Age of secession: The international and domestic determinants of state birth*. Cambridge: Cambridge University Press.

Griffiths, R. D. (2016b). States, nations, and territorial stability: Why Chinese hegemony would be better for international order. *Security Studies*, 25(3), 519–545.

Halperin, M. H., Scheffer, D., & Small, P. L. (1992). *Self-determination in the new world order*. Washington, DC: Carnegie Endowment for International Peace.

Jackson, R. (1993). The weight of ideas in decolonization: Normative change in international relations. In Judith Goldstein & Robert O. Keohane (Eds.), *Ideas and foreign policy: Beliefs, institutions, and political change* (pp. 113–138). Ithaca, NY: Cornell University Press.

Jackson, R. H. (1990). *Quasi-states: Sovereignty, international relations, and the third world*. Cambridge: Cambridge University Press.

Kadercan, B. (2015). Triangulating territory: A case for pragmatic interaction between political science, political geography, and critical IR. *International Theory*, 7(1), 125–161.

Kim, M., & Wolford, S. (2014). Choosing anarchy: Institutional alternatives and the global order. *International Theory*, 6(1), 28–67.

Krasner, S. (1999). *Sovereignty: Organized hypocrisy*. Princeton, NJ: Princeton University Press.

Krasner, S. (2013). Recognition: Organized hypocrisy once again. *International Theory, 5*(1), 170–176.

Kuperman, A. (2008). The moral hazard of humanitarian intervention: Lessons from the Balkans. *International Studies Quarterly, 52*(1), 49–80.

Manela, E. (2007). *The Wilsonian moment: Self-determination and the international origins of anticolonial nationalism*. Oxford: Oxford University Press.

Mayall, J. (1990). *Nationalism and international society*. Cambridge: Cambridge University Press.

Meetser, D. H. (2012). Remedial secession: A positive or negative force for the prevention and reduction of armed conflict. *Canadian Foreign Policy Journal, 18*(2), 151–163.

Mueller, D. C. (1989). *Public choice II*. Cambridge: Cambridge University Press.

Mylonas, H. (2013). *The politics of nation-building: Making co-nationals, refugees and minorities*. Cambridge: Cambridge University Press.

Norman, W. (1998). The ethics of secession as the regulation of secessionist politics. In Margaret Moore (Ed.), *National self-determination and secession* (pp. 34–61). Oxford: Oxford University Press.

Osiander, A. (2001). Sovereignty, international relations, and the westphalian myth. *International Organization, 55* (2), 251–287.

Osterud, O. (1997). The narrow gate: Entry to the club of sovereign states. *Review of International Studies, 23*, 167–84.

Radan, P. (2002). *The break-up of Yugoslavia in international law*. London: Routledge.

Ratner, S. R. (1996). Drawing a better line: Uti possidetis and the borders of new states. *The American Journal of International Law, 94*(4), 590–624.

Sandholtz, W., & Stiles, K. (2008). *International norms and cycles of change*. Oxford: Oxford University Press.

Shaw, M. N. (1996). The heritage of states: The principle of uti possidetis juris today. *British Yearbook of International Law, 67*, 75–154.

Spruyt, H. (1994). *The sovereign state and its competitors*. Princeton, NJ: Princeton University Press.

Tilly, C. (1975). *The formation of national states in Western Europe*. Princeton, NJ: Princeton University Press.

Wellman, C. H. (2005). *A theory of secession*. Cambridge: Cambridge University Press.

Zacher, M. (2001). The territorial integrity norm: International boundaries and the use of force. *International Organization, 55*(20), 215–250.

Territorial design and grand strategy in the Ottoman Empire

Burak Kadercan

ABSTRACT

Territorial design and grand strategy in the Ottoman Empire. *Territory, Politics, Governance*. How could the Ottoman Empire preserve intrastate peace and stability from its emergence in the 14th century until the 19th in regions – especially the Balkans and the Middle East – that later became hotbeds for ethnic, religious, and sectarian conflict while at the same time fighting numerous interstate wars? This paper offers a novel explanation for this puzzle, based on the notion of 'territorial design'. The Ottomans were able to preserve internal peace and stability thanks to their flexible and pragmatic approach to managing the space–society–politics nexus, which in fact followed from their grand strategy for expansion in a cost-effective fashion. The theoretical and historical analysis provided here also has implications for tackling macro-historical puzzles and patterns from an interdisciplinary perspective, positioning the Ottoman case vis-à-vis international relations theory, and motivating questions about the origins of the present-day territorial order.

摘要

奥图曼帝国的领土计划与宏观战略。*Territory, Politics, Governance*。奥图曼帝国如何从其自十四世纪兴起至十九世纪间，在特别是巴尔干和中东等区域中保持国内的和平与稳定—这些区域随后成为种族、宗教与教派冲突的温床—并同时进行无数的国际征战？本文根据'领土计划'的概念，对该谜题提供崭新的解释。奥图曼人由于对管理空间—社会—政治轴线採取弹性且务实的方法，因此能够保有内部的和平和稳定，而该方法实则遵循他们以符合成本效益的方式扩张的宏观战略。此处提供的理论与历史分析，同时对于以跨领域的视角处理巨观历史谜题和模式具有意涵，它将奥图曼的案例置放在国际关系理论的对面进行比较，并激发有关当前领土秩序的起源之问题。

RÉSUMÉ

La délimitation du territoire et la grande stratégie de l'Empire ottoman. *Territory, Politics, Governance*. Comment l'Empire ottoman a-t-il pu assurer la paix et la stabilité intra-étatique depuis sa naissance au 14e siècle jusqu'au 19e siècle - surtout aux Balkans et au Moyen-Orient – dans des régions devenues plus tard des foyers de conflits ethniques, religieux et sectaires, tout en faisant simultanément de nombreuses guerres inter-étatiques? Cet article fournit une réponse originale à cette question, fondée sur la notion de la 'délimitation du territoire'. Les Ottomans ont pu assurer la paix et la stabilité internes grâce à leur approche flexible et pragmatique pour gérer le lien spatialo-politico-sociétal, qui ressort en effet de leur grande stratégie en faveur d'une expansion efficace sur le plan des coûts. Cette présente analyse théorique et historique a aussi des implications pour la manière d'aborder les questions et les tendances macro-historiques d'un point de vue interdisciplinaire, la mise en place de l'étude de cas ottomane vis-à-vis de la théorie des relations internationales, et l'incitation à poser des questions au sujet des origines de l'ordre territorial en vigueur.

RESUMEN

Diseño territorial y gran estrategia en el Imperio Otomano. *Territory, Politics, Governance*. ¿Cómo pudo el Imperio Otomano mantener la paz y la estabilidad intraestatales desde su aparición en el siglo XIV hasta el siglo XIX en regiones – especialmente los Balcanes y Oriente Medio – que posteriormente serían hervideros de conflictos étnicos, religiosos y sectarios, luchando a la vez en numerosas guerras entre Estados? En este artículo se ofrece una nueva explicación a este enigma basada en la noción de 'diseño territorial'. Los otomanos fueron capaces de mantener la paz y la estabilidad internas gracias a su enfoque flexible y pragmático al gestionar el nexo entre espacio, sociedad y política, que de hecho era una herencia de su gran estrategia para una expansión de manera rentable. El análisis teórico e histórico que aquí se presenta también tiene repercusiones para los enigmas macro-históricos y los patrones desde una perspectiva interdisciplinaria, puesto que sitúa el caso otomano frente a la teoría de relaciones internacionales y provoca cuestiones sobre los orígenes del orden territorial de hoy día.

The association between territory, states, and war lies at the heart of the theory and practice of international politics. States are defined in terms of their relationship to territory and wars between and within states almost always have a territorial component, either as a cause or consequence. While territory can be seen as the linchpin that ties states and war to each other, the concept does not stand for an immutable 'object'. Instead, territory is best seen as a politically and culturally malleable institution that regulates interactions taking place within the space–society–politics nexus.[1]

Acknowledging that territorial practices show variance across time and space, in turn, motivates questions about the conventional wisdom involving the relationship between war-making and state-building. Best illustrated with Charles Tilly's (1990) dictum that 'the state made war, and war made the state', international relations (IR) scholarship has long recognized the existence of a coterminous and reflexive relationship between state-building mechanisms and efforts to produce as well as project military power. A 'territorial' interpretation of the said relationship, in turn, has to deal with at least two main questions: how does a state's approach to territory and territoriality affect its state-building and power projection mechanisms; and to what extent do different forms of institution-building and power projection affect a polity's territoriality?[2]

This paper aims to explore the relationship between territory and grand strategy as well as states' attitudes toward management of intrastate peace and stability in the context of an empirical puzzle. How could the Ottoman Empire preserve intrastate peace and stability from its emergence in the fourteenth century until the nineteenth century in regions – especially the Balkans and the Middle East – that later became hotbeds for ethnic, religious, and sectarian conflict while at the same time fighting numerous interstate wars? Conventional wisdom suggests that the Ottomans, who were supposedly driven by an innate penchant for territorial conquest, ruled the lands they conquered effectively as long as they remained a strong state.[3] The gradual decline of the Ottoman power accelerated by the nineteenth century and unleashed latent ethnic, religious, and sectarian tensions in these regions, triggering chronic intrastate and inter-communal conflict. Recent historical and sociological research on the Ottoman Empire, however, suggests that the conventional wisdom is misleading on both accounts. First, we have little, if any, reason to think that the Ottomans' penchant for territorial conquest differed from that of their European counterparts; Suleiman the Great's Ottoman Empire in the sixteenth century, for example, was not considerably more (or less) warlike than Louis XIV's France during the seventeenth century. Second, the 'timing' of the Ottoman decline and the rise of inter-communal and ethnic/sectarian/religious conflicts do not match: the Ottomans were able to rule the relevant lands with peace and stability even centuries after they were started to be seen as a 'sick man' among other great powers. The Ottoman rule, especially in the Balkans and Middle East, was built on the principle of institutional flexibility and pragmatism (which promoted a great deal of toleration for diversity), not on absolutism or systematic repression.[4]

I argue that both the drive for territorial conquest and the stability that the Ottoman Empire was able to provide within its domain can be best examined by scrutinizing the relationship between the Ottomans' territorial design and grand strategy. The early Ottoman grand strategy was built on expanding the territorial reach of the empire – not only in terms of direct governance but also defined in terms of 'spheres of influence' – in a rather 'cost-effective' fashion. This grand strategy involved three components: (1) a 'moving' frontier that would help the Ottomans to attract and motivate fighters while also placing continuous pressure on their neighbours, (2) 'co-opting' the social groups that were living on the edges of the empire by providing them with selective incentives, and (3) minimizing resistance and maximizing cooperation from the local populations in the newly acquired lands (which then could be used as stepping stones for further expansion). This three-pronged grand strategy, in turn, was built on a particular approach to territory and territoriality.

From a territorial perspective, most of the European absolutist states from the sixteenth century onwards showed a consistent preference for and a gradual inclination toward 'hardening' their borders and 'homogenizing' the space–society–politics nexus inside these borders.[5] The Ottoman Empire, conversely, consciously opted for a 'soft' and 'flexible' approach to demarcating space while also empowering a heterogeneous spatial-political dynamic within the lands it ruled over. Heterogeneous management of the territories they controlled made it possible for the Ottomans to establish inter-communal peace and effective conflict-resolution mechanisms, especially in regions that were vulnerable to religious, sectarian, and ethnic strife. The multilayered and context-dependent politicization of space allowed the Ottomans not only to rule over vast territories for centuries in a cost-effective fashion, but also to engage in territorial expansion well into the seventeenth century. At the end of Ottoman expansion, the territorial design that the Ottomans utilized to expand had already 'stuck'. This allowed the empire to govern with relative stability until the nineteenth century, even during numerous interstate wars, which were becoming increasingly defensive in nature.

The territorial interpretation of the Ottoman experience also provides insights about the gradual disintegration of the empire in the nineteenth and twentieth centuries. The Ottomans governed their domains through increasingly multifaceted and heterogeneous political-spatial arrangements for centuries, only to introduce, in a rather 'rushed' fashion, a Western-style territorial order from the nineteenth century onwards. Imposition of such a 'strict' territorial design was a function of the defeats the Ottomans suffered in the military and political sphere at the hands of their Western or 'Westernizing' competitors (most notably, Russia after Peter the Great's reforms). The centuries-old territorial design of the Ottoman Empire eventually clashed with the new order that the Ottoman modernizing elites tried to impose upon the space–politics–society nexus especially in the second half of the nineteenth century. The result was chronic intrastate and inter-communal violence as well as instability within the empire by the late-nineteenth and early-twentieth centuries.

Note that this article does not provide a conclusive empirical analysis on the subject. It is best seen as a theoretical as well as historical probe into the relationship between the Ottoman territorial design and grand strategy. In particular, the arguments presented here make four contributions to the relevant scholarly debates. First, it proposes a novel theoretical framework that explores the origins and consequences of different territorial arrangements from a macro-historical perspective. Second, it situates the Ottoman case vis-à-vis IR literature, which has yet to fully engage the Ottomans (Kadercan, 2015b).

Third, this paper provides a blueprint for a novel interpretation of the origins of the present-day territorial order. Conventional accounts provide a linear and Euro-centric narrative that starts from the birth of the territorial state in Europe during the course of the seventeenth century and ends with the global 'spread' of the Westphalian model in the twentieth century.[6] In these narratives, the extra-Westphalian territorial models are treated as if they are *a-territorial* or anomalies that, sooner or later, had to (or, have to) converge on the Westphalian baseline. However, as the exploration of the Ottoman case also confirms, the global territorial order itself is best conceptualized as a heterogeneous system co-constituted reflexively by different, and sometimes incompatible, territorial arrangements.

Finally, this study is an attempt to 'bring empires back in' with respect to IR theory and historiography. While IR, to a large extent, came of age after the First World War when much of the globe was still governed through imperial designs, it barely paid attention to the study of empires, consistently prioritizing the [ideal of] Westphalian state. As Barkawi (2010, p. 1361) forcefully argued, 'IR [as a discipline] was founded amidst empire, but discovered instead only a world of sovereign states and their collective action problems.' In this context, the Ottomans can be best thought of as an example of many imperial designs, the study of which may help students of international politics to grapple with not only the past, but also the present and future, of world politics. Put differently, this paper does not claim that the case of the Ottomans was an 'exceptional' one, but suggests that it was one among many other imperial designs that can be studied from a territorial perspective.

The remainder of this paper is organized into four sections. First, I introduce the research question. The second section outlines the 'modular' theoretical framework that aims to differentiate between 'master' territorial designs. The third section then delves deeper into the specifics of the Ottoman territorial design by examining its origins, associated practices, and consequences for grand strategy. In the fourth section, I elaborate on a number of implications that follow from this study.

THE CURIOUS CASE OF THE OTTOMAN EMPIRE: WAR ABROAD, [RELATIVE] PEACE AT HOME

The Ottoman Empire's origins can be traced to 1299. The House of Osman, at the time, was one of the smaller Turkic emirates in Asia Minor and not the most likely candidate for a future transcontinental empire. However, thanks to its rulers' firm grasp of power politics and dexterity in institution-building, the Ottomans became the single most powerful state in not only the Middle

East but also Europe by the sixteenth century, subduing the Mamlukes in Egypt (1517) and expanding as far as the gates of Vienna (1526). The Ottoman Empire fought numerous successful wars, which enabled it to build a vast empire comprised of various social groups hailing from different ethnic, religious, and sectarian backgrounds. The Ottomans of the early modern era were also able to rule their domains in relatively peaceful terms.[7] The question then becomes, how can we explain the peace and stability that the Ottomans were able to provide amidst frequent interstate war?

There exists no discernible answer in IR literature. Three factors can explain IR's 'silence' about the patterns of war and peace (or stability and instability) in the Ottoman case. First, IR as a subfield (or as a discipline) was born – and, to a large extent, still remains – a Western-centric enterprise. IR scholars have long taken the so-called modern state system as their starting point, barely paying attention to the polities and geographies that remained outside the Westphalian club. The second factor is 'timing'. The Ottoman Empire was formally admitted to the Westphalian system only by 1856, when the Ottomans had already lost their prominence (Bull, 1977).[8] As a result, in the very rare moments that the Ottoman Empire showed up in IR literature, it was seen and projected as a rather passive and weak – and most certainly doomed and moribund – actor that did not necessarily require special attention. The third factor that led to the invisibility of the Ottoman Empire in IR follows from the fact that the empire was never truly colonized. When the post-colonial approaches made their way into IR, scholars working in this vein spent little time dealing with the Ottoman Empire, since the frameworks they employed did not necessarily apply to it.

In the absence of rigorous scholarly engagement with the place of the Ottomans in theory and historiography of IR, conventional wisdom on the Ottoman Empire's approach to warfare has long been shaped by persistent biases that can be traced as far back as the fifteenth century. As Neumann and Welsh highlighted, the Ottomans, especially in the early modern era, served the role of a robust 'other' for the creation of a European identity (Neumann & Welsh, 1991). Posing the biggest geopolitical challenge to Christian hegemony in Europe from the fourteenth century onwards, the Ottomans were seen as the harbingers of Islamic conquest and unredeemable enemies of Christians everywhere. In European thinking, the lands occupied by the Ottomans also represented zones of complete submission (to despotic authority) and near-senseless brutality.[9]

In this geopolitical representation, the Ottoman Empire was portrayed either as a 'gunpowder empire' whose existence depended on territorial conquest and pillage or as a 'religious' entity driven by an unredeemable otherworldly zeal. According to conventional wisdom at the time, the Ottoman Empire perceived the world in Manichean terms, imagining itself to be in a Holy War against the infidels until *dar-al Islam* (the house of Islam) finally conquered *dar-al harb* (the house of war, which stood for the lands of the infidels).[10] However, conventional thinking – which was subsequently emboldened by a number of academic writings during the course of the twentieth century[11] – follows not from a holistic understanding of the Ottoman historiography, but from Orientalist prejudices.[12] In the words of Yurdusev (2004, p. 3), the relevant accounts do not 'do justice to the historical record'.

In reality, the Ottomans proved themselves to be sophisticated institution builders, synthesizing practices from the Turkic Seljuk Empire (1037–1194) as well as the classical Islamic empires, and, most notably, the Byzantine Empire. The claim that the Ottoman state's foreign policy was a function of religious beliefs and zeal, in turn, also finds little support from the historical and sociological research on the Ottomans.[13] While references to religion constituted an important part of the Ottoman court as well as the social-political life, pragmatism and a cunning understanding of Realpolitik played much more important roles in determining grand strategy than religious inclinations or beliefs did (Arı, 2004, p. 37; Yurdusev, 2004, p. 16).

In the absence of an informed answer to the puzzle in hand, the territorial design approach can help students of IR and political geography extract novel insights about the relationship between external conflict and internal (in)stability. The challenge for constructing a territorial interpretation of the Ottomans' grand strategy is two-fold. First, at the very minimum, IR scholars should be able to position the Ottomans' territorial system vis-à-vis other polities with which they are familiar. Put differently, a key aspect of such a framework would be its ability to 'speak to' the conventional Westphalian model that lies at the heart of IR.[14] It follows that such interpretation should avoid 'Ottoman exceptionalism', or the tendency to portray the Ottoman experience as a unique case that should be studied in its own right and in isolation. Second, the territorial interpretation of the Ottomans should also recognize the empire's particular characteristics. Therefore, the ideal territorial interpretation of the Ottoman experience would entail both 'modular' and 'specific' components.

In the next two sections, I develop such a 'two-level' interpretation. First, I differentiate between four key territorial designs (or 'master models'), positioning the Ottoman experience within the broader context of what can be referred to as 'imperial territorial governance'. Second, I examine some of the key characteristics of the Ottoman political system that gave the empire its particular territorial design. Together, these two components can shed light on the relationship between the Ottoman grand strategy and patterns in state-building as well as power projection from a territorial perspective.

THEORY: TWO FACES OF THE TERRITORIAL DESIGN

Following the territorial design framework, territory can be conceptualized in three dimensions: the physical features of space (or land), demarcation processes, and the constitution of demarcated space. The physical components of territory point toward the natural (or geographical) attributes of territory as well as economic and demographic resources attached to it. Demarcation, in turn, requires human agency and involves the process of delineating and compartmentalizing space, which can range from the Westphalian 'hard' borders to porous and fluid frontiers (Kratochwil, 1986). Demarcation processes will determine the modes of transaction across different political units, as well as their as proximity and contiguity vis-à-vis each other. The very constitutive properties of territory refer to the particular political and social functions as well as meanings assigned to demarcated space, which follow from the institutionalization of legal, administrative, political, and cultural practices that manage and regulate the relationship between society, state, and space.[15] Scrutinizing the interaction between the processes related with demarcation and constitution of territorial units allows for studying the variation in states' attitudes toward territory.

In this framework, geographical space would refer to physical features such as oceans, waterways, altitude as well as natural [read material] resources that may be attached to the space (or land) in question.[16] The impacts of geographical space on politics are not necessarily constant but can vary depending on environmental or technological change. While the first dimension of territory does not require territorialization, demarcation and constitution of territory follow from politicization of space and require human agency. Territorialization – by way of categorizing and delineating space – directly aims to organize and regulate individual and social behaviour. It does so by way of defining the scope and extent of authority and the cultural as well as emotive affiliations of human groups vis-à-vis space. For territories to exist in any meaningful sense, their demarcation and constitution also need to be reified periodically (if not continuously) and systematically through institutionalized practices.

Building on this three-pronged approach to territory and territoriality, I offer a two-dimensional framework that builds on demarcation processes and the different ways in which space within demarcated territories are constituted in both material and ideational dimensions. Figure 1 summarizes the interaction between the demarcation and constitution of territory. 'Hard' borders refer to cases where states have both the willingness and capability to commit to pre-defined as well as clearly demarcated borders and exercise near-absolute control over transactions taking

	Attitude Towards Territory's Constitutive Properties	
	Territorial Homogeneity	Territorial Heterogeneity
Hard Borders	"Rigid" Example: Western nation states (especially twentieth century)	"Contradictory" Example: Failing states, post-1945
Soft Borders	"Early Westphalian" Example: European states, 1648-1800s	"Flexible" Example: The Ottoman Empire, 1300s-1800s

(Left margin label: **Attitude Towards Territory's Demarcation Processes**)

Figure 1. Territorial design.

place across them. In the relevant cases, borders are 'tight' and resistant, if not impervious, to change. 'Soft' borders, in contrast, refer to cases where states neither commit to pre-defined boundaries nor (claim to) impose absolute control over exchange of goods and people across them. The softness of the demarcation mechanisms may have to do with the incentives of the relevant political actors, their capabilities to delineate territory in specific terms (and enforce such delineation), or both. In the relevant territorial orders, borders or boundaries are more likely to be subject to change.

In particular, the ideal Westphalian state is built on the notion of hard borders.[17] However, as Osiander (2001) and, more recently, Branch (2014) highlighted, hardening of borders became possible only in the nineteenth century, with the emergence of new political dynamics (such as the notion of popular sovereignty and nationalism) as well as technological advances (most notably in cartography). Therefore, while hard borders are usually associated with the Peace of Westphalia, such borders became more of a reality only by the nineteenth century. Even then, as the territorial exchanges of the nineteenth and twentieth centuries that usually followed interstate wars showed, the borders were still subject to occasional change. Arguably, it was the emergence of the so-called border fixity (or, territorial integrity) norm that eventually finalized the process of hardening of borders in the modern state system.[18]

Homogenous territorial designs, in turn, involve state efforts to unify legal, administrative, political, and cultural practices as well as institutions within demarcated space. The nation-state ideal of the twentieth century is an exemplar. In particular, world political maps in the present day can be taken as ideal (or, 'idealistic') representations of a world order made up of homogenous state territories. Each country is marked by a single shade of a colour, which is uniform within the borders of the state. Germany, for example, is represented by a single shade of blue, and while the 'colour' of Germany separates the German state territory from other countries, it also does not display variation within Germany's borders. Heterogeneous territorial design stands for institutions and practices that organize space–politics relationship in multilayered, context-dependent, and diverse forms. Most European states at least until the sixteenth and seventeenth centuries, the Ottoman Empire, and most European colonies could be named as examples where the political authorities institutionalized territorial heterogeneity.[19]

Building on this framework, we can talk about four variations with respect to how borders are demarcated and how they are constituted within the demarcated terrain. The first is what I refer to as 'rigid' territorial designs, which distinguish themselves with the 'marriage' of hard borders and homogenous spaces. This 'order' is in fact further emboldened by two dynamics. First, nationalism (or appeals to nationalism) leads to state-sponsored and domestically driven discourses and practices involving the inviolability of homelands. The second is the so-called border fixity norm that emerged in the second half of the twentieth century, which aimed to 'freeze' the borders by way of international norms and institutions.

While this master [rigid] territorial design is the baseline for modern imagery and thinking about territory, it can be misleading in two ways. The first is a temporal illusion. Students of international politics may read this territorial design back into the distant past, for example, imagining the politics of seventeenth and eighteenth centuries in terms of a relatively 'new' model. Such illusion can only lead to misleading interpretations of past territorial practices. Second, the geographical scope of this design is more limited than usually surmised. In many parts of the world, the notion of territorial heterogeneity is more representative of states' approach to society–space–politics nexus than territorial homogeneity.

The second master territorial design can be categorized as 'early Westphalian' and is marked by soft[er] borders and institutionalized attempts for homogenization of space–society–politics nexus. In such designs, borders or boundaries may exist in theory, but are either permeable or subject to change. Territorial homogeneity might be an aspirational or operational phenomenon, but what is important is the presence of, or a drive for, institutional mechanisms aiming to homogenize the space–society–politics nexus, or preserve existing homogeneity. From an historical perspective, homogenization in the Westphalian system was established in two stages. In the first aspirational stage, the monarchs aimed at diluting the local bases of power as well as curbing the influence of transnational actors such as the Church or the Empire with varying success.

The second 'operational' stage, in turn, was triggered by the French Revolution and subsequent Napoleonic rule. As Sewell (2004) highlighted, the Revolutionaries, trying to destroy the bases of power of the ancient regime, accelerated the process of 'rationalizing' space. Napoleon, in turn, had two interrelated impacts on the further homogenization of territorial practices in the European system. First, Napoleon's conquests triggered a process where the number of states in Europe (including princedoms) was reduced from almost 300 to around 30. Second, the spread of the Napoleonic code of law further established uniformity in space–society–politics nexus. In the words of Branch (2014, p. 33), 'the states that emerged in the post-Napoleonic period were transformed from their compost and weakly centralized precursors: rulers now wiped clean the remaining medieval complexities and overlapping claims in favor of exclusive territorial rule over clearly delineated states'. Therefore, the early Westphalian design is best applicable to European states between the seventeenth and nineteenth centuries.

The third master design is what I refer to as 'contradictory territorial designs'. These involve cases where the borders are 'hardened' externally but with little territorial homogeneity within the borders. Territorial systems such as these usually emanate from the contradictions between idealized European/Western 'rigid' designs and the local arrangements that predate the imposition of such models. As Horowitz (2004, p. 478) suggests, the dominance of the European/Western powers over the course of the nineteenth and twentieth centuries eventually made the 'rigid delineations observed in Europe' an aspirational master model to be employed by local actors. In many parts of the globe, in this reading, the process of establishing hard borders was 'rushed' (for states strove for hard borders before they established territorial homogeneity), with adverse effects on peace and stability.[20] In particular, as Atzili (2012) argues, the emergence of the border fixity norm, by way of hardening borders 'from the outside', led to chronic instability in regions ranging from the Middle East to Africa.[21]

The final master category refers to the imperial territorial designs, which are associated with soft demarcation principles and territorial heterogeneity. This territorial design reflects the logic of empires, which would be defined as 'a large, composite, multiethnic, and multireligious political [formations] in which relations between center and periphery are regulated through flexible and negotiated arrangements' (Barkey & Godart, 2013, p. 85). In empires, '[middle men] with a territorial base play a central role in key practices, and … [the] power bargains between the center and the middlemen are not uniform, neither ideally nor in practice' (Jordheim & Neumann, 2011,

p. 155). Operating through what Nexon and Wright (2007, p. 254) refer to as 'heterogeneous contracts', 'imperial systems' can be conceived as composite, as opposed to consolidated, polities. Such entities are not 'territorially consolidated because they were never territorially demarcated' (Yurdusev, 2004, p. 18). As Winichakul (1994, p. 79) highlighted in his study on the creation of the Siamese national identity as a geographical entity, such extra-Westphalian entities are comprised of 'numerous boundaries' and 'patchy arrangements of power units' which are intrinsically flexible.

Of the four categories sketched above, the Ottoman experience from the fourteenth until the nineteenth centuries falls neatly within the final one.[22] Positioning Ottoman territorial governance within the broader imperial territorial design is only the first step for charting out the Ottoman territorial design. In the next section, I delve into the particularities of the relationship between Ottoman territorial design and grand strategy as well as state-building efforts.

Ottoman territorial design and grand strategy

Early Ottoman grand strategy from the fourteenth century until the seventeenth century aimed at territorial expansion in a 'cost-effective' fashion. Given that sources of economic and military power were congruent with control of land at the time, the desire for expansion was hardly surprising.[23] Furthermore, the early Ottomans, especially until the mid-fifteenth century, were initially one of the smaller political entities in Asia Minor and had to survive in a very competitive environment, operating on relatively limited resources. In such an environment, the early Ottomans were also compelled to 'expand for security'.[24]

The Ottomans frequently invoked references to religious duty for continuous expansion (in the name of Islam) to galvanize support from Muslim populations. However, the early Ottoman rulers also remained pragmatic with respect to their approach to the relationship between war-making and religious affiliation. Put simply, 'in pursuit of territory, booty, and power' the Ottomans did not hesitate to 'attack co-religionists, ally with former enemies, or hire warriors from any background' (Darling, 2000, p. 138).

The Ottomans' notion of territorial expansion differed from modern European states with respect to the relationship between power projection, acquiring, and holding territory. While the early modern European experience usually associated territorial change via grand battles in war, the Ottomans were less concerned with grand battles as the primary expansion method. Instead, they conceived conquest as an ongoing enterprise that could also be carried out through continuous small-scale raids. Arguably, this had a lot to do with the ways in which the Ottomans thought of territory. Different from the ways in which the modern European states thought of territorial demarcation, the Ottomans did not consider land in terms of discrete pieces of real estate. Territory was seen more in terms of a 'fuzzy' continuum, with no real end-points or beginnings.

The Ottoman grand strategy for long-term expansion, which itself involved a 'great deal of pragmatism and flexibility' (Agoston, 2007, p. 77), was built on three components: (1) a 'moving' frontier that would help the Ottomans to attract and motivate fighters while also placing continuous pressure on their neighbors, (2) 'co-opting' the social groups that were living on the edges of the empire by providing them with selective incentives, and (3) minimizing resistance and maximizing cooperation from the local populations in the newly acquired lands (which then could be used as stepping stones for further expansion). The Ottomans' grand strategy was affected by, and in turn affected, the empire's particular territorial design.

The territorial design that was institutionalized by the Ottomans from the 1300s to the late seventeenth century (initially crafted as a cost-effective expansion method) was 'locked in' even after Ottoman expansion halted. In so many ways, this 'sticky' design played an important role in limiting the extent and scope of intrastate conflict and instability particularly in the Middle East well until the nineteenth century. The territorial design of the Ottomans can be analyzed vis-à-vis its four interconnected layers: (1) its overarching geopolitical principles, (2) territorial heterogeneity, (3) power projection mechanisms, and (4) appeals to co-opt those living in the newly acquired lands.

(1) Overarching geopolitical principles

The first component of the Ottoman territorial design entailed how the Ottomans envisioned the political-spatial nature of the globe, which separated them not only from the modern nation-states but also many Islamic empires. Conventional thinking holds that the Islamic empires thought of the spatial categorization of the world in binary terms. On the one hand, there was *dar-al Islam*, or the lands of Islam, where the society–politics–space nexus was administered through Islamic law and tradition. On the other hand, there was the so-called *dar-al harb*, the lands of war, which was terrain to be conquered in the name of Islam. While it is open to debate if the non-Ottoman Islamic empires actually envisioned the territorial division of the world in such crude terms, a closer look at Ottoman thinking reveals that the empire's geographical philosophy was much more sophisticated. In particular, the Ottomans consciously conceived a 'third' category, in addition to *dar-al harb* and *dar-al Islam*. *Dar al-sulh*, or the lands of peace, stood for the 'Ottoman vassal principalities and other tribute-paying administrations' (Arı, 2004, p. 41).

This spatial categorization suggests that the Ottomans did not think of the global territorial order in binary terms defined as spaces of war versus spaces of Islam, but were cognizant of the grey zones (with many shades of grey, that is) that were not amenable to religion-defined homogeneity. As will also be discussed, this macro-geopolitical perspective suggests that the Ottomans were intentionally trying to create lands of stability in areas where they conquered or were thinking of conquering down the road. This perspective is also compatible with their approach to territory in practice, which was built on a great deal of flexibility and pragmatism.

(2) Territorial heterogeneity

As mentioned above, until the nineteenth century, the Ottoman Empire's territorial design was built on flexible boundaries and a system of heterogeneous management with respect to the space–society–politics nexus. The flexibility and heterogeneity, in so many ways, were a function of the origins of the Ottoman institutions and the make-up of the populations they ruled.

While the Ottomans are usually depicted as primarily an Islamic empire, the Ottoman imperial system evolved or 'was derived' from numerous sources including the Byzantine Empire as well as Turkic and nomadic traditions, not to mention previous Near Eastern models of administration (Agnelov, Batsaki, & Bazzaz, 2013; Yurdusev, 2004, p. 17). Such diversity in design is not surprising given the temporal and spatial extent of the empire. In the words of Gocek (2013, p. 74), '[The Ottoman Empire's] temporal reign traversed the modern and pre-modern eras, and its geographical land mass covered parts of Eastern Europe, the Balkans, Asia Minor, the Arabian Peninsula, and North Africa.' The complexity of the Ottoman institutions only increased with further expansion, as the empire 'became increasingly heterogeneous as it spread over three continents' (Karpat, 1977a, p. 2).

The population over which the Ottomans ruled was also considerably diverse. Even Asia Minor, which is today highly homogenous with respect to religious and ethnic dimensions (thanks to the population transfers of the twentieth century) and usually accepted as the Turkish homeland, was marked by high levels of ethnic, religious, and sectarian differences. Such diversity and the mixed settlement of different social groups made it impractical, or at least very difficult, for the Ottoman state to impose a homogenous administrative and political system within their domain.

Note that while the Ottoman state was imperial in design and purpose, it also cannot easily be defined as colonial in the sense that the term is used in the context of European colonialism (Gocek, 2013, p. 79). There are at least two key differences. First, the Ottoman territorial possessions were largely contiguous. Second, while the Ottoman court was dominated by Sunni Muslims, the Ottomans were not necessarily 'alien' to the societies they ruled over. Additionally, they recognized as well as acknowledged the diversity of the populations within their domain. From an historical point, this is hardly surprising. The Ottomans 'started as the rulers of a predominantly Christian population' (Barkey 2014, p. 471) and 'owed great deal of their success to the cooperation of local Christian elements' (Veinstein, 2013, p. 121).

The early Ottoman state builders, accordingly, did not aim to transform the society–politics–space association by imposing a master 'one-size-fits-all' model of governance. Accordingly, the ideological and institutional structure employed by the Ottomans 'appealed as much to the Muslim as the non-Muslim peoples of the empire, refraining from the imposition of an absolute creed or understanding of one religion, one completely unified and cohesive system' (Barkey 2014, p. 472). In a landscape where 'the frontiers of faith were wide, moveable, and difficult to control' (Brummett, 2015, p. 75), the Ottomans opted for institutional flexibility and pragmatism. This also meant that they shied away from imposing 'hard' borders on the 'porous borderlands between Christianity and Islam' (Barkey 2014, p. 472).

As Karen Barkey recognized, as the Ottomans struggled to control this diverse terrain, they 'made decisions based on immediate concerns' (Barkey, 1991, p. 710). Different from the so-called divide-and-conquer strategy of the early modern European absolutist state, the Ottomans emphasized short term crisis management. In such a system, 'the state [created] conflict [of interest] within the provincial command structure, projecting a shifting rationale for provincial groups to remain loyal to the state' (Barkey, 1991, p. 700). This political system made it both expedient and necessary for the Ottomans to work through local networks of social and political authority. The local notables, in turn, 'found the imperial framework acceptable as long as its demands remained limited to the exercise of limited sovereignty', which was the case at least until the nineteenth century (Keyder, 1997, p. 32).

When compared with most of its counterparts in the West, especially those that can be classified as absolutist states, 'the Ottoman Empire was observably more pluralistic in its sociopolitical and imperial policies, at least judged by the norms of its era' (Iyigun, 2015, p. 30). The pluralistic and tolerant nature of the imperial policies followed the Ottomans' intentions to expand their spheres of influence while also ensuring the continuing obedience of both Muslims and non-Muslims. The result was a 'diverse and tolerant society based on the simultaneous division and integration of communities into the state, while providing them with internal autonomy to organize and lead their peoples in their own traditional ways' (Barkey 2014, p. 475). The reflection of such diversity was also present in what Al-Qattan refers to as 'territorialization of law' in the Ottoman Empire, which established a flexible and fluid system that mediated between *shariah*, *kanun* (traditional law), and local/religious practices (Al-Qattan, 2007, pp. 201–212).

The overall result was an 'institutionally flexible system that provided for domestic and political peace' (Barkey 2014, p. 475) where the likelihood of rebellion and conflict, when compared with the European states of the time, was very low.[25] In sum, the Ottoman approach to the space–society politics nexus was flexible, accommodating, and practical. This approach then contributed to the relatively peaceful governance Ottomans were able to provide in the lands they controlled.

(3) Territory and power projection: the *Ghazi* tradition

As mentioned above, the Ottoman conquest was based on a 'gradual' understanding of expansion.[26] This gradual approach to territorial conquest could be associated with the so-called *Ghazi* tradition. In the Islamic empires, the disregard for hard borders and the embracing of 'open frontiers' revealed itself best in the *Ghazi* order.[27] *Ghazi*, in its traditional interpretation, stood for the Islamic knight who served both for religious reasons as well as for the sake of bounty. *Ghazis* were utilized to expand the empire's frontiers by raiding enemy areas repeatedly, in order to soften up the populations and break down resistance. A cult of martyrdom was combined with a remarkably flexible and pragmatic approach not only to territorial expansion, but also to strategic retreats and territorial contraction. As Kafadar (1995) maintains, in the Ottoman state warfare was usually depicted in terms of desultory frontier raiding, not grand battles, which was in fact a major aspect of the *Ghazi* order.

The term *Ghazi* was at the centre of decades-long debate in the Ottoman historiography, which makes it necessary to elaborate further on the subject. While the early interpretations of the *Ghazi* tradition represented the institution as a religion-fueled war-like enterprise, more recent literature established the pragmatic and sophisticated nature of the tradition. To begin with, the *Ghazi* order was not strictly warlike. The frontier society that hosted and produced the majority of the *Ghazi* fighters was both tolerant and diverse. In fact, the *Ghazi* order acted as 'the most powerful and inclusive unifying device available to conquerors on the frontier, more so than tribalism, origin, religion, language, or culture' (Darling, 2000, p. 157). Furthermore, while the *Ghazi* practice had its roots in Islamic thought, it was not driven solely by religious concerns (Gürkan, 2012). The Ottoman sultans often invoked the *Ghazi* ideal, but 'the ideal served more as a legitimizing ideology than as an organizing principle of the state' (Dale, 2010, p. 55).

Put differently, *Ghazi* tradition, at least in the way that the Ottomans employed it, was built on pragmatism and aimed at integration of new territories to the imperial system in a cost-effective fashion. In the words of Darling (2000, p. 137), the *Ghazi* order was 'inclusive rather than exclusive, aiming at the attachment of new territories and new adherents by whatever means proved successful, whether violent or pacific'. As Inalcık (1973, p. 66) emphasizes, the *Ghazi* tradition had a distinct emphasis on keeping the subjects of the empire content with their everyday lives. For example, between 1299 and 1402, when the *Ghazi* order exerted its influence in newly conquered Christian-majority areas, especially in the Balkans (but also Asia Minor), it extracted only limited taxes and relieved the locals of personal tasks they had been held responsible for by their [former] Byzantine and Latin rulers (Karpat, 1977b, p. 86).

Once the Ottomans completed the 'infiltration' stage, the next step was to expand their authority by co-opting the locals, which required flexibility and pragmatism in managing the society–space–politics relationship.

(4) Co-optation and long-term pacification

The Ottoman territorial design was built on relatively mild interference with the local arrangements in the newly conquered areas, at least in the short term. According to Inalcik (1954, p. 103), the Ottoman conquests involved two stages. The first was a period of suzerainty, which then would be replaced by a more direct form of control following the elimination of native dynasties. This process took a long time and did not aim at transforming the social and political structure in the conquered lands, which were usually preserved in their pre-Ottoman administrative boundaries (Inalcik, 1954, p. 108). Second, 'the Ottomans often conquered territories without fundamentally transforming their own peculiar rules of reproduction be it legal, ideological, and even material' (Nisancioglu, 2014, p. 336). For example, the conquests in the Balkans did not lead to major disruptions in economic and social life and Ottoman rule 'provided room for the continuity of local traditions and life patterns' (Minkov, 2004, p. 34). Even when the Ottomans transitioned into Inalcik's 'second stage' of eventually liquidating the local nobility, such acts were 'not resented by the masses who had little in common with the [nobility] and had often suffered grievously from arbitrary rule' (Sugar, 1977, pp. 274–275). As a result, Ottoman rulers often succeeded in co-opting the masses in newly conquered areas.

Overall, while the spatial extent of the Ottomans expanded considerably between the fourteenth and seventeenth centuries, the Ottoman rulers refrained from remaking the spatial-political order in the lands they conquered. Such 'hands off' approach to governing people and space helped the Ottomans to preserve peace and stability in regions that were especially susceptible to conflict and instability for centuries, even in the face of frequent interstate war.[28] If that is the case, what does this framework tell us about the rise of violent conflict and instability in the Ottoman Empire during the course of the nineteenth and twentieth centuries?

The collapse of the traditional Ottoman territorial order followed the Westernization efforts initiated rapidly in the second half of the nineteenth century. These efforts involved efforts to remake the state institutions on the basis of the Western nation-state model. There were two interrelated motives behind such efforts. The first was the extent and scope of the military defeats suffered at the hands of European powers as well as Russia. Until the nineteenth century, Ottoman rulers considered military defeats primarily as a military problem and refrained from large-scale political and administrative reforms, focusing primarily on military reformation. By the early nineteenth century, however, the Ottomans' increasing inferiority on the battlefield eventually convinced their leadership to emulate the Western institutions not only in the military but also in administrative and political dimensions. Second, by the nineteenth century European states were able to interfere with the ways in which the Ottomans ran their institutions. In general, the Ottomans were asked for two contradictory transformations in their domestic order. On the one hand, the outside powers wanted the Ottomans to become more like a European nation-state with respect to managing their territories. On the other hand, the Ottomans were compelled to allow the external powers to project legal and political authority within the same domain.

These pressures culminated in the so-called Tanzimat Fermani of 1839 (also known as the Imperial Edict of Gulhane). The so-called Tanzimat reforms constituted the first major attempt at transforming the very fabric of the Ottoman state. The reforms aimed to impose uniformity in taxation, military service, property rights, and law.[29] Attempts to homogenize the space–society–politics nexus and impose 'harder' borders eventually led to numerous internal conflicts and rebellions within the empire (Makdisi, 2002; Zubaida, 2002, p. 205). A major driving factor was the clash between the traditional flexibility of the Ottoman territorial design and the rigidity of the new order that the Ottoman elites were trying to impose in a rather top-down and 'rushed' fashion. In the words of Gocek (2013, p. 88), 'Western European practices and institutions adversely impacted the fluidity of Ottoman identity' and eventually 'identities became more solid and stratified, introducing publicly visible inequality and enmity among social groups'. In such a landscape, the Westernization efforts, which involved uniformity and centralization in the space–society–politics nexus, 'was not congenial to autonomous provinces' (Gocek, 2013, p. 533) that were the heart of the traditional Ottoman territorial design. At the very extreme, the 'geographical claim' of such undertaking 'implied massive ethnic cleaning' (Keyder, 1997, p. 41), which also meant that the Westernization efforts turned the entire territorial design of the Ottomans on its head.

Overall, it can be concluded that the imperial territorial design, when combined with particular Ottoman practices, allowed the Ottomans to rule over expansive domains with relative peace and stability until the nineteenth century. Centralization and homogenization efforts then clashed with the territorialization of nationalistic and ethnic claims, facilitating the implosion of the entire system.

CONCLUSION

The relationship between state-building, war-making and territoriality remains a fertile ground that can lead to novel insights as well as new research questions for students of international politics and history. The territorial design framework, in this context, makes it possible to examine the Ottoman Empire's grand strategy as well as state-building efforts from a novel perspective and put the European/Western into a comparative perspective. Beyond the particular research question raised, this article has four further implications.

First, by building on the recent scholarship in political geography and critical studies on the socially and politically constructed nature of territories, this study proposes a novel theoretical framework that explores the origins and consequences of different territorial arrangements from a macro-historical perspective. As Andrew Phillips (2010, p. 304) argued,

> historical events as complex and protracted as transformation of international order are best understood through recourse to eclectic approaches that seek to tease out the knotty interconnections and co-constitutive relations between the material, ideational and institutional aspects of social reality.

The territorial design framework allows for tackling macro-historical puzzles from such an eclectic perspective while also building on an analytical linchpin – the study of territory and territoriality – that can potentially connect different disciplines such as political science, political geography, and history to each other.

Second, this paper is an attempt to situate the case of the Ottoman Empire vis-à-vis the broader IR understanding of political entities.[30] In relation, this study can also be seen as part of a recent trend in the literature that aims to expand the spatial and temporal scope of IR theory and historiography. For example, as Grygiel (2013) recently argued that students of IR and security studies have a lot to learn and benefit from scrutinizing cases from pre-modern history. Scrutinizing the early Ottoman experience, which lies at the heart of this essay, can potentially provide numerous insights for the students of international politics. Similarly, this article joins many others in making the case for bridging the gap between IR and the study of non-Western polities.[31]

Third, this paper seeks to provide a blueprint for a novel interpretation of the origins of the present-day territorial order. The conventional accounts provide a linear and Euro-centric narrative that starts from the birth of the territorial state in Europe during the course of the sixteenth and seventeenth centuries and ends with the global 'spread' of the Westphalian model in the twentieth century.[32] In these narratives, the extra-Westphalian territorial models are treated as if they are *a-territorial* or anomalies that, sooner or later, had to (or, have to) converge on the Westphalian baseline. The territorial design framework, when combined with the examination of the Ottoman experience, challenges this narrative, arguing – following scholars such as Agnew (2009) and Elden (2009) – that the Westphalian model is only one territorial design among many alternatives.

Finally, this study contributes to the debates about the importance of empires for a more complete understanding of the past and present of international politics (e.g., Barkawi, 2010). Coming out of age after the Second World War, mainstream IR has rarely taken up empires as a core subject of study. Regardless of this tendency,[33] partially due to the politically charged and sensitive nature of the term,[34] much of the globe was administered by European, regional, or transcontinental extra-Westphalian empires, well into the twentieth century. The territorial interpretation of the Ottoman case, in this context, aims to contribute to the emerging literature that seeks to position the study of the empires vis-à-vis IR theory in two ways. First, it explores an extra-Westphalian empire, suggesting that the study of imperialism could, and in fact should, extend beyond explorations of the Western empires operating in non-Western parts of the globe. Second, it offers a modular 'two-level' framework that can both accommodate different cases of imperial territorial design and recognize individual characteristics of particular polities. The case of the Ottomans, for example, is explored in two levels: the first level situates the Ottomans within the 'imperial design' category (a category that would include many other cases) and the second examines the particular characteristics of the Ottoman territorial design. This two-level framework can also be utilized to explore numerous potential cases ranging from other extra-Westphalian empires to Western colonialism, and even the Soviet Union, with respect to not only the Westphalian ideal, but also vis-à-vis each other. A research frontier in this context would be to examine the Ottoman territorial model in comparison with the Austrian and Russian imperial designs as well as European colonial presence in the non-Western world.[35]

The conventional thinking about the past and present of world politics tend to portray the global territorial order in terms of clearly demarcated and 'single-colour' spaces on a political map. A closer look at the extra-Westphalian systems including the Ottomans suggests that such thinking is simply misleading. Different territorial regimes – both across and within states – have existed side by side in the past and present of global political order (Agnew, 1994, 2009; Elden, 2013; Larkins, 2010; Vaughan-Williams, 2009). If, as students of international politics, our intention is to better understand the complexity of the present-day territorial order, a necessary next step would be to scrutinize the complexity of past and extra-Westphalian territorial orders and their long-term legacies.

DISCLOSURE STATEMENT

No potential conflict of interest was reported by the author.

NOTES

1. On this interpretation, see Jordan in this issue and Kadercan (2015a).
2. On this dynamic, see Atzili (2012).
3. For example, Finer (1997, p. 1173) and Findley (1980).
4. For example, Barkey (2008).
5. Note that there were considerable differences among European states at the time (Spruyt, 1996). The correct dichotomy should be between the 'ideal' European/Westphalian state and the Ottoman Empire, as Europe also has had its share of imperial designs, most notably the Austrian Empire, which survived well into the twentieth century, if in a different form (e.g., as a dual monarchy).
6. For a critique of this view, see Agnew (2009).
7. This is not to say that the Ottomans did not face rebellions. On the contrary, the seventeenth century experienced numerous rebellions, especially in the Asia Minor. However, 'rebellions in the Ottoman Empire were instigated, not by peasants on the land but by companies of demobilized soldier-brigands led by petty army officers who wanted territory to control and tax' (Barkey, 1991, p. 699). Also see Darling (1996, p. 13), Barkey (1994) and Goldstone (1991).
8. For an alternative view, see Acharya and Buzan (2010).
9. These initial 'constructed biases' against the Ottomans 'stuck,' at least until eighteenth and nineteenth centuries. On the 'construction' of the Ottomans as a barbarous race in Europe especially during Renaissance, see Meserve (2008). By the nineteenth century, the once-almighty Ottoman Empire was militarily checked and politically subdued, which eventually led to the 'domestication' of the once-untamed Ottoman lands from the eyes of the Westerners. The subjugation of the Ottoman lands was not merely a discursive exercise; from the nineteenth century onwards, the Western powers increasingly inserted their 'extra-territorial' authority into the Ottoman domain via legal exemptions as well as economic sanctions and privileges. On legal extra-territoriality in the Ottoman Empire, see Kayaoglu (2010).
10. On the imagery/fear of the Ottomans in Europe, see Lewis (2004, pp. 115–116) and Brummett (2015, p. 2).
11. Most notably, Wittek (1938). Also see Coles (1968, p. 34). On Euro-centric portrayals of the Ottomans, see Abou-El-Haj (2005, pp. 3–5).
12. On 'military orientalism', see Porter (2009).
13. For example, Faroqhi (2004).
14. The rationale here is not one of reification of the analytical (or normative) primacy of the Westphalian territorial model. Instead, the rationale simply follows from the established heuristic

value of the said model; the students of international politics are inherently familiar with the Westphalian territorial design, which also makes it the most natural reference point.

15. Note that while demarcation will influence the very constitutive properties of territory, the latter do not automatically follow from the former. Put differently, similar demarcation practices do not guarantee that territories 'inside' the borders will be socially and politically constructed in identical ways.

16. On 'land', resources, and territory, see Rosecrance (1986) and Agnew (2009, p. 35).

17. See Krasner (1999) for the idealized nature of this territorial system.

18. For a similar argument, see Zacher (2001).

19. It is also possible to trace heterogeneous designs beyond such examples, both geographically and temporally. Imperial territorial designs, for example, were projected not only by European states into extra-European lands, but also within Europe (see Kearns, this volume). Furthermore, while heterogeneous territorial designs associated with European colonialism can be traced well into the second half of the twentieth century, there are also more recent and non-European models. For example, as Suny (1993) documented, the Soviet Union managed the territories it controlled through numerous and context-dependent mechanisms, behaving [territorially] more like an empire than a nation-state. Similarly, present-day Pakistan's territorial design, especially when the Federally Administered Tribal Areas (FATA) are taken into consideration, displays characteristics that reveal considerable heterogeneity. For similar lines of research, see Barfield (2001), Adelman and Aron (1999) and Spruyt (2005).

20. For a compatible view, see Atzili (2012).

21. One contradiction, for example, is that while borders are 'fixed', they can remain 'permeable', as is the case with a number of Sub-Saharan states.

22. Note that the Ottoman case would not be the sole representative of this category, but merely one example that would be associated with it.

23. On this logic, see Rosecrance (1986).

24. On this dynamic, see Mearsheimer (2001).

25. See Barkey (1991, p. 712).

26. Also, see Veinstein (2013, p. 173).

27. Ottomans were not the only polity using the *ghaza* ideology in Asia Minor (Colak, 2014, p. 18). On *Ghaza* (or *ghazawat*) tradition before the Ottomans, see Haug (2011).

28. This does not mean that the Ottoman rule emphasized respect for the local arrangements for their own sake. When faced with opposition from the local lords, 'in order to make their new conquests secure the Ottomans used an elaborate system of colonization and mass deportation' (Inalcik, 1954, p. 122). Also see Doumanis (2013, p. 23).

29. On Tanzimat Fermani, see Shaw and Shaw (1976, pp. 55–272).

30. Note that concerns about putting the Ottoman Empire in a comparative perspective are shared by historians as well. On the relevant debates, see Abou-El-Haj (2005, p. 2).

31. For example, Neumann and Wigen (2013), Zhang (2001), Buzan and Little (2000) and MacKay (2013).

32. For a critique of this view, see Agnew (2009).

33. Notable exceptions include Spruyt (2005) and Nexon and Wright (2007).

34. Barkawi and Laffey (2002) and Buzan and Lawson (2013).

35. Of course, such comparisons may extend to inter-imperial comparisons between the Ottomans and ancient China. For a similar approach, see Hui (2005).

REFERENCES

Abou-El-Haj, R. A. (2005). *Formation of the modern state: The Ottoman empire, sixteenth to eighteenth centuries.* Syracuse, NY: Syracuse University Press.

Acharya, A., & Buzan, B. (2010). *Non-Western international relations theory perspectives On and beyond Asia.* New York, NY: Routledge.

Adelman, J., & Aron, S. (1999). From borderlands to borders: Empires, nation-states, and the peoples in between in north American history. *The American Historical Review, 104*(3), 814–841.

Agnelov, D., Batsaki, Y., & Bazzaz, S. (2013). Introduction. In S. Bazzaz, Y. Batsaki, & D. Angelow (Eds.), *Imperial geographies in byzantine and Ottoman space* (pp. 1–22). Washington, DC: Center for Hellenic Studies.

Agnew, J. A. (1994). The territorial trap: The geographical assumptions of international relations theory. *Review of International Political Economy, 1*(1), 53–80.

Agnew, J. A. (2009). *Globalization and sovereignty.* Lanham: Rowman & Littlefield.

Agoston, G. (2007). Information, ideology, and limits of imperial policy: Ottoman grand strategy in the context of Ottoman-Habsburg rivalry. In V. Aksan & D. Goffman (Eds.), *The early modern Ottomans: Remapping the empire.* Cambridge: Cambridge University Press.

Al-Qattan, N. (2007). *Inside the Ottoman Courthouse: Territorial law at the intersection of state and religion.* na.

Arı, B. (2004). Early Ottoman diplomacy: Ad Hoc period. In A. N. Yurdusev (Ed.), *Ottoman diplomacy: Conventional or unconventional* (pp. 36–65). New York: Palgrave Macmillan.

Atzili, B. (2012). *Good fences, bad neighbors: Border fixity and international conflict.* Chicago: University of Chicago.

Barfield, T. J. (2001). The shadow empires: Imperial state formation along the Chinese-nomad frontier. In S. E. Alcock (Ed.), *Empires: Perspectives from archaeology and history* (Vol. 122, pp. 10–41). Cambridge: Cambridge University Press.

Barkawi, T. (2010). Empire and order in international relations and security studies. In R. A. Denemark (Ed.), *The international studies encyclopedia* (Vol. III, pp. 1360–1379). Chichester: WileyBlackwell.

Barkawi, T., & Laffey, M. (2002). Retrieving the imperial: Empire and international relations. *Millennium – Journal of International Studies, 31*(1), 109–127.

Barkey, K. (1991). Rebellious alliances: The state and peasant unrest in early seventeenth-century France and the Ottoman Empire. *American Sociological Review, 56*(6), 699–715.

Barkey, K. (1994). *Bandits and bureaucrats: The Ottoman route to state centralization.* Ithaca, NY: Cornell UP.

Barkey, K. (2008). *Empire of difference: The Ottomans in comparative perspective.* Cambridge: Cambridge University Press.

Barkey, K., & Godart, F. C. (2013). Empires, federated arrangements, and kingdoms: Using political models of governance to understand firms' creative performance. *Organization Studies, 34*(1), 79–104.

Barkey, K. (2014). Political legitimacy and Islam in the Ottoman Empire lessons learned. *Philosophy & Social Criticism, 40*(4–5), 469–477.

Branch, J. (2014). *The cartographic state: Maps, territory, and the origins of sovereignty.* Cambridge, UK: Cambridge University Press.

Brummett, P. (2015). *Mapping the Ottomans.* New York: Cambridge University Press.

Bull, H. (1977). *The anarchical society: A study of order in world politics.* New York: Columbia University Press.

Buzan, B., & Lawson, G. (2013). The global transformation: The nineteenth century and the making of modern international relations. *International Studies Quarterly, 57*(3), 620–634.

Buzan, B., & Little, R. (2000) *International systems in world history: Remaking the study of international relations.* Oxford: Oxford University Press.

Colak, H. (2014). Tekfur, Fasiliyus, and Kayser: Disdain, negligence and appropriation of byzantine imperial titulature in the Ottoman world. In M. Hadjianastasis (Ed.), *Frontiers of the Ottoman imagination* (pp. 5–28). Boston, MA: Brill.

Coles, P. (1968). *The Ottoman impact on Europe.* New York: Harcourt, Brace & World.

Dale, S. F. (2010). *The Muslim empires of the Ottomans, Safavids, and Mughals.* New York: Cambridge University Press.

Darling, L. T. (1996). *Revenue-Raising and legitimacy: Tax collection and finance administration in the Ottoman Empire, 1560–1660.* New York: E. J. Brill.

Darling, L. T. (2000). Contested territory: Ottoman Holy War in comparative context. *Studia Islamica, 91*, 133–163.

Doumanis, N. (2013). *Before the nation: Muslim-Christian coexistence and its destruction in late-Ottoman Anatolia.* Oxford: Oxford University Press.

Elden, S. (2009). *Terror and territory: The spatial extent of sovereignty.* Minneapolis: University of Minnesota.

Elden, S. (2013). *The birth of territory.* Chicago: University of Chicago Press.

Faroqhi, S. (2004). *The Ottoman Empire and the world around it.* London: I.B. Tauris.

Findley, C. V. (1980). *Bureaucratic reform in the Ottoman Empire: The Sublime Porte, 1789–1922.* Princeton, NJ: Princeton University Press.

Finer, S. E. (1997). *The history of government from the earliest times.* Oxford: Oxford UP.

Gocek, F. M. (2013). Parameters of a postcolonial sociology of the Ottoman Empire. *Political Power and Social Theory, 25,* 73–104.

Goldstone, J. A. (1991). *Revolution and rebellion in the early modern world.* Berkeley: University of California Press.

Grygiel, J. (2013). The primacy of premodern history. *Security Studies, 22*(1), 1–32.

Gürkan, E. S. (2012). Batı Akdeniz'de Osmanlı Korsanlığı Ve Gaza Meselesi. *Kebikeç: İnsan Bilimleri İçin Kaynak Araştırmaları Dergisi, 33,* 173–204.

Haug, R. (2011). Frontiers and the state in early Islamic history: Jihad between caliphs and volunteers. *History Compass, 9*(8), 634–643.

Horowitz, R. S. (2004). International law and state transformation in China, Siam, and the Ottoman Empire during the nineteenth century. *Journal of World History, 15*(4), 445–486.

Hui, T. H. (2005). *War and state formation in ancient China and early modern Europe.* New York: Cambridge University Press.

Inalcik, H. (1954). Ottoman methods of conquest. *Studia Islamica, 2,* 103–129.

Inalcık, H. (1973). *The Ottoman Empire; the classical Age, 1300-1600.* New York: Praeger.

Iyigun, M. (2015). *War, peace, and prosperity in the name of God: The Ottoman role in Europe's socioeconomic evolution.* Chicago: University of Chicago Press.

Jordheim, H., & Neumann, I. B. (2011). Empire, imperialism and conceptual history. *Journal of International Relations and Development, 14*(2), 153–185.

Kadercan, B. (2015a). Triangulating territory: A case for pragmatic interaction between political science, political geography, and critical IR. *International Theory, 7*(1), 125–161.

Kadercan, B. (2015b). Bringing the 'Other' empires back In: The case of the Ottoman Empire. *American Political Science Association's International History and Politics Newsletter, 1*(1), 2–4.

Kafadar, C. (1995). *Between two worlds: The construction of the Ottoman state.* Berkeley: University of California Press.

Karpat, K. (1977a). Introduction. In K. Karpat (Ed.), *The Ottoman State and its place in world history.* Leiden: E. J. Brill.

Karpat, K. (1977b). The stages of Ottoman History: A structural comparative approach. In K. Karpat (Ed.), *The Ottoman state and its place in world history.* Leiden: E. J. Brill.

Kayaoglu, T. (2010). *Legal imperialism: Sovereignty and extraterritoriality in Japan, the Ottoman Empire, and China.* Cambridge: Cambridge UP.

Keyder, C. (1997). The Ottoman Empire. In K. Barkey & M. V. Hagen (Eds.), *After Empire: Multiethnic societies and nation-building: The Soviet Union and the Russian, Ottoman, And Habsburg Empires.* Boulder, CO: Westview Press.

Krasner, S. D. (1999). *Sovereignty: Organized hypocrisy.* Princeton, NJ: Princeton UP.

Kratochwil, F. (1986). Of system, boundaries, and territoriality: An inquiry into the formation of state system. *World Politics, 39*(1), 27–52.

Larkins, J. (2010). *From hierarchy to anarchy: Territory and politics before Westphalia.* New York: Palgrave Macmillan.

Lewis, B. (2004). *From Babel to Dragomans: Interpreting the Middle East.* New York, NY: Oxford University Press.

MacKay, J. (2013). International politics in eighteenth and nineteenth century Central Asia: Beyond anarchy in international-relations theory. *Central Asian Survey, 32*(2), 210–224.

Makdisi, U. (2002). Ottoman orientalism. *The American Historical Review, 107*(3), 768–796.

Mearsheimer, J. J. (2001). *The tragedy of great power politics.* New York: Norton.

Meserve, M. (2008). *Empires of Islam in renaissance historical thought*. Cambridge, MA: Harvard University Press.

Minkov, A. (2004). *Conversion to Islam in the Balkans: Kisve Bahas petitions and Ottoman social life, 1670–1730*. Boston, MA: Brill.

Neumann, I. B., & Welsh, J. M. (1991). The other in European self-definition: An addendum to the literature on international society. *Review of International Studies, 17*(4), 327–348.

Neumann, I. B., & Wigen, E. (2013). The importance of the Eurasian steppe to the study of international relations. *Journal of International Relations and Development, 16*(3), 311–330.

Nexon, D. H., & Wright, T. (2007). What's at stake in the American empire debate. *American Political Science Review, 101*(2), 253–271.

Nisancioglu, K. (2014). The Ottoman origins of capitalism: Uneven and combined development and Eurocentrism. *Review of International Studies, 40*(2), 325–347.

Osiander, A. (2001). Sovereignty, international relations, and the Westphalian myth. *International Organization, 55*(2), 251–287.

Phillips, A. (2010). *War, religion and Empire: The transformation of international orders*. New York: Cambridge University Press.

Porter, P. (2009). *Military orientalism: Eastern War through Western eyes*. New York: Columbia UP.

Rosecrance, R. N. (1986). *The rise of the trading state: Commerce and conquest in the modern world*. New York: Basic.

Sewell, W. (2004). The French revolution and the emergence of the nation form. In M. Morrison & M. Zook (Eds.), *Revolutionary currents: Transatlantic ideology and nation-building* (pp. 91–127). Lanham, MD: Rowman and Littlefield.

Shaw, S. J., & Shaw, E. K. (1976). *History of the Ottoman Empire and modern Turkey*. Cambridge: Cambridge UP.

Spruyt, H. (1996). *The sovereign state and its competitors: An analysis of systems change*. Princeton, NJ: Princeton University Press.

Spruyt, H. (2005). *Ending empire: Contested sovereignty and territorial partition*. Ithaca, NY: Cornell University Press.

Sugar, P. F. (1977). *Southeastern Europe under Ottoman rule, 1354-1804*. Seattle, WA: University of Washington Press.

Suny, R. (1993). *The revenge of the past: Nationalism, revolution, and the collapse of the Soviet Union.* . Stanford, CA: Stanford University Press.

Tilly, C. (1990). *Coercion, capital, and European States, AD 990-1990*. Cambridge, MA: B. Blackwell.

Vaughan-Williams, N. (2009). *Border politics: The limits of sovereign power*. Edinburgh: Edinburgh UP.

Veinstein, G. (2013). The Great Turk and Europe. In J. V. Tolan, G. Veinstein, & H. Laurens (Eds.), *Europe and the Islamic world: A history* (pp. 111–253). Princeton, NJ: Princeton University Press.

Winichakul, T. (1994). *Siam mapped: A history of the Geo-body of a nation*. Hawaii: University of Hawaii Press.

Wittek, P. (1938). *The rise of the Ottoman Empire*. London: Royal Asiatic Society.

Yurdusev, A. N. (2004). Introduction. In A. N. Yurdusev (Ed.), *Ottoman diplomacy: Conventional or unconventional* (pp. 5–35). New York: Palgrave Macmillan.

Zacher, M. (2001). The territorial integrity norm. *International Organization, 55*(2), 215–250.

Zhang, Y. (2001). System, empire and state in Chinese international relations. *Review of International Studies, 27* (5), 43–63.

Zubaida, S. (2002). The fragments imagine the nation: The case of Iraq. *International Journal of Middle East Studies, 34*(2), 205–215.

The territory of colonialism

Gerry Kearns

ABSTRACT

The territory of colonialism. *Territory, Politics, Governance*. Stuart Elden writes of territory as a specific form of sovereignty, and has provided its genealogy through a study of European texts. These texts drew upon a Roman legacy and engaged the practical issue of the relations between papal and monarchical powers. This paper argues that colonialism was at least as important a context for the elaboration of territory as a strategy of sovereignty. Furthermore, and as the example of Ireland shows, this colonial practice was not only a matter external to Europe.

摘要

殖民主义的领土。*Territory, Politics, Governance*。斯图尔特．埃尔登将田野书写为主权的特定形式，并透过研究欧洲的文本提供领土的系谱学。这些文本引用罗马的遗产，并涉入教皇和君权间的关系之实际议题。本文主张，殖民主义作为阐述领土的脉络，至少和主权的策略一样重要。此外，如同爱尔兰的案例所示，此般殖民实践并非仅是欧洲外部之事。

RÉSUMÉ

Le territoire du colonialisme. *Territory, Politics, Governance*. Stuart Elden a traité le territoire comme une forme spécifique de la souveraineté, et a fourni sa généalogie au moyen d'une étude des documents européens. Ces documents-ci puisent dans un héritage romain et se livrent dans la question pratique des relations entre le pouvoir pontifical et le pouvoir monarchique. Ce présent article affirme que le colonialisme était du moins aussi important comme cadre pour la délimitation du territoire que pour une stratégie de souveraineté. Qui plus est, et comme le montre l'exemple de l'Irlande, cette pratique coloniale n'était pas tout simplement une question externe pour l'Europe.

RESUMEN

El territorio del colonialismo. *Territory, Politics, Governance*. Stuart Elden describe el territorio como una forma específica de soberanía, y ha presentado su genealogía mediante un estudio de textos europeos. Estos textos se inspiraban en un legado romano y trataban la cuestión práctica de las relaciones entre los poderes papales y monárquicos. En este artículo argumento que el colonialismo no solo representaba una estrategia de soberanía, sino también un contexto importante para la elaboración de territorio. Asimismo, y como muestra el ejemplo de Irlanda, esta práctica colonial no fue solamente una cuestión externa a Europa.

In their editorial, Atzili and Kadercan (2017) invite political scientists and political geographers to a conversation about territory. In sketching matters of common concern, they distinguish between studies of the limits of territory and studies of its constitution, and between those identifying factors internal to states and others that stress the significance of external forces, such as the pressures exerted by other states or by multilateral institutions. They suggest that political geographers and political scientists approach these shared topics in rather different ways, with political scientists developing hypotheses for empirical testing and geographers problematizing concepts and explicating the genealogy of territorial discourse. There are differences of epistemology at stake here, as well as those differences in approach and emphasis that come from divergent traditions of academic formation. Post-structuralism (Dews, 1987) has had a strong impact upon Political Geography as have various other critiques of positivism (Keat, 1981). The result has been the development, initially by Ó Tuathail (1996) and by Dalby (1991), of a research project they called Critical Geopolitics.

Much of this work has been inspired by the scholarship of Michel Foucault and it does indeed bear some of the marks that Atzili and Kadercan identify. However, the separation between discourse studies and empirical work is not as necessary as might appear. I take Foucault's genealogical method to include examining the conditions of existence of various discursive formations (Kearns, 2007). A discursive formation is a set of institutions together with the texts, laws, and ideologies that sustain and animate them. Thus, any particular discursive formation will have material as well as textual circumstances that must be met before it can persist. For example, one might explore the emergence and selection of the concepts that allow a specific type of governance (biopolitics) that takes the biological material of the population as a focus of policy (Kearns & Reid-Henry, 2009). The influencing of birth rates through the adjustment of welfare regimes is certainly imagined in the population theory advanced by Malthus (1798), but it is can only be realized in the context of a suite of welfare policies, laws, buildings, employees, and so on (Dean, 2015). It is a very obvious point, but discursive formations include more than just texts and thus the study of the genealogy of concepts must needs move into materialist and historical analyses.

For example, in previous work, I have looked at the inter-states system as the essential, if under-theorized, context for explicating the changes in state strategy that Michel Foucault identified as biopolitics (Kearns, 2014a). I suggested that there had been a tendency to understand the development of biopolitics through an evolutionary model of the state considered as an entity in isolation. In taking up the inter-states system as the vital setting for the elaboration of biopolitics, I am, of course, identifying an opportunity for scholars of international relations, at least those with historical interests, to engage with one of the central themes in the academic field that straddles the social and the life sciences (Hirst & Woolley, 1982).

My concern in this paper is with the concept of territory, or to be more specific, with territorial sovereignty (Agnew, 2013). I want to understand the material as well as the textual conditions of emergence of a form of sovereignty that rules through the presumed control exercised over a determinate space. I want to develop my argument by engaging with Elden's (2013) recent work, *The Birth of Territory*. This magisterial review of the emergence of precisely this variety of sovereignty has already gathered significant commentary, including several responses from Elden himself (2014, 2015a, 2015b). Some people have faulted Elden for paying too little attention to practices and too much to texts alone (Bryan, 2015; Cox, 2014; Koch, 2014). Others have questions about his particular reading of Foucault, either on 'birth' (Charron, 2014; Heffernan, 2015) or on the historicity of categories (Legg, 2015). Still others ask about the articulation of territory with matters such as enclosure (McDonagh, 2015), non-state relations (Sassen, 2015), diplomacy (Murphy, 2015), and property (Cox, 2014).

In *The Birth of Territory*, Elden distinguishes between land (a matter of ownership), terrain (a field of military activity), and territory (a geographical area that is made the object of sovereignty). As I have commented elsewhere, there is a certain unevenness in his treatment of these three concepts with the first two treated as quasi-universals that may receive specific form in different periods, whereas the third, alone, is understood to have a distinct birth, its conditions of existence being met only, it would seem, with the establishment of the European absolutist states from the late seventeenth century (Kearns, 2014b). I will explicate these questions of method in a brief discussion of the historical specificity of land and territory. Broadly speaking, I think that it is only by narrowing territory to a specific type of territorial sovereignty (Agnew, 2013) that Elden separates it from land or terrain as a category of greater historical specificity. Even, then, I will go on to suggest, this specifically territorial form of sovereignty also emerged in contexts other than the one that Elden highlights, in particular that it was born again and again under different circumstances as part of the spatial tactics of colonialism.

In explaining the birth of territory, Elden proposes that the absolutist forms of European sovereignty were shaped in part by opposition to the interference of the pope in matters of internal sovereignty and, relatedly, against the claims of the Holy Roman Emperor. In terms of the framework proposed by Atzili and Kadercan in their Introduction, then, Elden is concerned with the interaction between domestic and interstate/external determinations of the constitution of territory. Elden asks, in effect: when is sovereign power exercised as territorial control? He operationalizes this question by looking for the moment when conceptual studies of sovereignty give it this territorial form? Although this question, and its restating as a specific research project, may not look like the sort of hypotheses that Atzili and Kadercan consider characteristic of political science, it could be suggestive of some such hypotheses.

I will not attempt this translation here but instead develop a slightly different argument. I want to suggest that colonialism was an important context in which a specifically territorial form of sovereignty was elaborated. The critical colonial condition was perhaps the colonial state's failure to interpellate the sub-altern population as subjects. The economy of the metropole was projected into the colony but, in the absence of loyal institutions constituting a civil society for the colony, the colonial state very often extended its claim in a territorial fashion, almost as a sort of shorthand for designating a set of entities, resources, and relations about which it otherwise knew or mastered very little. I am emphasizing, then, the significance of the external relations of colonialism for stimulating territorial practices that produced the colony as a space of colonial revenue extraction.

The idea that colonialism was an important context for the development of ideas of international law and of sovereignty more generally has been argued by a number of scholars from former colonies (Anand, 1972; Elias, 1972). Scholars of international relations theory have also taken up this theme. Bowden (2009) has described how international law has repeatedly re-inscribed the colonial encounter as a distinction between civilized and uncivilized states. In an important study, Anghie (2004, pp. 2–3) argued, not only that 'colonialism was central to the development of international law, [but] that sovereignty doctrine emerged out of the colonial encounter'. Anghie proposes that theories of sovereignty emerge in a context where the urgent task is to distinguish between states whose sovereignty must be respected, European, and places which lacking properly sovereign states can be made subject to external rule. Bowden and Anghie imply that sovereignty is in some sense a marker of difference between the core and the periphery of the world system. Keene (2002) puts this claim in a broader historical and geographical context, suggesting that the claim that Europe was made of properly sovereign states was originally more normative than descriptive. In what they were remaking as the world's periphery, European colonial powers established a sort of divided sovereignty for many colonies and dependencies, allowing some autonomy to native rulers while reserving to European discretion martial, tax, and property regimes. Keene points out that a system of divided sovereignty was already characteristic of parts of Europe, particularly within the framework of the Holy Roman Empire. I admire the way Keene integrates the development of sovereignty for Europe and its overseas colonies into a single narrative.

There are four elements of this analysis that merit greater attention. In the first place, and as I will develop further below, divided sovereignty shares much with the notion of parcelized sovereignty that Bloch (1962) understood as central to feudal governance. Secondly, and again I will develop this a little more below, the development of an ideology of undivided sovereignty was part of a struggle against papal interference in matters of dynastic succession and the settlement of domestic property and tax regimes. Thirdly, although for Europe at least, the reference to feudal and papal contexts for divided sovereignty might make it seem an atavism, in fact, colonial forms of governance *within* Europe were a crucible for the development of the most advanced styles of public administration to such an extent that, from at least the seventeenth century, places like colonial Ireland bid fair to be classed among the more advanced examples of contemporary capitalist state development.

Despite the way they elaborate a colonial context for discussing the development of notions of sovereignty, neither Bowden nor Anghie make a specifically territorial form of sovereignty a focus of their work although in each case there are some suggestions that might be developed further. For example, in Bowden's (2009, pp. 56, 60) account of how, from work on the Iroquois Confederacy, Morgan (1877) elaborated a stages-theory of the evolution of civilization, the object of human organization goes from family, to property, to territory. Since the Confederacy was a territorial organization, this case hardly helped to establish the Eurocentric superiority assumed by civilization theory. Similar difficulties are raised by one of the few discussions of territory in Anghie's work. Anghie (2004, pp. 57–59) notes that Western positivist theorists of international law suggested that civilized sovereignty rested upon the notion of territorial control and that, as such, neither the societies of pirates nor of nomads could be admitted to the society of civilized states. However, Anghie also remarks that historical scholarship upon the societies of Africa and Asia had clearly established that territorial states existed in both places at various times both before and during European colonialism. In these circumstances, international jurists, such as Cambridge professor Lawrence (1895), argued that territory was a necessary but not sufficient indicator of civilized status and that African and Asian states failed on other grounds. In the cases considered by Bowden and Anghie, then, territorial sovereignty had been first proposed as a marker of difference between civilized and uncivilized states, and then largely ignored when it was found among peoples of the periphery and thus could no longer serve as an efficient diviner. These are important studies and they highlight some of the troubling relations between concepts of territory and concepts of civilization. However, I want to return to territory as part of the practice of colonial sovereignty.

By taking up the question of individual titles to land alongside his interest in divided sovereignty, Keene comes much closer to my concerns. Across a large part of North America, the establishment of a system of states and territories by the federal government of the United States not only used a cadaster voided of native claims in order to lay down a new set of spaces for Euro-American settlement, but also used a specific form of federal and divided sovereignty to manage these spaces while simultaneously undertaking an ambitious project of state building. Keene points out that projected into the spaces seized from native peoples were property arrangements that in European terms were relatively modern, being a title fee simple rather than subject to any feudal qualification. Keene goes further and points out that this use of unencumbered property titles was already part of the promotion of cultivation on difficult lands within Europe, as where new land was made by reclamation and maintained by continual, collective drainage-works.

Elden, himself, recognizes the territorial aspects of colonialism but suggests that it is not really part of project because his 'is a study of a European question' (Elden, 2015a, p. 99). Yet, colonial practices were developed also inside Europe as Meinig (1986) shows in presenting the reconquest of the Iberian peninsula from the Moors as something of a dress rehearsal for the methods deployed in the subjugation of swathes of South America, just as Canny (1976) finds the English to have used Ireland as a place wherein they prepared the techniques of the later British colonial project in North America. In other work, I have argued that that colonialism was central to the development of modern forms of sovereignty, suggesting that the 'state of exception' (Agamben, 2005) was often invoked for colonial circumstances where sovereignty was claimed, but only very limited local legitimation was enjoyed (Kearns, 2006). In a somewhat different context, Rabinow (1995) highlighted the importance of the colony as a site where a new political technology of environmental modernism was developed. MacDonagh (1958) showed how the colony might serve as a laboratory for social policies that would only later be attempted in the metropole. Barder (2015) has argued that the subjugation of colonial rebellion may involve the crafting of new techniques of surveillance and management that later serve as exemplars of social control in the homeland of the colonizer.

This paper considers the European case of Ireland suggesting that even by confining attention to Europe, it is impossible to evade the signal importance of colonialism as the laboratory of territorial sovereignty. In Ireland, the British crown elaborated forms of sovereignty that drew a space within which it claimed specific authority over colonial subjects. It chose territory rather than persons as the primary object of sovereignty in part because it lacked the local control that could establish a subject population by census or allegiance. The nature of the authority that was claimed related to the economic mechanisms of exploitation projected into the space of the colony. Feudal and capitalist colonies, then, projected very different sovereign claims but in each case the sovereignty was specified as extending to subjects captured within a definite spatial grid.

GENEALOGY AND HISTORICAL MATERIALISM

Elden writes that 'property in land' is not a suitable object for a genealogical analysis because it features in diverse societies across time and space, and thus must 'fail the historically specific test' (Elden, 2013, p. 10). I am reminded of Marx's discussion of historical versus universal categories in the early pages of his *Grundrisse*. But Marx was not concerned with origins, or at least he was not concerned with, say, the birth of the commodity, or the birth of property. He was interested, instead, in the historically specific circumstances under which certain economic forms became dominant. Furthermore, Marx took up precisely the concept, property in land, that Elden discards and used it to explicate the relations between states and economies, between superstructure and base.

Origins and generality

Elden begins with Rousseau and the argument that modern justice and thus civilization has emerged from modern property rights and that these, in turn, have been produced over a long period during which the cultivation of land created a more general demand for elaborate systems of ownership. Elden (2013, p. 2), proposes that: 'Similar questions can be asked about a very particular understanding of property and political power over land, that of the relation between the state and its territory.' Note, here, the emphasis upon a 'particular understanding', rather than upon, say, a particular set of empirical relations. Note, also, the emphasis upon the state, for this leads Elden to his criticism of perhaps the best known elaboration of territoriality in geographical scholarship. Sack's (1986) *Human Territoriality* is an influential text in Political Geography but because Sack treats territoriality as a spatial tactic applicable alike to the parent trying to keep the child from danger by forbidding it to go into the kitchen where the water is boiling, and to the Roman Catholic church organizing its power through a hierarchical system of nested parishes, dioceses, and archdioceses, Elden argues that Sack fails to theorize the historically specific understanding of territoriality as the relation between a state and its spatial extent.

Elden's exploration of categories, then, may seem rather like the way *Grundrisse* begins, where Marx (1973, p. 100) asked himself what might be a good point of departure for the study of the specificity of modern society:

> It seems to be correct to begin with the real and the concrete, with the real precondition, thus to begin, in economics, with e.g. the population, which is the foundation and the subject of the entire social act of production. However, on closer examination this proves false. The population is an abstraction if I leave out, for example, the classes of which it is composed. These classes in turn are an empty phrase if I am not familiar with the elements on which they rest. E.g. wage labour, capital, etc. These latter in turn presuppose exchange, division of labour, prices, etc.

Marx went on to show that in following this method, political economists break the modern economy down into acts of commodity exchange. Are these, then, the universal building blocks of all economies, or in Marx's (1973, p. 102) exposition: '[D]o not these simpler categories also have an independent historical or natural existence predating the more concrete ones? That depends'; in some cases yes, in others no.

In the case of commodity exchange, suggested Marx, the political economists were wrong to hypostasize exchange as a universal, as had Smith (1993, p. 21) in the famous passage from *The Wealth of Nations*, where he explained the division of labour as proceeding from 'a certain propensity in human nature [...]; the propensity to truck, barter, and exchange one thing for another'. Marx argued that, in contrast, the historical record featured many societies where cooperation predominated and in which commercial exchange occurred only at their margins, in the interactions between separate communities. In the Roman Empire, for example, commodity exchange was a feature of economic life at its limits, propelled by the needs of the army, a feature which may explain the great density of Roman coin that modern archaeologists had recovered from the fringes of the former Empire. On the other hand, in modern society, commodity exchange is pervasive. What was once marginal was now central.

Likewise, with the category 'possession' which Hegel had treated as a universal condition of humanity. In fact, proposed Marx, modern property was a juridical relationship, very unlike the forms of personal use of times long ago. In earlier times, it made sense to say that an individual held things for personal use without implying that any legal system existed by which this was formalized. Such a legal system had developed at first for certain special categories of possession, for which contracts were produced. These contracts set out the particular sets of uses that attended a particular legally enforceable form of ownership. Once again the form that once was an exception had now become the rule. The student of modern society, according to Marx, must needs explain the generality of commodity exchange and of juridical relations of ownership, rather than treating them as systems established time out of mind and thus as having origins lost in the mists of the past. The historical materialist method enjoins us to ask, not, when is a particular category emergent or first fully conceptually elaborated, but, rather, what does it do?

Concepts and relations

Marx's materialism is readily caricatured. Nevertheless, I am persuaded by its central claim. In each historical period, the historically dominant ways of thinking about society, politics, and economy are in close relation to the historically specific ways society, politics, and economy are conducted. In his *Introduction to the Critique of Political Economy*, Marx (1975a, p. 351) wrote: 'Thought and being are indeed distinct, but they are also in unity.' Echoing Heidegger's discussion of being-in-the-world, Butler (2012, p. 9) has commented upon ethical reflection as a state of 'being comported beyond oneself [...] in response to the claims made by those one [...] did not fully choose'. This notion of being tumbled into social relations we have not chosen has a family relation with Marx's (1975b, p. 425) notion of materialism: 'In the social production of their existence, [people] inevitably enter into definite relations, which are independent of their will, namely relations of production appropriate to a given stage of development of their material forces of production.' In short, the problems that are given to speculation are precisely those encountered in practice.

It might seem, again, that Elden (2013, p. 8) shares this last ambition for he describes his approach as giving attention to 'texts that reveal concepts that inform [...] practices'. Certainly many of the texts that Elden (2013, p. 10) examines, 'privileging the legal and the technical', are a commentary upon ideal state practice and are thus suggestive of the concepts that might be said to inform, or at best describe, state practice. However, Elden (2013, p. 10) rarely takes us up close to practices, rather, as he himself notes, he 'begins to fold the analysis of practices into its genealogical narrative'. Elden is interested in some contexts more than in others. In short, attending quite brilliantly to the long story of the relations between papal and monarchical powers, Elden underplays a vital series of other economic contexts, particularly where they implicate colonialism.

GENEALOGIES OF THE ABSOLUTIST STATE

Jurisdiction and papacy

Elden wants to show that modern discussions of territory, as state power over a determined space, emerged from earlier discussions of related terms. The conditions of existence of the modern concept, then, comprehend the older elaboration of related terms. Elden proposes that the rediscovery of Roman law in sixteenth- and seventeenth-century Europe informed a discussion of sovereignty that effectively asserted the right of the monarch to act as emperor within its own lands, thereby devaluing the overarching political legitimation asserted over monarchs by the Bishop of Rome and, by association, the Holy Roman Emperor. Elden's (2013, p. 321) conclusion is that: 'Leibniz's suggestion that the sovereign is he "who is master of a territory" is a fundamental moment in the development of Western political thought.'

Elden goes further in arguing for the importance of Leinbiz and does so in a way that, again, is very suggestive of the political practices that, as I would phrase it, the concept of territory was intended to justify. Elden (2013, p. 321) takes a swipe at the more usual suspects in the genealogies of the absolutist state: 'While it might appear that Hobbes's absolute sovereignty and Newton's absolute space defined modern politics and geography, Leibniz's relational view of both are closer to how politics was actually practiced.' Elden's reasons are good ones. Leibniz, notes Elden, saw sovereignty as a continuum rather than as absolute, and as asserted in relation to the powers of external contending sovereignties rather than in isolation. The ideology of the monarch, or later the state, might be that it was 'master of a territory', but in reality this mastery was conditioned by the possibility of external interference. This relativity inheres in the distinction Elden describes Leibniz as having drawn between the force of jurisdiction and the force of territory. The first comprehends the relatively mild force of law usually affirmed over a limited terrain, whereas the second deploys the more severe force of the military and can be asserted over a wider terrain. A territory is held, then, by force of arms.

Elden only gets to this at the end of his book, with, it would seem, territory having been born out the renegotiated terms of the body of Roman law that related to the Empire and its limits. But here there is a tension between Leibniz's forces of jurisdiction and of territory. The practical problem that concerned the theorists upon whom Elden draws, particularly Leibniz and Chemnitz, was the assertion of monarchical sovereign power against the imperial claims of the Holy Roman Empire, as distantly legitimated by its relation to the papacy. Elden points out that the criticisms of the Holy Roman Empire developed by Chemnitz (notably that its abuses proceeded from its imperial forms and its virtues from the autonomy of the constituent estates, or principalities) were used by the French negotiators to the Treaty of Westphalia (1648).

The new interest in Roman law was part of an argument within Europe about the ways a monarch should be sovereign within its own lands. Building upon the monarchical rights asserted by the Diet of Augsburg (1555), where wars of religion were foresworn leaving to each monarch the right to determine the religious affiliation of its subjects, and thus the related right of the prince to determine the legality of succession without reference to the Pope, the Treaty of Westphalia went further and confirmed the powers of the monarch over the lands under its control, specifically the right to dissolve ecclesiastical property should it so wish. These were essentially about the force of jurisdiction. The relations between jurisdiction and territory may be close, and the decline of the martial force of the Holy Roman Empire altered the parallelogram of forces within which sovereigns operated, but the rights asserted in 1555 and 1648 look more like jurisdiction than territory. The claims made in these treaties were made against the Pope and against the Holy Roman Emperor. They applied equally to all the neighbouring principalities that were parties to the treaty. They were essentially rights exercised within a space and concerned the qualities of sovereignty. In Leibniz's terms they did not concern the qualitative change in force that accompanied the extension of power beyond a prescribed realm, within which something close to consent might have been established. It was rather a confirmation of jurisdiction than an extension to territory by military might. Perhaps I make too much of Leibniz's distinction but the idea of territory as a projection of force by military means is suggestive of a rather different set of practices than those Elden prioritizes.

Land and territory in the feudal colony

At one point, Elden (2013, p. 244) asks of a set of sixteenth- and early-seventeenth-century writers, including Shakespeare: '[W]hat is the relation between place and power in their thought?' The issue arises from a discussion of conquest and of the New World, but the theme runs into the sand before it matures. This might suggest we need to attend to different forms of feudal and early-capitalist colonialism; alternative genealogies of absolutism. For example, Elden describes Machiavelli as setting out to explain how an empire or state might hold lands it had taken in conquest. In this respect, we might see Machiavelli as having devised a textbook for colonialism. Yet, for Elden (2013, p. 252), this is not a particularly modern treatment because '[g]eographical questions are underplayed in his work, territory was not the object of rule'. For Machiavelli, then, people were the object of rule.

This distinction between ruling over people and ruling over territory needs closer examination. Under one of the forms of the parcellization of sovereignty that was, as Bloch (1962, p. 251) noted, a central feature of the feudal system, a monarch might grant to a baron certain jurisdiction over a defined piece of land, perhaps as a barony, and the baron in turn could divide out this land granting manors and villages to individual lords (Anderson, 1974a, p. 150). In return, the monarch and the baron could require in return from the baron and lord respectively, the economic benefits of hospitality and tax, and the military benefit of equipped and trained soldiers from those resident on the parcel of land. At certain times and in certain parts of Europe, the economic rights devolved to baron or lord included a right to the labour of those residents in the neighbourhood and these people were required to continue to live there, as serfs or *villeins*. At the heart of feudalism, then, was a state practice that prescribed control over people in the form of control over an area. It was, at least in Sack's terms a form of territoriality.

Within a given territory, then, the monarch secured the loyalty of powerful barons by making concessions to them in the form of territorial grants. But this reduced the resources of the monarch and increased those of the barons who were thus enabled to imagine challenging the authority of the monarch. The fissiparity of feudalism was, as Kiernan (1980) described, rebalanced by periodic *redaction* whereby the monarch dissolved existing grants reclaiming them to itself before reallocating some of them to a new set of allies, which would out of loyalty and self-interest sustain the rule of the monarch.

Colonialism offered an alternative way to retain the loyalty of the barons. Ireland was in this sort of relation with England. The French style of manorial system was, as all English schoolchildren know, extended to England with the Norman Conquest of 1066. By 1171, the Norman-English king Henry II looked to Ireland for new lands so that he might make conquest there and establish lands on which to settle his two sons, thereby diverting them from challenging him for land and authority in England. Within a few years, one of the sons, Richard, now established on Irish estates, found himself in similar relation with the knights under him:

> [N]ot being able to subsist by plunder as they were wont, [they] came in a body to the earl, and loudly declared that unless Raymond was appointed their commander they would at once quit his service, and either return to England, or, what was worse, desert to the enemy. (Gerard of Wales, 1894, p. 255)

These knights asked for Raymond as commander because he had promised to lead them beyond the existing English settlement into those lands of the Irish that yet remained unsubdued. Military adventures beyond the established feudal baronies, to establish new estates or simply for plunder, were an essential dynamic of the feudal system. But, note also that a historically specific form of land-as-property, the feudal estate, is at the heart of this territoriality.

I call this form of the feudal estate a feudal colony because the asymmetry between English and Irish was retained in law and reinforced by territorial distinctions. We can see this very clearly in the areas Pratt (1991) calls the contact zone. For example, in the fourteenth century, Kilkenny was a frontier town, planted in the Irish midlands and the funnel for the Midlands trade down south towards Cork, then a more significant export centre than was Dublin. In Kilkenny, as in several English settlements in Ireland, there was a distinction between Englishtown and Irishtown. No Irish were allowed to live, work, or trade in the English (or new) town. Furthermore, no Irish had any legal protection within English town should they be there on sufferance in the hours before curfew. Thus, when, in 1344 and in the streets of Englishtown within the city of Kilkenny, Bartholomew Foly killed a man calling himself Adam Walsh (an English name deriving from Welsh), and the court heard that the victim was in fact one 'Adam Omolgane, an Irishman and not an Englishman', then it was 'adjudged that the said Bartholomew is quit thereof' (Otway-Ruthven & Smithwick, 1961, pp. 18–20). In 1372 when asserting a new town charter, the English burgesses of Kilkenny insisted that they 'shall not be compelled to go outside the bounds of [the town of Kilkenny] for military service or to parley against the Irish or whatsoever enemies [...] unless they freely wish to do this' (Otway-Ruthven & Smithwick, 1961, p. 13). The distinction between the Irish and the English is framed not only in ethnic but also in territorial terms.

Following one of many sets of rebellions, in 1367, the English held a parliament in Kilkenny and passed a set of laws to regulate relations between the English and the Irish. These Statutes of Kilkenny included a ban on intermarriage between English and Irish, excluded the Irish from such professions as law, military or church, and also attempted to inoculate the English in Ireland against Irish culture ordaining that

> every Englishman do use the English language, and be named by an English name, leaving off entirely the manner of naming used by the Irish; and that every Englishman use the English custom, fashion, mode of riding and apparel, according to his estate. (s. 3; Hardiman, 1843, p. 11)

The status of the English in Ireland was of course intended to be higher than the Irish but it is a feature of the colony that the status of the metropolitan settlers in the colony is better than it might have been back in the home country. So, in this case, the crisis of feudalism that followed the mass mortality of the Black Death (perhaps one-third of the population died in the four years 1348–1351), harsh new forms of labour discipline were enacted in England with brutal punishment for those wandering poor who did not choose settled and gainful employment. In Ireland, wages and conditions of employment were likewise regulated by the Statues of Kilkenny, but only for the Irish. Irish labour was not allowed to leave the country: '[N]o labour shall pass beyond sea; and in case that he shall do so and shall return, he shall be taken and put in prison for a year, and afterwards make fine at the King's will' (s. 33; Hardiman, 1843, p. 145). There really was one law for the Irish and another for the English. In fact, there were three sets of law: and English common law for the English, a different set of English laws for the Irish, and the self-regulation of the Irish according to their own Brehon law (significantly about compensation rather than about deterrent pain). No English person was to resort to local Irish forms of justice:

> [N]o Englishman, having disputes with any other Englishman, shall henceforth make caption, or take pledge, distress or vengeance against any other, whereby the people may be troubled, but that they shall sue each other at the common law; and that no Englishman be governed in the termination of their disputes by March law nor Brehon law, which reasonably ought not to be called law, being a bad custom. (s. 4; Hardiman, 1843, p. 17)

The marches (and hence 'march law') was a geographical and a colonial term, meaning the lands beyond English law, as in the Welsh marches or marchlands. This territorial term recurs in the Statutes of Kilkenny, for example, in this regulation of the sports to be allowed the English settlers (the commons) of Ireland:

> The commons of the said land of Ireland, who are in the different marches at war, do not, henceforth, use the plays which men call horlings, with great sticks and a ball upon the ground, from which great evils and maims have arisen, to the weakening, of the defence of the said land, and other plays which men call coiting; but that they do apply and accustom themselves to use and draw bows, and throw lances, and other gentlemanlike games, whereby the Irish enemies may be the better checked by the liege people and commons of these parts'. (s. 6; Hardiman, 1843, p. 23)

Note here, that the English settlers are described as living in these marginal areas under state of war. Note also the conflation of land and persons in the term commons, which at the time could refer to English persons of low status but also to the lands of which such people had collective use. It is clear from these Statutes that the English feudal estates in Ireland are maintained under conditions of radical legal separation between Irish and English, a condition that deserves to be called feudal colonialism. It is a system that regulates people but does so in an explicitly territorial manner.

Land and terrain in the early-capitalist colony

The feudal state was no more than the collection of estates claimed by the monarch. This could be an archipelago of detached entities and, in the case of the English kings, included during the period c.1330–1500, properties in France, Britain, and Ireland. This political geography was unstable, not only because peripheral barons might establish local monarchies, but also because rival monarchs might pick off remoter possessions. As the scale and cost of warfare increased with canon rather than crossbow, and sieges became ever more prolonged and deadly, the political geography of monarchy changed. The new military technologies caused terrain to be understood in a new way. Mercenaries could no longer be sent hither and yon to take and hold remote estates. Rather, there was now, as Anderson (1974b) argued, a focus upon concentrating holdings to make the collective more easily defensible from a common heartland. Monarchs now travelled less and instead of visiting themselves upon various barons in turn, they centralized authority in capital cities and taxed more intensively the lands that they claimed. They now had to draw to a central location a much larger share of the national product, the better to sustain their capital city.

Elton (1953) called this a Tudor revolution in government, and Hoskins (1988) has described the new forms of statecraft that were developed in England, preparing the way for the mercantilist state of the eighteenth century. But the colonies were central to this new science of the state, with its novel statistics. It was no longer useful to follow the feudal practice of treating the colonial periphery as a place under weak control to be plundered or farmed by adventurous sons, earls, or barons who might otherwise cause trouble at home. Instead, the Irish possessions were expected to yield more for the English crown: more timber for ships, more corn for the English towns, and more soldiers for the English army. This required a new territorial project in Ireland: the shiring of the Irish lands. Under Poynings Law of 1495, Ireland was made subject to all British statute law and the English monarch asserted the right of veto over all legislation proposed by the Irish parliament. Ireland was now to be divided into shires, each administered by a sheriff appointed by the English crown and answerable in the first instance to an English administrator, the Lord Deputy of Ireland. All Irish lords, with lands claimed under whatsoever authority, were to surrender those lands to the English crown and to plea for the same to be re-granted with the understanding that all would now come under English common law and English statute law. Gaelic forms of property, marriage, and inheritance were to be dissolved.

This was a colonial and a territorial project because it comprehended Ireland as a single territorial entity and because it recognized within Ireland very different statuses for the English and Welsh, and soon the Scots, in contradistinction to the Irish. Indeed the early-capitalist colonial adventure in Ireland perhaps forges the British state of England, Wales, and Scotland. Colonialism makes British the English, Welsh, and Scots and it does so against the Irish. The Irish resisted this colonialism and the religious conversion that went with it. In response, the British waged successive wars of reconquest and entrenched still deeper the distinction between Irish native and British settler.

Before I spend a little time on these new territorial strategies of attainder, exile, and plantation, I want to underline the essentially virtual nature of colonial sovereignty. The ideology of the early modern state, as absolute or constitutional monarchy, was that it rested upon the loyalty of its subjects, what Locke described as the 'tacit consent' of the people (Elden, 2013, p. 308). Its ideology was in the form that Leibniz described as a force of jurisdiction. In Ireland and other colonies, it was more akin to the force of territory, sustained only by repeated and brutal use of military force. There is a more general point that one could develop about the relations between the imaginary and the lived. Capitalism, for example, is imagined and defended in the form of petty commodity production, whereas it is practiced through monopoly powers, vested interests, and special concessions. For the colonial state at least, the distance between ideal and reality allowed projection to serve as legitimation.

COLONIAL TERRITORY

When Elden moves on, in the 'Coda', to a brief explication of territory as a political technology, he shifts geographical frame, no longer writing about Leibniz and the Treaty of Westphalia, he writes about colonialism and the New World. Asserting that territory precedes nation, Elden notes that surveying was particularly important in the colonies. This picks up a thread that he had dropped earlier. The internal and external geopolitics of European states co-mingle. However, the issues arising from the relations between sovereignty and papacy are somewhat different from those secreted by the colonial fix. First, the comingling. Elden suggests that when the Pope published the Treaty of Tordesillas, dividing the future Spanish territories to the west, from the projected Portugese territories to the east, of a line 378° west of the established European settlements on the Cape Verde islands, he carved a caesura that bore no relation to contemporary patterns of exploration, occupation, or settlement (Elden, 2013, p. 22). Yet, the relation between internal and external is clear. The authority exercised by the Pope in determining dynastic succession within Europe was likewise asserted in separating the realms of those same princes outside Europe.

The papal, if not the religious, form of this legitimation seems like special pleading. Indeed, when Elden describes the consolidation of the Reformation, he remarks that a late-sixteenth-century English political philosopher, Richard Hooker, had sketched a compound church-polity where the authority of the secular over the ecclesiastical could be justified because, as historical fact, the state had first taken the land militarily before it could ever have been filled with religious mission (Elden, 2013, p. 280). Elden cites several commentators who remarked upon the belatedness of the ecclesiastical authority, yet the general argument of his book treated the translation of authority from clerical into secular geopolitics. It is the ambition of the normative that matters here, and that bridges the normative and the political. Hobbes' argument, as Elden describes it, is that, while the basis of sovereignty was the consent of the people, this implied, in turn, that all property rights should affirm the legitimacy of the government protecting those rights. In the colonies, if nowhere else, property was theft. More than this, the theft had been organized geographically.

Which brings me back to Ireland, and to the plantations. In the late fifteenth century, then, and with Poynings Law, the English state asserted the inclusion of Ireland within the state-territorial structure of England: Thou shalt have no law but ... By their own lights, the English now depicted Irish resistance as treason. Once it was accepted, having been asserted, that property titles in Ireland rested upon loyalty to the English crown, one could conclude that resistance was treachery. And, thus did property pass between Irish Catholic and settler Protestant. Yet this transfer was evidently colonial and manifestly both dramatic and violent.

Territoriality and theft

Each re-conquest of Ireland had a distinct territoriality: a specific set of relations between violence, theft, and reallocation. In the two centuries following 1500, 90% of Irish land became British property. In all cases, the Irish were treated as non-persons. On each occasion, the tactics were territorial. The reconquest of Ireland was clearly both colonial and territorial.

Over the period 1579–1583, a violent campaign by the British prepared the plantation of Munster. About one-in-three of the people living in the province died, of whom one-third perished by force of arms and two-thirds by pestilence and famine. The British destroyed the crops in the field and thereby produced this supplementary mortality. After the clearance, good English folk were invited to settle Munster. The instrument of dispossession chosen by the British assumed and projected the virtual sovereignty of colonialism. Asserting that the Irish had vowed allegiance to the English monarch, the English found the rebels guilty of treason. This instrument of attainder was, I would suggest, a territorial tactic of colonialism. On behalf of the English Queen, the Lord Deputy of Ireland put through a parliament in Dublin, an Act for the Attainder of the executed Earl of Desmond and numerous other rebels 'convicted and attainted of high treason', so that they should all 'forfeit to your Highnesse, and to your heires and successors, all and every such honours, castles, mannors, messuages, lands, tenements, rents reversions, remainders, possession rights, conditions, interests, offices, fees, annuities, and all other their hereditaments, goods, chattels, debts', and anything else of use to them (28 Eliz. I c. 7, 1586, p. 420). A set of commissioners were appointed 'to survey the lands of such as have been in rebellion within the last four years in Ireland and have no lawful pardons for their lands' and their instructions from the English Privy Council were quite detailed, requesting to know of these forfeited estates, their annual profit under very many categories, as well as a determination of their area (quoted in Murphy, 2013, p. 36). Once again, then, we see a set of people organized by managing the space, or lands, to which they are linked. Or, rather, we find their social status devalued by redefining the association between land and people. This was one more territorial form of colonialism.

Some of the older territorial tactics continued, including various forms of the spatial ban, and the Lord Deputy for Ireland, Sir John Perrot, charged with subduing the province, proposed a series of measures that had clear territorial form. He retained the old distinction between the small part of Ireland, the Pale, within which the English writ ran without too much resistance, and the remainder beyond, which was effectively under belligerent occupation. He sought to disarm the Irish within the territory under English control. In 1584, Perrot endorsed a proposal that:

No man [was] to wear weapons within the English Pale, either by day or by night, unless he be of the Pale, and in English habit or else it shall be lawful for any of the army to kill him. (Brewer & Bullen, 1868, p. 399)

The pacification failed and, within a decade, the British deployed one of the largest armies yet seen in the western hemisphere when they sent 18,000 troops to subdue Ulster. This was more numerous than the army the Spanish sent to take South America. This time the destruction of the Irish people was even more savage and Mountjoy's scorched earth policy full earned its infamy: perhaps 40,000 souls perished, one half the population of Ulster. We must appreciate just how much mortality and displacement was necessary for plantation to be given a chance. The British had to dispose of half the population of Ulster to give the Presbyterian Scots a fair chance to establish a new, and loyal, society. The secretary to Mountjoy saw it all without any seeming remorse:

And no spectacle was more frequent in the Ditches of Townes, and esepciallie in wasted Countries, than to see multitudes of these poore people dead with their mouthes all coloured greene by eating nettles, docks, and all things they could rend up above ground. (Moryson, 1907, p. 283)

This was no natural catastrophe but rather biological warfare, a recurring tactic of colonial repression.

Surpassing both these in infamy was the re-Conquest directed by Oliver Cromwell. Smyth (2014, p. 4) has noted that:

In the Irish Folklore Commission archives only Daniel O'Connell–Catholic Ireland's greatest politician of the nineteenth century–surpassed Oliver Cromwell in number of references. Clearly for the Catholic Irish the memory of this perceived 'demon-destroyer' and his actions had burned deep into their psyche.

The military campaigns of the 1640s and 1650s produced mortality and emigration equivalent to about one-quarter of the Irish. The Act of Settlement that followed the Cromwellian campaign offered this evidently necessary assurance:

Whereas the Parliament of England, after the expense of much blood and treasure for suppression of the horrid rebellion in Ireland, have by the good hand of God upon their undertakings, brought that affair to such an issue, as that a total reducement and settlement of that nation may, with God's blessing, be speedily effected, to the end therefore that the people of that nation may know that it is not the intention of the Parliament to extirpate that whole nation. (Act for the Settlement of Ireland, 1652, p. 598)

Some 50,000 Irish were exiled to the Caribbean and the remaining rebel families were to surrender their lands to the British crown and be given back in the province of Connacht new lands to the extent of one-third of their former possessions.

Matters in Ireland bore no relation to Lockean ideas of property. None could claim that in Ireland property was the reward for cultivation; rather, it was straightforwardly the spoil of conquest. The space of Ireland was reorganized so that in the agriculturally most productive provinces, Leinster, Munster, and Ulster, Irish Catholic property was translated into British Protestant property. This plantation of a new society was a massive undertaking; fully 11 million acres were taken after the Cromwellian wars. From this enterprise came Petty's *Political Anatomy of Ireland, with the Establishment for the Kingdom and Verbum Sapienti* (1672; published posthumously in 1691). As Cronin shows, Petty took the tabular method of his Political Arithmetic, confining his description of the state to matters 'of Number, Weight, or Measure', and allied it to a more geographical perspective that came directly from his time in Ireland (Petty, 1691; quoted in Cronin, 2014, p. 63). Petty was director of the survey of the lands confiscated from the Irish in the 1640s and 1650s. These surveys were part inventory and part projection. As inventory, they described the condition of various parcels of land, their resources, and likely economic yield. As projection, these surveys presented a land fit for English and Protestant settlement. In large part, this meant erasing the Irish from their own lands. It was a projection of a void where in fact there were people, history, and a cultivated landscape. This erasure and projection is a common territorial strategy of colonialism. Despite the violence required to take the land, the ideology of colonialism was that now there was simply extensive possibility.

Territory was made the object of colonial governance, at least in its ideological form. This was done because a new geography could be offered as the starting point for a new society. Thus, Petty could insist that: 'The parishes of Ireland do much want Regulation, by uniting and dividing them; so as to make them fit Enclosures wherein to plant the Gospel' (Petty, 1662; quoted in Cronin, 2014, p. 61). Ireland was now Eden, and Petty claimed that he chose Ireland as the case study for his new science of *Political Anatomy* because it was a 'Political Animal, who is scarce Twenty years old; where the Intrigue of State is not very complicate and with which I have been conversant from an *Embiricon*' (Petty, 1691; quoted in Cronin, 2014, p. 63). Elden finds the 1494 Treaty of Tordesillas somewhat lacking as an example of territory, the exercise of sovereignty through mastery of space, precisely because it projected control without regard to existing patterns of exploration, occupation, or settlement. However, it is precisely in this form that territory does much of its most important work. It projects a blank space for colonial powers, erasing indigenous claims and legitimating new and colonial ones.

ACKNOWLEDGEMENTS

My thanks to Burak Kadercan for the invitation to contribute to a session on Territory at the International Studies Association annual meeting, New Orleans, February 2015. Thanks also to Stuart Elden for the generosity of our exchanges.

DISCLOSURE STATEMENT

No potential conflict of interest was reported by the author.

REFERENCES

28 Eliz. I c. 7. (1586). An act for the Attaindor of the Late Earl of Desmond, and others mentioned in this act. In J. G. Butler (Ed.), *The statutes at large, passed in the parliaments held in Ireland: From the third year of Edward the second, A.D. 1310, to the twenty sixth year of George the third, A.D. 1786 inclusive* (Vol. I [1786], pp. 418–422). London: Authority.

Act for the Settlement of Ireland. (1652). *Acts and ordinances of the interregnum: 1642–1660. Volume II: Feb., 1649 to March, 1660* (pp. 598–602) (C. H. Firth and R. S. Raith, Eds.) (1911). His Majesty's Stationery Office, London.

Agamben, G. (2005). *State of exception* [2003] (K. Attell, Trans.). Chicago, IL: Chicago University Press.

Agnew, J. (2013). Territory, politics, governance. *Territory, Politics, Governance, 1*(1), 1–4.

Anand, R. P. (1972). *New states and international law*. Delhi: Vikas.

Anderson, P. (1974a). *Passages from antiquity to feudalism*. London: New Left Books.

Anderson, P. (1974b). *Lineages of the absolutist state*. London: New Left Books.

Anghie, A. (2004). *Imperialism, sovereignty and the making of international law*. Cambridge: Cambridge University Press.

Atzili, B., & Kadercan, B. (2017). Territorial designs and international politics: The diverging constitution of space and boundaries. *Territory, Politics, Governance.* doi:10.1080/21622671.2016.1266962

Barder, A. (2015). *Empire within: International hierarchy and its imperial laboratories of governance*. New York, NY: Routledge.

Bloch, M. (1962). *Feudal society. Volume 1. The growth and ties of dependence* [1939] (L. A. Manyon, Trans.). London: Routledge and Kegan Paul.

Bowden, B. (2009). *The empire of civilization: The evolution of an imperial idea*. Chicago, IL: University of Chicago Press.

Brewer, J. S., & Bullen, W. (Eds.). (1868). *Calendar of the Carew manuscripts preserved in the archiepiscopal library at Lambeth, 1575–1588*. London: Longmans, Green, Reader, and Dyer.

Bryan, J. (2015). Reading Stuart Elden's 'The Birth of Territory'. *Political Geography, 46*, 96–97.

Butler, J. (2012). *Parting ways: Jewishness and the critique of Zionism*. New York, NY: Columbia University Press.

Canny, N. P. (1976). *The Elizabethan conquest of Ireland: A pattern established, 1565–1576*. Hassocks: Harvester Press.

Charron, A. (2014). Putting territory in context. *Dialogues in Human Geography, 4*(3), 343–345.

Cox, K. (2014). A review of 'Birth of Territory'. *Dialogues in Human Geography, 4*(3), 351–353.

Cronin, N. (2014). Writing the 'New Geography': Cartographic discourse and colonial governmentality in William Petty's *The Political Anatomy of Ireland. Historical Geography, 42*, 58–71.

Dalby, S. (1991). Critical geopolitics: Discourse, difference, and dissent. *Environment and Planning D: Society and Space, 9*(3), 261–283.

Dean, M. (2015). The Malthus effect: Population and the liberal government of life. *Economy and Society, 44*(1), 18–39.

Dews, P. (1987). *Logics of disintegration: Post-structuralist thought and the claims of critical theory*. London: Verso.

Elden, S. (2013). *The birth of territory*. Chicago: University of Chicago Press.

Elden, S. (2014). 'The Birth of Territory': A response. *Dialogues in Human Geography, 4*(3), 353–356.

Elden, S. (2015a). 'The Birth of Territory': A response. *Political Geography, 46*, 99–101.

Elden, S. (2015b). Author's response. *Journal of Historical Geography, 50*, 116–118.

Elias, T. O. (1972). *Africa and the development of international law*. Leiden: A. W. Sijthoff.

Elton, G. R. (1953). *The Tudor revolution in government: Administrative changes in the reign of Henry VIII*. Cambridge: Cambridge University Press.

Gerald of Wales. (1894). The vaticinal history of the conquest of Ireland [1189] (T. Wright, Trans.). In *The historical works of Giraldus Cambrensis* (pp. 165–324). London: George Bell and Sons.

Hardiman, J. (Ed.). (1843). *A statute of the fortieth year of King Edward III. Enacted in a parliament held in Kilkenny, A.D. 1367, before Lionel Duke of Clarence, Lord Lieutenant of Ireland* (J. Hardiman, trans.). In *Tracts relating to Ireland* (Vol. II, pp. 1–121 [175–295]). Dublin: Irish Archaeological Society.

Heffernan, M. (2015). Genealogies, choices, consequences and languages. *Journal of Historical Geography*, *50*, 110–112.

Hirst, P., & Woolley, P. (1982). *Social relations and human attributes*. London: Routledge.

Hoskins, W. G. (1988). *The age of plunder: The England of Henry VIII, 1500–1547*. London: Longmans.

Kearns, G. (2006). Bare life, political violence and the territorial structure of Britain and Ireland. In D. Gregory & A. Pred (Eds.), *Violent geographies: Fear, terror and political violence* (pp. 9–34). New York, NY: Routledge.

Kearns, G. (2007). The history of medical geography after Foucault. In S. Elden & J. Crampton (Eds.), *Space, knowledge and power: Foucault and geography* (pp. 205–222). Aldershot: Ashgate.

Kearns, G. (2014a). Governing vitalities and the security state. *Environment and Planning D: Society and Space, 32* (5), 762–778.

Kearns, G. (2014b). Review of Elden, 'The Birth of Territory'. *Environment and Planning D: Society and Space. Blog.* Retrieved September 1, 2015, from http://societyandspace.com/reviews/reviews-archive/elden/

Kearns, G., & Reid-Henry, S. (2009). Vital geographies: Life, luck and the human condition. *Annals of the Association of American Geographers*, *99*(3), 554–574.

Keat, R. (1981). *The politics of social theory: Habermas, Freud and the critique of positivism*. Oxford: Basil Blackwell.

Keene, E. (2002). *Beyond the anarchical society: Grotius, colonialism and order in world politics*. Cambridge: Cambridge University Press.

Kiernan, V. (1980). *State and society in Europe, 1550–1650*. Oxford: Basil Blackwell.

Koch, N. (2014). 'The Birth of Territory': Should political geographers do conceptual history? *Dialogues in Human Geography*, *4*(3), 348–351.

Lawrence, T. J. (1895). *The principles of international law*. London: Macmillan.

Legg, S. (2015). The birth of territory: A review forum. *Journal of Historical Geography*, *50*, 109–118.

MacDonagh, O. (1958). The nineteenth-century revolution in government: A reappraisal. *Historical Journal*, *1*, 52–67.

Malthus, T. (1798). *An essay on the principle of population, as it affects the future improvement of society*. London: J. Johnson.

Marx, K. (1973). *Grundrisse* [1939] (M. Nicolaus, Trans.). London: Pelican Books.

Marx, K. (1975a). Economic and philosophical manuscripts (1844) (G. Benton, Trans.). In K. Marx (Ed.), *Early writings* (pp. 277–400). London: Pelican Books.

Marx, K. (1975b). Preface (to 'A contribution to the critique of political economy') (1859). In K. Marx (Ed.), *Early writings* (pp. 424–428). London: Pelican Books.

McDonagh, B. (2015). Property, land and territory. *Journal of Historical Geography*, *50*, 112–113.

Meinig, D. W. (1986). *The shaping of America: A geographical perspective on 500 years of history, volume 1, Atlantic America*. New Haven, CT: Yale University Press.

Morgan, L. H. (1877). *Ancient society: Or, researches in the lines of human progress from savagery, through barbarism to civilization*. New York, NY: Henry Holt.

Moryson, F. (1907). *An itinerary: Containing his ten years travel through the twelve dominions of Germany, Bohemia, Switzerland, Netherland, Denmark, Poland, Italy, Turkey, France, England, Scotland and Ireland, vol. II [1617]*. Glasgow: James Maclehose and Sons.

Murphy, A. (2015). Reading Stuart Elden's 'The Birth of Territory'. *Political Geography*, *46*, 94–96.

Murphy, J. A. (Ed.). (2013). *The Desmond survey*. Cork: University College Cork. Retrieved from October 29, 2015 http://www.ucc.ie/celt/published/E580000-001/index.html

Ó Tuathail, G. (1996). *Critical geopolitics: The politics of writing global space*. Minneapolis: University of Minnesota Press.

Otway-Ruthven, A. J., & Smithwick, W. A. (1961). *Liber primus Kilkenniensis*. Kilkenny: Kilkenny Journal.

Petty, W. (1662). *A treatise of taxes and contributions*. London: N. Brooke.

Petty, W. (1691). *Political anatomy of Ireland*. London: D. Brown and W. Rogers.

Pratt, M. L. (1991). *Imperial eyes: Travel writing and transculturation*. London: Routledge.

Rabinow, P. (1995). *French modern: Norms and forms of the social environment*. Chicago, IL: University of Chicago Press.

Sack, R. D. (1986). *Human territoriality: Its theory and history.* Cambridge: Cambridge University Press.

Sassen, S. (2015). Making territory work analytically beyond its connection to the state. *Journal of Historical Geography, 50*, 115–116.

Smith, A. (1993). *An inquiry into the nature and causes of the wealth of nations [1776]. A selected edition* (K. Sutherland, Ed.). Oxford: Oxford University Press.

Smyth, W. J. (2014). Towards a traumatic geography of Ireland 1530–1760 and beyond: The evidence of Irish language texts. *Historical Geography, 42*, 30–57.

Drone strikes, ephemeral sovereignty, and changing conceptions of territory

Katharine Hall Kindervater

ABSTRACT

Drone strikes, ephemeral sovereignty, and changing conceptions of territory. *Territory, Politics, Governance*. One of the questions posed about contemporary US drone strikes is to what extent these strikes, particularly those occurring outside of Iraq and Afghanistan, are reshaping our conceptions of territory and sovereignty. It appears that geographies of war and of the use or projection of force are radically changing. This article examines the US legal frameworks for drone-targeting operations, and in particular the conceptions of territory they draw upon, to argue that contemporary strikes reflect less a disappearance of the importance of territory and sovereignty to justifications of the use of force than a reconfiguration of their meanings. Grounded in an understanding of territory that is more networked and dynamic, drone strikes reflect the emergence of a new landscape of mobile and ephemeral sovereignty.

摘要

无人机攻击，短暂的主权，以及改变中的领土概念。*Territory, Politics, Governance*。有关当代美国的无人机攻击的问题之一，特别是那些发生在伊拉克和阿富汗之外的地区，是这些攻击在什麽程度上重塑我们对于领土和主权的概念。战争的地理，以及投入与规划兵力的地理，似乎正在经历大幅变革。本文检视美国使用无人机瞄准操作的法律架构，特别是他们所援引的领土概念，主张当代的攻击反映出领土和主权之于合理化武力使用的重要性并未消失，而是其意义受到重构。无人机攻击植基于对领土更为网络化且动态的理解，反映出崭新的动态与短暂的主权地景的浮现。

RÉSUMÉ

Les attaques de drones, la souveraineté éphémère et des notions de territoire changeantes. *Territory, Politics, Governance*. L'une des questions posées à propos des attaques de drones contemporaines par les É-U c'est la suivante: jusqu'à quel point ces attaques, surtout les attaques qui se défèrlent à l'extérieur de l'Iraq et de l'Afghanistan, est-ce qu'elles modifient les notions de territoire et de souveraineté? Il semble que les topographies de la guerre et l'emploi ou la projection de la force sont en pleine mutation. Ce présent article examine les cadres juridiques américains des opérations menées à partir des drones, et notamment les notions de territoire auxquelles ils peuvent faire appel, pour affirmer que les attaques contemporaines reflètent moins la disparition de l'importance des notions de territoire et de souveraineté face aux justifications pour l'emploi de la force que plutôt une recomposition de leur signification. Bien fondées sur une compréhension du territoire qui est plus interconnectée et dynamique, les attaques de drones constituent un reflet de la naissance d'un nouveau paysage de souveraineté mobile et éphémère.

RESUMEN

Ataques de aviones teledirigidos, soberanía efímera y cambios en los conceptos de territorio. *Territory, Politics, Governance*. Una de las cuestiones planteadas sobre los actuales ataques de aviones no tripulados estadounidenses es en qué medida estos ataques, en particular los que ocurren fuera de Irak y Afganistán, están transformando nuestros conceptos de territorio y soberanía. Parece que las geografías de la guerra y el uso o la proyección de fuerza están cambiando radicalmente. En este artículo analizamos los marcos legales en Estados Unidos para las operaciones con aviones teledirigidos, y en particular los conceptos de territorio en los que se basan, para argumentar que los actuales ataques no reflejan tanto una desaparición de la importancia de territorio y soberanía para justificar el uso de la fuerza sino más bien una reconfiguración de sus significados. Los ataques de aviones no tripulados se basan en una comprensión de territorio más interconectada y dinámica, y reflejan la aparición de un nuevo entorno de soberanía móvil y efímera.

The message is that we will shrink the world to find you, we will shrink the world to bring you to justice ...
(FBI Director James Comey – Hudson, 2014)

As the FBI Director's comments about shrinking the world made at a Minneapolis press conference indicate, space is an important figure in today's discourse surrounding the US government's use of drones and the ever-evolving war on terror.[1] Proponents and critics alike stress that the drone allows for shrinking space or distance and overcoming territorial limits, enabling targeting at increasingly large distances and extending the spatial reach of the military with limited risk to US soldiers. Further, perhaps in part because of these characteristics, the drone has become a weapon and surveillance tool (Kindervater, 2016) that is increasingly deployed in territories outside of war zones and met with relatively little resistance[2] – examples of which can be found in Libya, Somalia, Pakistan, and Yemen.[3]

If the contemporary global drone wars raise questions about the changing space of war, they also produce related questions about the meaning of territory, and more specifically the relationship between territory and the projection of force. For example, as drone strikes exceed the 'traditional' limits of the battlefield, does the relevance or salience of the territory of the nation-state fall away, especially as it relates to sovereignty and sovereign jurisdiction? Have new or different conceptions of territory emerged in the war on terror and contemporary drone wars? This article examines the role of territory in the United States' deployment of lethal drones, and does so by looking at two publicly available documents that provide legal justifications for drone targeting operations. Focusing on these legal justifications throws into relief the malleable, dynamic, and multiplicitious character of territory, as well as how territory and authority are mobilized and constructed in relation to the law and the projection of force. I argue that territory is mobilized in these documents to legally justify the use of force and the reach of US sovereign power. By drawing on conceptions of territory that are dynamic and malleable, the Obama Administration attempts to place drone strikes squarely within the law, effecting a new landscape of mobile and ephemeral sovereignty that stands in contrast to conventions of state sovereignty that are fixed to static demarcations of territory.

The first section of the article is devoted to a close reading of a Department of Justice memorandum and white paper, which outline the US government's justification for drone strikes outside war zones as well as against US citizens. In these documents, how the space of war is characterized becomes important for determining the legality of a strike. Here, law/legal justification and territory work together to produce a shape-shifting field of state violence and the use of force. Territory and the space of the battlefield become important bolsters to the United States' authority to strike, yet the concept of territory that underpins these documents is far from fixed and static. Thus, the second section turns to recent efforts by critical geographers to develop dynamic and networked concepts of territory and how this might help us to think through the significance of territory to the execution of drone strikes, leading to the emergence of a more ephemeral and fluid form of sovereignty. The article concludes by revisiting the concept of territorial design advanced in this special issue in light of this engagement with US drone strikes. As I discuss, looking at territory through the lens of the contemporary drone strike allows us to see the tensions and connections between the constitution and demarcation processes of territory as well as the multiplicity of state territory.

DRONE STRIKES, LAW, AND TERRITORY

Since 11 September 2001, two public government documents provide the most comprehensive account of the government's justification of the use of drone strikes outside of Iraq and Afghanistan, extending state power and the projection of force outside of delineated battle spaces. The 2010 Memorandum for the Attorney General from the Department of Justice Office of Legal Counsel ('Memorandum') and the 2011 draft of a Department of Justice White Paper ('White Paper') each outline a legal argument in support of drone strikes, with particular focus on the lawfulness of targeting American citizens abroad. Together, the documents reveal not so much the rationales for drone strikes, but the – sometimes contradictory and conflicting – frameworks of authority and power that the Obama administration places these strikes within. Territory is a central figure in these frameworks. In what follows, I introduce the arguments made in these documents and then look more closely at the roles of territory and the law in producing the spaces of contemporary drone wars.

The 2010 Memorandum specifically focuses on affirming the legality of a drone strike targeting Anwar al-Awlaki, an American citizen in Yemen, by assessing whether or not the strike would violate federal criminal laws or the Constitution of the United States. The conclusion of the document – that these strikes are legal – is supported by three main arguments, which the Memorandum moves through in order, yet also keeps fairly distinct from one another. This has the effect of making it difficult for the reader to distinguish exactly what the legality of the strikes hinges on – a difficulty compounded by redacted portions of the text.[4]

The first consideration of the Memorandum is whether, in the case of targeting al-Awlaki, the actions of the government would fall under a public authority justification for the criminal codes it would otherwise violate.[5] If the targeting of al-Awlaki fell under the public authority justification, it would not be considered an 'unlawful killing' or murder by the state. The Memorandum argues that this justification would apply for either Department of Defense or Central Intelligence Agency (CIA) drone strikes because it would constitute a 'lawful conduct of war' (Office of Legal Counsel, U.S. Department of Justice, 2010, p. 20). To make this argument, which is the most detailed section in the Memorandum, the authors argue that al-Awlaki as an individual falls within the scope of the 2001 Authorization for Use of Military Force (AUMF).[6] The

Memorandum authors argue, ' ... the AUMF itself does not set forth an express geographic limitation ... ' (Office of Legal Counsel, U.S. Department of Justice, 2010, p. 24). What is important, therefore, is the status of those involved in the conflict, not the location of the conflict, which is seen to extend globally and to move with the individuals involved. Following this, and in what begins to feel like circular reasoning to the reader, the Memorandum concludes that because the military would follow the rules of International Humanitarian Law in its targeting procedures, these actions would be under the conduct of war and thus fall under the public authority justification.[7]

The second and third major justifications put forward in the Memorandum rely on evidence that al-Awlaki is actively taking part (or planning to take part) in hostile actions directed against the United States. It first determines that the United States would not fall subject to the War Crimes Act because of al-Awlaki's legitimate status as a target. Second, the Memorandum demonstrates that there are no constitutional limitations placed on killing al-Awlaki as a US citizen because the threat he poses is greater than the violation of his constitutional rights. The argument that the US government would prefer to capture him, but deems it infeasible, is used to bolster this claim. Any evidence presented that the United States had tried to capture him, if it exists, has been redacted.

Focused also on the targeted killing of a US citizen more generally, and not directly referencing al-Awlaki, the 2011 Department of Justice White Paper parallels many of the arguments and conclusions outlined in the 2010 Memorandum, with sections focused on Constitutional limitations, the public authority justification, and war crimes. The 2011 White Paper, however, adds a more specific legal framework for when lethal force is justified. It states that:

> ... where the following three conditions are met, a U.S. operation using lethal force in a foreign country against a U.S. citizen who is a senior operational leader of al-Qa'ida or an associated force would be lawful: (1) an informed, high-level official of the U.S. government has determined that the targeted individual poses an imminent threat of violent attack against the United States; (2) capture is infeasible, and the United States continues to monitor whether capture becomes feasible; and (3) the operation would be conducted in a manner consistent with applicable law of war principles. (Department of Justice, 2011, p. 1)

These three stipulations represent the most concise guidelines across available government documents for the authority to strike, and they centre on an official within the US government making the determination of a threat.[8] Once this determination is made, and the individual target in question is associated with a terrorist group,[9] killing this individual is deemed lawful as long as capturing him/her is seen as difficult and the 'laws of war' are followed.[10]

Focusing on the first stipulation, a central component of the target determination is whether or not the individual poses an *imminent* threat. Much of the justification for this stipulation that follows in the White Paper deals with what constitutes an imminent threat and how norms of sovereignty and territory are taken into consideration. According to its authors, the possibility of an imminent threat authorizes the United States to target an individual under the justification of self-defence (Department of Justice, 2011, p. 1). This targeting practice also does not violate another state's sovereignty, such as Yemen or Pakistan's sovereignty; either the lethal action is undertaken with the consent of that state, *or* that state is unwilling to accept or take action on its own, rendering US action justified by the immediacy of the threat. In other words, imminent threat trumps other states' control of their own territories.[11] In addition to self-defence, the White Paper also draws on the AUMF for justification of targeted killing outside of Iraq and Afghanistan, arguing that under the AUMF the United States is involved in a 'non-international conflict' with terrorist groups whose nature (as per the AUMF remit) has no geographical limitation. The categorization here of 'non-international conflict' is a legal term found in the laws of armed conflict and refers to a conflict between a state and non-state organized armed groups. This is contrasted to an 'international' conflict between two states. The White Paper thus essentially defines the drone strike as an act of war in two ways, or from two angles. The first is through the AUMF – that these strikes fit within the scope of this authorization of force. The second is through the definition of a non-international conflict – that the nature of the US engagement against terrorist groups puts it within this type of conflict, and therefore expands it globally. While this might be redundant (the 2011 White Paper is no more clear and no less circular than the 2010 Memorandum), the authors clearly seek to emphasize the lack of geographical limits and territorial boundaries to the potential scope of drone strikes and US projection of force and authority.

The self-defence and AUMF/non-international conflict justifications come together in a peculiar way around the idea of a threat's imminence. In the White Paper the authors are working with a general and fairly broader concept of imminence, one that is tied more to the longer temporality of the war on terror (Department of Justice, 2011, p. 7). An imminent threat is not a 'ticking time bomb' scenario, but rather signalled by participation in a terrorist group that is continuously planning attacks. At first glance, it is unclear why the argument of imminent threat is necessary to the legal framework if, as the 2010 Memorandum (along with parts of the 2011 White Paper) makes clear, attacks against Al-Qaeda members and affiliates are justified globally under the AUMF and the existence of a 'non-international conflict'. The broad concept of imminence seems unnecessary and redundant, perhaps even adding further confusion. Yet the emphasis on imminence reflects the importance of temporality to the justification of lethal force. This is not a long-standing or permanent justification, but rather one that is temporary, ephemeral, and must be repeatedly renewed for the individual/threat in question, wherever they are located.

Connected to this particular understanding of imminent threat, in both the Memorandum and the White Paper the drone strike is also justified spatially. The interpretation of the AUMF as having no geographical limits and the definition of 'non-international conflict' as not tied to states gives the legal framework of drone strikes global reach. Indeed, the landscape of force projection that emerges out of these documents renders 'non-international conflict' sort of a misnomer: it might be better described as a hyper-international or global conflict. In this understanding of conflict, 'traditional' or 'fixed' international boundaries do not matter in the way they seem to have in the past (as containers or delimiters of violence, reach of power, etc.), at least when it comes to determining where force can or cannot be used. In this legal view, drones strikes outside of Afghanistan and Iraq are not beyond the battlefield; they rather are incorporated in a redefined battlefield. Furthermore, this is a battlefield tied less to territorial space and more to the individual who produces that battlefield through his/her associations or actions.

Recent critical scholarship in geography seeks to make sense of this redefined battlefield or battle space as it relates to the use of drones, and a common theme in this scholarship is the role that law plays in justifying and extending the use of force: it is through law that geographies of war are expanding and changing. This emphasis on law seems to fit with the US government's selection of the law as the avenue through which to justify strikes, even if the legal arguments themselves are incomplete, fuzzy, or debatable. While there is a rich and growing set of literature on war and law, here I focus on three prominent examples from this scholarship in geography that address drone strikes and the space of contemporary war specifically and demonstrate how law and violence are intertwined in different ways: (1) Derek Gregory's writings on the geography of drones strikes, particularly as it relates to his concept of the 'everywhere war', (2) Ian Shaw and Majed Akhter's exploration of the relationship between law and technology, and (3) John Morrissey's mobilization of the term 'lawfare'. Taken together, these scholars help us to think about the role of law in producing contemporary geographies of war, but also point the way forward from the analysis of the Memorandum and White Paper above to understanding the role of territory as a political technology (Elden, 2010) in shaping the Obama administration's legal justifications for drone strikes.

In 'Drone Geographies', Derek Gregory argues that drones must be understood within a matrix of military violence that is connected to and producing new visualities and experiences of the battlefield (Gregory, 2014, p. 7). Running through his discussion of various components of this matrix (which includes the development of homeland security, techniques of viewing at a distancing, and the emergence of global threats) is a sense that a new spatiality of war is emerging. War is no longer 'over there' or contained within a defined geographical area; rather the 'there' of war is 'everywhere'. The concept of everywhere war captures not only the endless nature of war today – its persistent temporality – but also its spatial scope, where it is increasingly difficult to delineate spaces of war from spaces of peace (Gregory, 2011, pp. 238–239). In everywhere war, the global spatiality of war is tied to its temporality, which has become increasingly 'event-ful'. Violence can now happen anywhere, at any time:

> Violence can erupt on a commuter train in Madrid, a house in Gaza City, a poppy field in Helmand or a street in Ciudad Juarez: such is the contrapuntal geography of the everywhere war. It is also to claim that, as cartographic reason falters and military violence is loosed from its frames, the conventional ties between war and geography have come undone .... (Gregory, 2011, p. 239)

Gregory explores three cases of the everywhere war: US drone attacks in Pakistan, the drug war between the United States and Mexico, and cyberwar. These examples show the blurring of the boundaries of war and violence more generally. Furthermore, Gregory finds that the question of legality features prominently in each case. It 'runs like a red ribbon throughout the prosecution of late modern war' (Gregory, 2011, p. 247). For Gregory, the everywhere war spreads largely because war is framed in a seemingly neutral and objective legal language.[12] For example, when drone strikes, even those carried out by the CIA, are justified through an urgent and legal language of 'self-defence' – as we saw, for example, in the Memorandum and White Paper – little attention is given to civilian casualties or to the strikes' ever-expanding nature. The legal framework thus serves to mask the effects of its violence, at least from a Western point of view. For Gregory, framing this violence within a legal apparatus is key to enabling the everywhere war, and involves an intensifying relationship between legality, security, and war. As Gregory concludes:

> The invocation of legality works to marginalize ethics and politics by making available a seemingly neutral, objective language: disagreement and debate then become purely technical issues that involve matters of opinion, certainly, but not values. The appeal to legality – and to the quasi-judicial process it invokes – thus helps to authorize a widespread and widening militarism of our world. (2011, p. 247)

Ian Shaw and Majed Akhter take up how this legal apparatus works more explicitly in their investigation of the relationship between law and technology in drone strikes in the Federally Administered Tribal Areas (FATA) region of Pakistan. Looking at the increase of drone strikes in FATA as well as the history of the region, Shaw and Akhter argue that FATA is produced as an exceptional place – justifying continuing violence and violation of Pakistan's sovereignty – through the region's legal status and through the object of the drone itself. FATA has been an exception within Pakistani law (here they draw on Agamben's concept of the space of exception) since at least the 1901 Frontier Crimes Regulation, which rendered the area outside of the reach of the law. The Pakistani government has continued this designation in one form or another up to the present. While FATA long has been a frontier region where law is suspended, what is significant about contemporary drone strikes in FATA is how law (as the suspension of law) works along with the object of the drone to create FATA also as a space of exception *for* the United States (Shaw & Akhter, 2012, p. 1497). They suggest that the drone itself acts as an exception of sorts, making certain actions inside FATA acceptable. As Shaw and Akhter argue, the drone is an object that has been fetishized by the military so that its human element or relations are rendered invisible (2012, p. 1492).[13] It is, in other words, the drone that can be used in FATA, not other military technologies:[14]

... the legal-historical geography of the terrain acts in concert with the object itself to produce drone warfare in FATA: it is not simply a matter of drones operating over an undifferentiated enemy landscape. Rather, uneven geo-legalities of war, state, and exception make drone warfare a reality in certain spaces and not others. (Shaw & Akhter, 2012, p. 1500)

In examining the intersections of law, geography, and technology in FATA, Shaw and Akhter provide insight into the specificities of the FATA region, yet it is not clear how their argument holds up when other kinds of incursions into Pakistan are considered, such as the Navy Seal raid that killed Osama bin Laden, or when the lens is turned to other drone strikes around the globe, such as those in Yemen or Somalia. Something more fundamental seems to be happening in the relationship between law, territory, and expanding spaces of killing.

Trying to understand the more general relationship between war, space, and law (Jones & Smith, 2015), some geographers have turned to the concept of 'lawfare' – a term describing the waging of war through law or the weaponization of law.[15] John Morrissey argues that the United States has deployed two forms of lawfare in waging the war on terror. The first is through detention and rendition, creating exceptional spaces where individuals lose their legal status. The second is through the protection of military personnel in forward deployed areas, where soldiers and individuals connected to the military are granted legal status in expanding new spaces of war.[16] Both of these ways that law is extended or negated are biopolitical, Morrissey argues, and involve the regulation of life and management of populations (2011, p. 285). In other words, war and violence expand through lawfare, understood by Morrissey as a technique of biopolitics, implying that biopolitics merges with geopolitics (2011, p. 290). As Morrissey writes, 'The US military's liberal lawfare reveals how the rule of law is simply another securitization tactic in liberalism's "pursuit of security"; a pursuit that paradoxically eliminates fundamental rights and freedoms in the "name of security"' (Morrissey, 2011, p. 297).

Morrissey and others thus provide a way to understand how law functions as a fundamental component of contemporary war. Law is central across this scholarship, albeit in different ways, to understanding the expanding deployment of drones. Drone strikes are not exceptions to the law, but rather the law is an important factor in the production of contemporary drone wars. A chief way that this works in the Obama administration's legal justifications is through a reimagining of territory. The mobilization of territory in these legal texts, and in particular a reworking of state power in relation to territory, is a key aspect supporting the use of drone strikes. Bringing a more dynamic concept of territory to bear on this legal framework reveals not just that war and state violence are expanding through lawfare, but that both the meaning of state sovereignty and the spatiality of the projection of force is changing similarly as well.

THE MEANING OF TERRITORY AND EPHEMERAL SOVEREIGNTY

One of the difficulties of understanding the expansion of drone strikes outside of war zones is the strong association between state sovereignty and territory as it relates to the reach of state power and the projection of force and authority. Two decades ago, John Agnew observed that the end of the Cold War and an increasingly globalized economy, among other factors, required questioning the assumption that the basis of the state, its limit of power, is clearly demarcated territory (Agnew, 1994, pp. 55–56). The target of his intervention was primarily international relations theory, which he felt retained an antiquated concept of territory, for which he identified three geographic assumptions of a territorial conception of the state that needed interrogation. One could argue that the following assumptions have not changed much in mainstream political science scholarship: (1) the territory of the state is the basis of sovereign space, (2) there is a definitive territorial demarcation between inside and outside the state, and (3) the territorial state contains society and exists before it (Agnew, 1994, p. 59). As Agnew (1994, p. 77) warned, 'In idealizing the territorial state we cannot see a world in which its role and meaning change.'

Writing more recently, Nisha Shah argues that we remain within this territorial trap, despite efforts to reconceptualize the state and processes of globalization. In her view, the territorial trap that lingers is the assumption equating territory with the physical land of the state (Shah, 2012, p. 58). Seeing territory not just as this physical realm but also a normative and productive concept, Shah argues that

> globalization theories must not only focus on whether goods, people, and information move through – permeate – territorial borders, but also focus on whether and how notions of global space are providing a new political theory that stands in contradistinction to territory. (2012, p. 58)

In other words, globalization theorists, and theorists of state power, need new conceptions of territory and space that are adequate to processes of globalization (Shah, 2012, p. 71).[17]

Agnew and Shah point to the inadequacy of thinking state power and sovereignty only through a 'traditional' fixed and physical conception of territory. In response, geographers have led an effort to think about territory in a different way.[18] Arguing that territory is historically produced as a concept, Stuart Elden reminds us that much is missed when territory is thought only in its physical-land register.[19] He suggests that territory is thought and produced in other ways. For example, drawing on geographers writing on vertical geopolitics and aerial geographies,[20] as well as theorists such as Peter Sloterdijk, Elden proposes thinking about territory in volumetric terms (2013b). Using the example of tunnels that cross Israel's borders, Elden shows how territory needs to be understood not only above and below the surface of the earth, but also between and through these spaces. Thus territory is not simply a plane or surface, it is three-dimensional; and also is dynamic and constantly changing (Elden, 2013b, p. 36).

Joe Painter similarly advocates a shift to understanding territory as continuously in process. Because of this emphasis on becoming, territory is seen by Painter to be more networked than a homogenous planar space. As he writes, 'Territory is not the timeless and solid geographical foundation of state power it sometimes seems, but a porous, provisional, labour-intensive and ultimately perishable and non-material product of networked socio-technical practices' (Painter, 2010, p. 1116).[21] Furthermore, we might think of territory also as felt and embodied. In *Aerial Life*, Peter Adey provides a useful study in the affective nature of territory. For him, territory is not only not rooted to the ground but also is produced in part through and on the body. One example of this is the Air Scouts in Britain at the beginning of the twentieth century, essentially a training programme and camp for young men who were not flying planes but participated in simulations, games, and drills. As Adey describes, through the physical routines of the Air Scouts, aerial life begins to emerge as 'a body readied for performance, prepared for war; a body militarized and posed to step into action; a citizen-body militarized attaining stronger links with the body of the nation' (2010, p. 53).

As the space of state power, then, territory is a less a physical thing or demarcated space than it is a complex outcome and an ongoing process – a political technology (Elden, 2010). Territory both reflects and is productive of state power, rather than simply a container in which state power is exercised. Understanding territory as a political technology, one that emerges in many registers (e.g. volumetric, aerial, or embodied), opens up the question of the relationship between territory and sovereignty. This challenges us to think about the ways that sovereignty has not always been 'fixed' to physical territory in the traditional sense, but also how sovereign power is projected in a more fluid and dynamic manner today. Being more attuned to the productive and dynamic nature of territory enables us to see sovereign power working in ways that might otherwise remain out of sight.

While focused primarily on the biopolitical character of drone strikes, and in particular on pattern of life analysis, Ian Shaw's formulation of the 'Predator Empire' is a useful starting point. Geographically, the drone wars of the Predator Empire (a term he uses to describe the global proliferation of drones) must be understood topologically. Space, here, is no longer fixed to physical territory, but is shape-shifting and especially tied to aerial mobility. As he writes:

> Predators 'fold' space with an unparalleled level of aeromobility, reducing the importance that geographic distance and obstacles have in separating 'there' from 'here'. This power topology is not strictly exercised *across* space then, but rather, in its capacity to crumple an environment by *digitizing* it. (Shaw, 2013, p. 15)

Thinking of the drone strike topologically allows us to think differently about the spaces in which sovereign power acts and how the use of force is justified. Following Foucault's description of sovereign power as akin to a siege,[22] Mbembe shows how sovereign power (and what he calls necropower) and biopower are combined in late-modern colonial occupation. Drawing on the example of the Israeli occupation of Palestine, he writes, 'The *state of siege* is itself a military institution. It allows a modality of killing that does not distinguish between external and internal enemy. Entire populations are the target of the sovereign' (Mbembe, 2003, p. 30). Similarly, with the drone strike we can identify a kind of mobile state of siege – one that crisscrosses the globe and is continuously changing, folding into new configurations.

What happens in these moments of folding? In a sense, the spatiality or territory of sovereign power is reconfigured, and the zone of the drone strike is incorporated into the scope and extent of state power. It is seized in the lens of the drone. Evoking topology also attunes us to the temporality of this reach of sovereign power. It is not permanent and fixed but tied to the temporality of the war on terror, as we have seen with the mobilization of a broad concept of imminence in the Obama administration's legal justifications for targeted killing. Seen this way, the global foldings of sovereignty are ephemeral, temporary, and always possible.[23] As exemplified in contemporary drone wars, sovereign power is always potentially expanding, shifting, folding, and being reconfigured.

The ephemeral sovereignty of the drone strike, therefore, is supported and produced in part through the mobilization of territory in the legal justifications – an understanding of territory as dynamic and multiple supports this projection of force and renders moot, at least in the eyes of the Obama administration, any contradiction between the strikes and other states' sovereignty. The reach of state power is clearly not tied to the fixed territory of the state, but rather with the drone strike it becomes mobile and global, tied to the assumed actions and movements of individuals. Looking at the justifications of force and the actual deployment of drone strikes shows how sovereignty operates in practice – effective sovereignty – and how it can change. And especially, as Agnew writes, '... *effective* sovereignty is not necessarily so neatly territorialized' (2005, p. 437).

This idea of ephemeral and fluid sovereignty is not unique to contemporary drone strikes. As Ann Laura Stoler shows, when sovereign power is delinked from the idea of the bounded, physical state, it emerges as multiplicitous and dynamic. For her, sovereignty is better understood through a range of degrees: 'We can think of [imperial formations] better as scaled genres of rule that produce and count on different degrees of sovereignty and gradations of rights. They thrive on turbid taxonomies that produce shadow populations and ever-improved coercive measures to protect the common good against those deemed threats to it' (Stoler, 2006, p. 128). Stoler's primary target is mainstream scholarship on colonialism, which she argues retains a concept of sovereignty tied to the nation-state and thereby misses the way that state power, especially imperialistic state power, has always exceeded these boundaries. What is especially poignant about Stoler's analysis is that 'extra-territorial' exercises of state power are themselves not exceptions, but rather form the very basis of the state:

Ambiguous zones, partial sovereignty, temporal suspensions of what Hannah Arendt called 'the right to have rights', provisional impositions of states of emergency, promissory notes for elections, deferred or contingent independence, and 'temporary' occupations – these are conditions at the heart of imperial projects and present in nearly all of them. (2006, p. 139)

A concept of ephemeral sovereignty rooted in a understanding of territory as dynamic and multiple[24] helps us to better understand two important aspects of contemporary drone wars. The first is that it helps us to make sense of the drone strike's direct action on life and how this is justified by the government to extend outside of 'traditional' contexts of war. Unhinging sovereignty from an understanding of fixed territory opens up space for us to see how this can work 'outside' of the state. As Mbembe reminds us, ' ... it makes little sense to insist on distinctions between "internal" and "external" political realms' (2003, p. 32), divisions that are continuously recreated, mobile, and, in the case of the drone strike, tied to the perceived imminent threat from individuals around the globe. Second, and related, ephemeral sovereignty marks the emergence of new spatialities of power. Viewing power topologically reframes debates over how drone strikes violate the sovereignty of Pakistan or Yemen, for example. We can see how multiple foldings of sovereignty might exist at the same time and how, in the Memorandum and White Paper, a dynamic and fluid conception of territory helped to support these claims to authority and the use of force. This is to say that the United States' and Pakistan's claims to sovereignty might look very different and operate within both overlapping and competing registers. Any challenge to these claims or effective critiques of drone strikes cannot ignore the role here of territory as a productive political technology to expanding the scope and spaces of state power.[25]

CONCLUSION: DRONES AND TERRITORIAL DESIGN

An understanding of state territory as networked and dynamic is a key element in the US government's justification for the global expansion of drone strikes. Here these legal frameworks not only serve to enable the expansion of violence and the 'everywhere war', but the concepts of territory mobilized in these texts also reveal the emergence of ephemeral sovereignty and shape-shifting landscapes of state power and the use of force. Critiques of contemporary drone strikes, therefore, need to engage with how the strikes operate within and are productive of the law and the functioning of the state, and are not outside and exceptional to it. This analysis further demonstrates the important role that territory plays in shaping these new geographies of power.

The concept of 'territorial design' that Atzili and Kadercan put forward in this special issue emphasizes three important dimensions of territory: its physical features, its demarcation processes, and the constitution of demarcated or territorial space. The second and third dimensions highlight the productive and changing nature of territory – what we might parallel to Elden's formulation of territory as a political technology. This examination of contemporary drone wars through the context of the US government's legal justification for extra-territorial strikes illustrates the need for a more dynamic understanding of territory as well as the importance of territory to the formulation of foreign policy and the extension of state violence and authority.

In particular, this 'case' of part of the legal apparatus supporting the expansion of drone strike contributes to a better understanding of four aspects of the intervention of territorial design made in this issue. First, the mobilization of territory in the Memorandum and the White Paper reveal a complex relationship between the demarcation and constitution processes of territory (the second and third dimensions). In the case of the drone strike, the meaning of territory (as fluid, global, and tied to imminent threat) serves to support a continual process of territorial demarcation as the landscape of state power and authority is folded and refolded. Second, and related, we can begin to see clearly how territory is multiple. Its meanings change, co-exist, and overlap. This multiplicitous character of territory is crucial for understanding the varying degrees of importance and recognition given to state sovereignty in the government's documents. Third, the drone strike helps us begin to think through the role of technology and knowledge in the production of territory and territorial design. The drone itself is an important factor in constructing and demarcating territory, not as much in the sense of patrolling territory but in how territory and state authority are imagined and evoked through the justification of the use of drones. As I have shown, shifting conceptions of territory are a key aspect of the emergence of global drone strikes. Finally, this broader examination of the law and territory has brought important work by critical geographers into the conversation about production of territory in international relations, providing a framework for thinking territory as a dynamic and complex political technology.

ACKNOWLEDGEMENTS

The author would like to thank the editors of this special issue, Boaz Atzili and Burak Kadercan, as well as the anonymous reviewers, for their comments on earlier drafts of this article.

DISCLOSURE STATEMENT

No potential conflict of interest was reported by the author.

NOTES

1. This article is based in part on a chapter from my dissertation, *Lethal surveillance: Drones and the geo-history of modern war*, University of Minnesota (May 2015).
2. At least in the eyes of the US government and mainstream Western media. The large pushback against drones in Pakistan, for example, has received relatively limited media attention in the United States.
3. By using drones in Libya, for example, the Obama administration was able to argue that US engagement in Libya was not actually war. The lack of ground troop deployment and limited engagement with enemy forces were two of the justifications given for not applying the War Powers Resolution to Libya (Savage & Landler, 2011).
4. Legal scholars have commented on the circular logic and thin reasoning of the 2010 Memorandum. As Van Buren (2014) noted:

> Here's the terrifying part: ostensibly the result of some of the best legal thinking available to the White House on a issue that couldn't be more basic to the American system, it wouldn't get a first-year law student a C-. The arguments are almost bizarrely puerile in a document that is a visibly shaky attempt to provide cover for a predetermined premise. No wonder the administration fought its release for so long. Its officials were, undoubtedly, ashamed of it.

5. The two codes considered are 18 U.S Code S1119 ('Foreign murder of United States nationals') and 18 U.S. Code S956 ('Conspiracy to kill, kidnap, maim, or injure persons or damage property in a foreign country').
6. The 2001 AUMF, enacted on 18 September 2001, reads:

> That the President is authorized to use all necessary and appropriate force against those nations, organizations, or persons he determines planned, authorized, committed, or aided the terrorist attacks that occurred on September 11, 2001, or harbored such organizations or persons, in order to prevent any future acts of international terrorism against the United States by such nations, organizations or person. (S.J. Res. 23. 107th Congress, 2001)

7. The section on the CIA's inclusion under the public authority justification is more redacted, but draws on a similar logic: that targeting would be a part of the AUMF tied to the conflict that the United States is currently involved in. It should also be noted that the Memorandum's evocation of International Humanitarian Law is essentially an empty argument. Under International Humanitarian Law, a 'non-international conflict' (which, as I discuss further below, the Memorandum classifies the AUMF conflict to be) falls *only* under the Geneva Convention Common Article Three, which is extremely short and has been argued to be very open to interpretation (Rivkin, Casey, & Stimson, 2009).

8. These stipulations parallel those outlined in President Obama's 2013 speech at the National Defense University (Office of the Press Secretary, The White House, 2013) and a fact sheet release by the White House in 2016 (Office of the Press Secretary, The White House, 2016).

9. The wording of this criteria of association is vague and thus left open to wide interpretation. The US government has claimed to primarily focus on senior leaders, although this has clearly not been the case. The targets of drone strikes have been primarily either low-level operators or those engaging in activities deemed connected to or reflective of terrorist operations (Entous, 2010; Landay, 2013).

10. The 'laws of war' here likely refers to International Humanitarian Law (called Laws of War or Laws of Armed Conflict by the United States), which consists of the 1949 four Geneva Conventions and the 1977 Additional Geneva Protocols. Only the four original conventions are universally accepted and ratified. As mentioned in note 8, because this conflict is classified as a 'non-international conflict' only Common Article III (under the Additional Protocol II) would apply. Not only is Common Article III short and open to interpretation, the United States has not ratified Additional Protocol II and is only a signatory to it. See https://www.icrc.org/ihl/INTRO/475?OpenDocument. This claim to following the laws of war is therefore mostly a hollow one. Furthermore, it is not clear in the White Paper how and by whom capture is determined infeasible.

11. It is interesting to note that this discussion of state sovereignty is not addressed explicitly (at least in the publicly available version) in the 2010 Memorandum. While it is only briefly discussed in the 2011 White Paper, perhaps its addition reflects growing international concern and conversation over the violation of state sovereignty by US drone strikes.

12. Note that this argument has affinities with Weizman's (2011) analysis of humanitarian law.

13. While my argument ultimately moves away from the idea of the drone strike as a suspension of the law and instead shows how these strikes are mobilized and are expanding fully within the realm of the law and normal functioning of state power, Shaw and Akhter's analysis illustrates one of the ways that the law and the technology of the drone are productive of the proliferation of drone strikes.

14. This parallels the argument made by Obama in reference to Libya. See note 3.

15. For one of the key texts on 'lawfare', see Kennedy (2006). For Kennedy, law is more than just the letter of the law, it must also be understood through its practice and discourse. In his words, 'Warfare has become a modern legal institution' (Kennedy, 2006, p. 5). See also Jones (2016).

16. Steve Niva makes a parallel argument to Morrissey, but does not focus on the law. Niva argues that changes in the organizational structure of the military, especially with the creation of the Joint Special Operations Command (JSOC), led to the emergence of a more networked and decentralized battlefield. As he writes:

> The extension of the networked shadow warfare to Pakistan, although officially directed by the CIA, marks the crystallization of the networked intelligence and targeting model of warfare originally developed by JSOC into a modular form of war that could be delinked from the conventional military battlespace and extended across new cartographies. (Niva, 2013, p. 196)

17. Globalization, of course, is by no means a new phenomenon or problem – what is important here, as we will see moving forward, is that the conception of territory as fixed land over which the state rules has always been a fiction of power. When understood as the space of sovereign power, territory is at once multiple, contested, and continually changing.

18. Note that the following discussion of efforts to think territory with different conceptual tools leaves out a large body of interdisciplinary literature focused on critiquing the concept of the border. Much of this literature, while opening up the concept of the border, does not engage with the concept of territory explicitly, often retaining the notion that territory is the physical extent of the state. See, for example, Andreas (2003) or Rajaram and Grundy-Warr (2007).

19. Elden has written extensively on this topic. For the most thorough overview, see his recent book *The birth of territory* (Elden, 2013a).

20. See, for example, Graham (2004).

21. There are significant parallels between Painter's conception of territory and Massey's (2005) critique of Cartesian/modern space.

22. 'Power in this instance was essentially a right of seizure: of things, time, bodies, and ultimately life itself; it culminated in the privilege to seize hold of life in order to suppress it' (Foucault, 1990, p. 136).

23. This differs from Gregory's eventful violence mentioned earlier, where violence can happen anywhere. Rather, it is state power that becomes eventful. This is also different from Elden's discussion of 'contingent sovereignty', which is more in line with blurred boundaries rather than the reconfiguration of the space of sovereignty (2009).

24. The idea of ephemeral sovereignty also resonates with efforts to see sovereignty, especially in relation to war and humanitarian intervention, as multiple, competing, and historically contingent. See, for example, Dunn and Cons (2014), Reid-Henry (2007), and Kleinfeld (2015).

25. Tyler Wall (2016) provides an excellent example of why drone strikes need to be understood within the scope of expanding state power (rather than exceptional to it) through his comparison of drone strikes and police violence within the United States.

REFERENCES

Adey, P. (2010). *Aerial life: Spaces, mobilities, affects.* West Sussex: Wiley-Blackwell.

Agnew, J. (1994). The territorial trap: The geographical assumptions of international relations theory. *Review of International Political Economy, 1*(1), 53–80. doi:10.1080/09692299408434268

Agnew, J. (2005). Sovereignty regimes: Territoriality and state authority in contemporary world politics. *Annals of the Association of American Geographers, 95*(2), 437–461. doi:10.1111/j.1467-8306.2005.00468.x

Andreas, P. (2003). Redrawing the line: Borders and security in the twenty-first century. *International Security, 28* (2), 78–111. doi:10.1162/016228803322761973

Department of Justice. (2011). *Department of justice white paper: Lawfulness of a lethal operation directed against a U.S. Citizen who is a senior operational leader of Al-Qa'ida or an associated force* (Draft November 8). Retrieved from http://www.fas.org/irp/eprint/doj-lethal.pdf

Dunn, E. C., & Cons, J. (2014). Aleatory sovereignty and the rule of sensitive spaces. *Antipode, 46*(1), 92–109. doi:10.1111/anti.12028

Elden, S. (2009). *Terror and territory: The spatial extent of sovereignty.* Minneapolis: University of Minnesota Press.

Elden, S. (2010). Land, terrain, territory. *Progress in Human Geography, 34*(6), 799–817. doi:10.1177/0309132510362603

Elden, S. (2013a). *The birth of territory.* Chicago, IL: The University of Chicago Press.

Elden, S. (2013b). Secure the volume: Vertical geopolitics and the depth of power. *Political Geography, 34*, 35–51. doi:10.1016/j.polgeo.2012.12.009

Entous, A. (2010, May 3). Drones kill low-level militants, few civilians: U.S. *Reuters.* Retrieved from http://www. reuters.com/article/2010/05/03/us-pakistan-usa-drones-idUSTRE6424WI20100503

Foucault, M. (1990). *The history of sexuality: An introduction, volume 1.* (R. Hurley, Trans.). New York, NY: Vintage Books.

Graham, S. (2004). Vertical geopolitics: Baghdad and after. *Antipode, 36* (1), 12–23. doi:10.1111/j.1467-8330. 2004.00379.x

Gregory, D. (2011). The everywhere war. *The Geographical Journal, 177*(3), 238–250. doi:10.1111/j.1475-4959. 2011.00426.x

Gregory, D. (2014). Drone geographies. *Radical Philosophy, 183*(January/February), 7–19.

Hudson, B. (2014, June 17). FBI Director Tours Mpls. Division, hails capture of Benghazi attacker. *CBSLocal Minnesota.* Retrieved June 17, 2014, from http://minnesota.cbslocal.com/2014/06/17/fbi-director-visits-minneapolis-division/

Jones, C. (2016). Lawfare and the juridification of late modern war. *Progress in Human Geography, 40*(2), 221–239. doi:10.1177/0309132515572270

Jones, C., & Smith, M. D. (2015). War/law/space notes toward a legal geography of war. *Environment and Planning D, 33*(4), 581–591. doi:10.1177/0263775815600599

Kennedy, D. (2006). *Of war and law.* Princeton, NJ: Princeton University Press.

Kindervater, K. H. (2016). The emergence of lethal surveillance: Watching and killing in the history of drone technology. *Security Dialogue, 47*(3), 223–238. doi:10.1177/0967010615616011

Kleinfeld, M. (2015). Too difficult to protect: A history of the 1934 Monaco draft and the problem of territory for international humanitarian law. *Environment and Planning D: Society and Space, 33*, 592–608. doi:10.1177/0263775815598102

Landay, J. S. (2013, April 9). Obama's drone war kills 'others', not just al Qaida leaders. *McClatchy Newspapers.* Retrieved from http://www.mcclatchydc.com/2013/04/09/188062/obamas-drone-war-kills-others.html

Massey, D. (2005). *For space.* Los Angeles, CA: Sage.

Mbembe, A. (2003). Necropolitics (L. Meintjes, Trans.). *Public Culture, 15*(1), 11–40. doi:10.1215/08992363-15-1-11

Morrissey, J. (2011). Liberal lawfare and biopolitics: US juridical warfare in the war on terror. *Geopolitics, 16*, 280–305. doi:10.1080/14650045.2010.538872

Niva, S. (2013). Disappearing violence: JSOC and the Pentagon's new cartography of networked warfare. *Security Dialogue, 44*(3), 185–202. doi:10.1177/0967010613485869

Office of Legal Counsel, U.S. Department of Justice. (2010, July 16). *Memorandum for the attorney general re: Applicability of federal criminal laws and the constitution to contemplated lethal operations against Shaykh Anwar al-Aulaqi.* Released through Savage, C. (2014, June 23). Justice Department Memo approving targeted killing of Anwar Al-Awlaki. *New York Times.* Retrieved from http://www.nytimes.com/interactive/2014/06/23/us/23awlaki-memo.html

Office of the Press Secretary, The White House. (2013, May 23). *Remarks by the president at the National Defense University.* Retrieved from https://www.whitehouse.gov/the-press-office/2013/05/23/remarks-president-national-defense-university

Office of the Press Secretary, The White House. (2016, July 1). *Fact sheet: Executive order on the US policy on pre & post-strike measures to address civilian casualties in the US operations involving the use of force & the DNI release of aggregate data on strike outside area of active hostilitie* [sic]. Retrieved from https://www.whitehouse.gov/the-press-office/2016/07/01/fact-sheet-executive-order-us-policy-pre-post-strike-measures-address

Painter, J. (2010). Rethinking territory. *Antipode, 42*(5), 1090–1118. doi:10.1111/j.1467-8330.2010.00795.x

Rajaram, P. K., & Grundy-Warr, C. (Eds.). (2007). *Borderscapes: Hidden geographies and politics at territory's edge.* Minneapolis: University of Minnesota Press.

Reid-Henry, S. (2007). Exceptional sovereignty? Guantánamo Bay and the re-colonial present. *Antipode, 39*(4), 627–648. doi:10.1111/j.1467-8330.2007.00544.x

Rivkin, D. B., Casey, L. A., & Stimson, C. (2009, February 19). Common Article 3 of the Geneva conventions and U.S. detainee policy. WebMemo #2303. *The Heritage Foundation Website.* Retrieved from http://www.heritage.org/research/reports/2009/02/common-article-3-of-the-geneva-conventions-and-us-detainee-policy

Savage, C., & Landler, M. (2011, June 15). White house defends continuing U.S. role in Libya operation. *New York Times*. Retrieved from http://www.nytimes.com/2011/06/16/us/politics/16powers.html

Shah, N. (2012). The territorial trap of the territorial trap: Global transformation and the problem of the state's two territories. *International Political Sociology*, *6*(1), 57–76. doi:10.1111/j.1749-5687.2011.00144.x

Shaw, I. G. R. (2013). Predator empire: The geopolitics of US drone warfare. *Geopolitics*, *18*(3), 536–559. doi:10.1080/14650045.2012.749241

Shaw, I. G. R., & Akhter, M. (2012). The unbearable humanness of drone warfare in FATA, Pakistan. *Antipode*, *44*(4), 1490–1509. doi:10.1111/j.1467-8330.2011.00940.x

S.J. Res. 23. 107th Congress. (2001). *Authorization for use of military force*. Retrieved from https://www.govtrack.us/congress/bills/107/sjres23

Stoler, A. L. (2006). On degrees of imperial sovereignty. *Public Culture*, *18*(1), 125–146. doi:10.1215/08992363-18-1-125

Van Buren, P. (2014, July 24). How one piece of paper destroyed your right to a trial. *The Nation*. Retrieved from http://www.thenation.com/article/180768/how-one-piece-paper-destroyed-your-right-to-trial

Wall, T. (2016). Ordinary emergency: Drones, police, and geographies of legal terror. *Antipode*, *48*(4), 1122–1139. doi:10.1111/anti.12228

Weizman, E. (2011). *The least of all possible evils: Humanitarian violence from Arendt to Gaza*. London: Verso.

Between land and sea: spaces and conflict intensity

Ehud Eiran

ABSTRACT

Between land and sea: spaces and conflict intensity. *Territory Politics Governance*. Do different levels of sovereignty affect the intensity of international conflicts that unfold there? The paper answers this question by comparing territorial conflicts between Israel and Lebanon in two spaces: land and sea. These spaces are subject to different levels of sovereignty. On land, sovereignty is understood to be full and indivisible. In the portion of the sea under dispute between Israel and Lebanon – the exclusive economic zone – sovereignty is only partial and refers primarily to the right to extract resources. The paper concludes that a partial form of sovereignty is indeed associated with a less intense conflict.

摘要

陆地与海洋之间：空间与冲突强度。*领土，政治，统治*。不同程度的主权，是否会影响该处发生的国际冲突的强度呢？本文透过比较以色列和黎巴嫩在陆地与海洋两个空间中的领土冲突来回答此一问题。这些空间受制于不同层级的主权。在陆地上，主权被认为是完整且不可分割的。在以色列和黎巴嫩之间具冲突的部分海洋—排外的经济区—主权仅是部分的，并且主要指涉采集资源的权利。本文于结论中指出，部分的主权形式，的确与强度较低的冲突有关。

RÉSUMÉ

Entre la terre et la mer: l'espace et l'intensité du conflit. *Territory Politics Governance*. Est-ce que les divers niveaux de souveraineté influencent l'intensité des conflits internationaux qui s'y déroulent? Cet article répond à cette question en comparant les conflits territoriaux entre l'Israël et le Liban dans deux espaces: à savoir la terre et la mer. Ces espaces-ci sont soumis à des niveaux de souveraineté différents. Pour ce qui est de la terre, on considère la souveraineté comme pleine et indivisible. Dans la partie de la mer entre l'Israël et le Liban qui est en litige – une zone économique exclusive – la souveraineté n'est que partielle et concerne principalement le droit d'exploiter des ressources. Pour conclure, l'article affirme qu'une forme partielle de souveraineté s'associe en effet à un conflit moins intensif.

RESUMEN

Entre la tierra y el mar: espacios e intensidad de los conflictos. *Territory Politics Governance*. ¿Afectan los diferentes niveles de soberanía en la intensidad de los conflictos internacionales que se desarrollan? En este artículo se responde a esta cuestión al comparar los conflictos territoriales entre Israel y Líbano en dos espacios: tierra y mar. Estos espacios están sujetos a diferentes niveles de soberanía. En tierra, se entiende que la soberanía es total e indivisible. En la parte del mar en disputa entre Israel y Líbano – la zona económica exclusiva – la soberanía es solamente parcial y se refiere sobre todo al derecho a extraer recursos. Se concluye el artículo constatando que una forma parcial de soberanía está efectivamente relacionada con un conflicto menos intenso.

INTRODUCTION

Constructivists have long held that social meaning ascribed to a space affects conflict dynamics there. Hassner, for example, showed that holy spaces are prone to beget intractable conflict over them (2010). Continuing this line of inquiry, the paper asks whether different levels of sovereignty over spaces, affects the intensity of conflicts that unfold there. The portion of the sea that is adjacent to states' sovereign boundaries is perhaps the most malleable of current national boundaries. This, not only because of its physical features in which the mass of water shifts constantly across national borders, but also because it is the most dynamic arena in which sovereignty has been reshaped, with significant impact on current interactions in world politics. Territorial designs relating to land mass and bodies of water are not uniform. While the notion of sovereignty over land mass was consolidated in the seventeenth century with the Peace of Westphalia (Philpott, 2001), sovereignty over bodies of water was reshaped only a few decades ago, following the 1958 and 1982 United Nations Conventions on the Seas (UNCLOS I and UNCLOS III). Most notably, in contrast to the binary or dichotomous perception of land-based sovereignty – states are either sovereign or not – UNCLOS created two partial forms of sovereignty in the seas beyond the twelve nautical miles, which compose its *territorial sea* and are considered part of states' territory (UNCLOS III, Article 1).

The first is the *contiguous zone*, which extends twelve more miles beyond a coastal state's territorial waters. In this area, the coastal state can take action to prevent infringement of some of its laws and regulations, and punish those who infringe on these laws and regulations. The second is an *exclusive economic zone* (EEZ) of up to 200 nautical miles into the sea in which the coastal state has limited sovereignty regarding economic resources such as fisheries and energy. The state maintains the right to enforce its own rules and regulations regarding these resources, including the right to board foreign vessels, conduct arrests, and subject persons to judicial proceedings (UNCLOS III, Articles 56, 58, 59). However, it lacks there all other aspects of sovereignty.

This notion of partial sovereignty is not without historical precedent. It somewhat mirrors that in pre-Westphalian European states where, in the process of state formation, rulers bestowed certain privileges and advantages upon officials in return for maintaining law and order in their jurisdictions, collecting revenue and forming armies. Effectively, the officials were rulers of their own states within the larger structure. These officials then had substantial influence and advantage over the government (Ertman, 2005; Kadercan, 2014). This ceding of power, whether by design or accident, was similarly seen in the Ottoman Empire where the military, a cohesive and powerful institution with its own mores and practices, as well as a central role in decision-making vis-a-vis state-waged war, developed as a separate and counter-power to the government. It was therefore able to exert its influence and will over the actions of the state (Kadercan, 2014). Partial sovereignty existed, too, in the compromise of power between Church and State in Medieval Europe, both acting as centres of power (Agnew, 2005). The church had its own enforcers of moral and political authority, its own laws and tithes, to which the state and subjects were bound (Witte, 2006). However, in all these cases partial sovereignty was a result of the sharing of legal rights between the state and other actors. In the maritime domain, partial sovereignty is a result of limited state powers in an area that extends beyond its territory, in a non-sovereign space.

The normative regime institutionalized by UNCLOS is unique in its treatment of sovereignty in the nation-state order of the modern world. In all other instances, state sovereignty is conceived normatively as complete, integrated and dichotomous. By contrast, in UNCLOS sovereignty is unintegrated and granted only partially.

This paper investigates an important aspect of partial sovereignty. It asks: how does partial sovereignty affect the dynamics and intensity of inter-state conflict when compared to complete sovereignty. In order to explore this question the paper compares a dyadic conflict between two states in the East Mediterranean, Israel and Lebanon, between which there are both land and maritime boundary disputes. Selecting the same parties for both domains allows us to control for differences in other variables such as regime type, power symmetry, leading ideology, domestic dynamics and economic development. In the land domain, where complete sovereignty is the norm, the paper explores the Lebanese claims for Shebaa Farms and a small region that comprises the remains of seven villages that are located in Northern Israel. In the sea, where partial sovereignty is the norm, both countries make conflicting claims about their respective EEZs, especially with regards to ownership of potential natural gas reserves that are located in a disputed area between them.

The paper proceeds as follows: In the first section, the paper establishes that sovereignty is perceived as a binary concept. Further, the paper suggests that the normative allocation of partial sovereignty in maritime spaces is fundamentally different from empirical manifestations of compromised sovereignty, which might stem from state capacity or voluntary transfer of authority to international bodies. In the second section, the paper explains the value of investigating the possible distinct effect of complete or partial sovereignty on inter-state conflicts. This inquiry is novel because it adds another layer to our understanding of the relationship between sovereignty and conflict. Territorial disputes have been responsible for a majority of international conflicts and wars (Diehl, 1996; Rasler & Thompson, 2006; Vasuqez & Valeriano, 2010), yet the dominant focus has been on ones that evolved around conflicting claims over land territory that represent a traditional Westphalian notion of sovereignty. The study of dispute over maritime spaces, in which only partial sovereignty is allocated, requires us to revisit basic claims about the relationship between sovereignty and conflict. In the next section, the paper provides background to the Israeli-Lebanese conflict, though the comparison that follows will investigate only the post 2000 period. In the fourth section, the paper presents the methodology of the comparison of severity of conflicts. The paper uses a revised version of Brecher and Wilkenfeld (1989). Their model offers an effective set of variables that allow us to measure cases when a crisis erupts in the framework of a protracted conflict. The model was selected because the territorial conflicts on land and at sea represent an escalation of the long protracted conflict between Israel and Lebanon that began in 1948. In the fifth section, the paper applies the model and investigates Israeli-Lebanese/Hezbollah conflicts over land and sea since 2000. In the last section, the paper explores alternative explanations, mostly of the material kind. This last section concludes with a discussion of the results and the potential contributions of this inquiry and outlines possible paths for future research.

SOVEREIGNTY: OLD AND NEW NOTIONS

Sovereignty is a foundational building block of the international system. It has evolved in the last four hundred years since it was formally crystalized in the set of agreements known as the Westphalia Peace in 1648 (Brus, 2002; Krasner, 1999; Philpott, 2001; Ruggie, 1986). The evolution of sovereignty was awarded much attention in recent decades by scholars of international relations of different schools, spanning from international law to structural realism (Hashmi, 1997; Jacobsen, Sampford, & Thakur, 2008; Kreijen, 2002; Philpott, 2001). Stephan Krasner (1999, 4) famously explained that the term sovereignty holds four different but interrelated dimensions: First, international/legal sovereignty refers to the recognition of a sovereign state by other states; second, Westphalian sovereignty that refers to the principle of non-interference from external sources; third, domestic sovereignty that refers to the execution of authority within the borders of the polity; and finally interdependent sovereignty that refers to the capacity of authority to regulate the flow of people, information, ideas, capital, and pollutants across its borders.

In all four dimensions, sovereignty is framed as dichotomous, or binary: a state either possesses sovereignty in a certain space, or lacks it completely. Admittedly, beginning in the last quarter of the twentieth century, some central aspects of sovereignty have come under threat. Economic globalization and new information technologies challenge most states' ability to control flows of capital and trade. This weakening of interdependent sovereignty further challenges states as they exercised their domestic sovereignty (Sassen, 2015). Furthermore, the rise of international humanitarian law, and in particular the idea of humanitarian intervention, challenges Westphalian and domestic sovereignty (Kreijen, 2002).

Contrary to the strengthening of international regimes and transnational actors at the expense of national authority, in the maritime domain states expanded their sovereignty. In 1982, the United Nations Convention on the Law of the Seas (UNCLOS III) was concluded. The convention soon became the dominant legal norm for the governance of the maritime domain. The convention came into force in 1994, and by 2015, it was ratified by 167 states. Most states that did not sign the convention, or did not ratify it, still embrace it as international customary law. In addition to the long recognized authority of states in their territorial waters, which extends to 12 nautical miles from the baseline, the convention awards coastal states exclusive privileges and authority in two areas that stretch out to the sea from the same baseline: (1) *contiguous zone* that extends up to 24 miles from the baseline (Part 2, Section 4, Article 33, UNCLOS), and (2) *exclusive economic zone* (EEZ) that extends up to 200 nautical miles from the baseline (Part 5, Article 55, UNCLOS). UNCLOS's provision of partial sovereignty (of varying gradation) to the coastal state in these areas constitutes a precedent in the normative understanding of sovereignty. In all other instances in international law, sovereignty is either fully granted or not granted at all. Despite the abovementioned contemporary challenges to sovereignty and its erosion in certain realms it remains, fundamentally, a binary concept.

This is not to say that the exercise of complete sovereignty is common or even possible. On the contrary, in many instances states may possess certain dimensions of sovereignty while failing to possess others (Krasner, 1999). Weak or failed states are often incompetent in exercising their sovereignty in realms such as border protection or law enforcement (Gros, 1996; Jackson and Rosenberg, 1982). Libya and Somalia are good examples. Further, states often willingly give up some aspects of their sovereignty when committing to international conventions, joining international organizations, or in accepting a restrictive legal norm. The various international conventions on the environment or on the proliferation of weapons of mass destruction are instances of this category. These examples, however, differ from the essence of UNCLOS in one fundamental element: none of them challenges the normative perception of sovereignty as complete. The former is a case of empirical lack of capacity and the latter is a case of voluntarily waiving the exercise of sovereignty in order to be part of a beneficial international regime. Even when the erosion of sovereignty is acknowledged as an empirical fact, it is still viewed as a unified concept. Pressures against sovereignty might result in 'suspended sovereignty', 'interrupted sovereignty', or 'conditional sovereignty', (Jacobsen et al., 2008, pp. 3–4) but never as partial, unintegrated, or divided.

In that regard, the normative regime institutionalized by UNCLOS is fundamentally distinct in that it purposefully assigns the coastal state merely partial sovereignty in its contiguous waters and EEZ.

THE IMPACT OF PARTIAL SOVEREIGNTY ON CONFLICT DYNAMICS

The difference between complete and partial sovereignty raises a myriad of questions that merit a comparative empirical inquiry. One important question relates to the relationship between partial sovereignty and conflict dynamics. Empirically, the paper investigates whether there exists a divergence in conflict dynamics between conflicts over regular, that is, complete sovereignty, and conflicts in which the disputed right is partial. In other words, the paper asks what is the effect of partial sovereignty on inter-state conflict. This inquiry can facilitate new insights about the relationship between forms of sovereignty and conflict dynamics as well as point towards further paths for future research on sovereignty.

ISRAELI-LEBANESE BORDER DISPUTES: HISTORICAL BACKGROUND

Lebanon rejected Israel's legitimacy even before the latter gained independence in 1948 (Erlich, 2000, p. 166). Despite hesitations among the country's Maronite elite, Lebanon assisted the Arab Liberation Army (formed by volunteers from various Arab states) in its January 1948 invasion into British-controlled Palestine. Lebanon organized volunteers for the Arab League-led force. It supplied it with arms, and allowed it to operate from its territory (Erlich, 2000, pp. 167–72). Though the Lebanese leadership declared that its own forces had invaded the Jewish state, in reality Beirut limited itself to participating in a single battle in June 1948 where its forces fought alongside Syrian and Arab Liberation forces (Barak, 2001; Ma'ayan & Erlich, 2000; Morris, 2003, p. 226). By late October 1948, Israeli forces had invaded Lebanon and occupied fifteen villages in the southern part of the country (Erlich, 2000, p. 210). The hostilities ended formally when Lebanon and Israel signed an armistice agreement in March 1949 (S/1264/Corr.1, 1949). Consequently, Israel withdrew to an armistice demarcation line (ADL) that was supposed to follow the international boundary between Lebanon and mandatory Palestine (S/RES/72, 1949). The United Nations Truce Supervision Organization (UNTSO) began delineating the international border. The parties did not complete the process, because of disagreements between Israel and Lebanon about the correct interpretation of the 1923 colonial map that served as the basis for the border delineation (Kaufman, 2006a, p. 60). To date, only 40% of the Israeli Lebanese line is delineated (Eshel, p. 79). In the following years, Lebanon continued to oppose Israel's legitimacy, but was careful not to engage it militarily. It did not participate in the three major Arab-Israeli wars in 1956, 1967, and 1973. However, it did allow the Palestinian national movement to use its territory, since the late 1960s, as a launching pad on Israeli targets. In the 1970s these attacks led to dozens of casualties on the Israeli side. Following an attack by Lebanon-based Palestinians in which thirty-five Israeli citizens were killed, Israel invaded Lebanon in March 1978. Following the invasion, Israel remained in control of a small portion of South Lebanon for about three weeks before it withdrew back to the international border. The Israeli operation also begat two Security Council resolutions: UNSCR 425 and 426 that called for Israeli withdrawal. The resolutions further created a new UN force, United Nations Interim Force in Lebanon (UNIFIL), which was to supervise the Israeli withdrawal and help the government of Lebanon, torn by then in vicious civil war, to assert its authority in the region (UNSCR 425, 426, 1978). In

1982, Israel invaded Lebanon again, in an effort to remove the Palestinian military and political infrastructure there and install a pro-Israeli regime in Beirut. Israel achieved its first goal, but failed in the second. A pro-Israeli President, Bashir Gemayel, was assassinated a few days after his election in September 1982 (Campbell, 1982). A peace accord signed by the two countries in 1984 was never ratified by Lebanon, because of Syrian pressure. By early 1985, Israeli-Lebanese talks about security arrangements failed, and Israel withdrew to a self-declared security zone in the South of Lebanon. It remained there until 2000 (CNN, 2006). Israel stated all along that it had no territorial claims in Lebanon, and that the sole purpose of its deployment in the country's Southern part between 1985 and 2000 was to hold a buffer zone against possible attacks by Palestinians. Israel deployed a small number of soldiers in the region and set up a local militia to help it control the region.

Though the Israeli military control in the South of Lebanon was meant to repel potential Palestinian penetrations into Israel, it led to the evolution of a new foe – Hezbollah. The Shiite organization used the Israeli occupation to solidify its leadership over the Shiite Lebanese, and eventually its rise to dominance among the many non-state actors that competed for supremacy in the chaotic environment of the Lebanese civil war. Hezbollah began attacking Israeli forces in South Lebanon. By the mid-1990s, this was provocation enough that Israel launched two massive military operations against Hezbollah to the north of its self-declared security zone. The second operation, Grapes of Wrath, in 1996, led to the loose agreement between Israel, Lebanon, the United States, and France that eventually set the 'rules of the game' for the armed conflict between Israel and Hezbollah (BBC, 2016). The agreement reflected a reality that continues to date: Hezbollah was the actual party that drove the conflict from the Lebanese side, but the formal party dealing with Israel was the Lebanese state. The organization is the country's most effective political actor by virtue of the privileges granted to it in the 1989 Taif accords and because of its position in Lebanon's Parliament and government.

By 1998–99, Israeli public opinion turned against Israel's control of the region, mostly because of the continued casualties Israel suffered at the hands of Hezbollah. Ironically, public opinion turned (Sela, 2007) just as the Israel defence force changed its operational posture in the area and had become more effective in responding to the challenge posed by Hezbollah. As noted, Israel maintained all along that it had no territorial claims in Lebanon, announcing in 1998 that it accepted UNSCR 425, thus indicating that it would eventually retreat from the area (Globes Service, 1998). In 1999, during his election campaign, labour candidate Ehud Barak, promised to leave the area, either as part of a peace accord with Lebanon and Syria, or unilaterally. Barak was elected later that year. Once the negotiations with Syria collapsed in early 2000, Barak ordered a unilateral withdrawal, which was completed in May 2000 (Orme Jr, 2000).

Those in Israel who opposed the withdrawal were concerned that Hezbollah would use South Lebanon as a base for future attacks on the Jewish state. The Shiite organization, after all, led an effective armed resistance against Israel, and held to an ideology that rejected Israel's legitimacy. Those who opposed withdrawal were also affected it seems by the memories of Palestinian attacks on Israel from South Lebanon during the 1970s and early 1980s (Sebag, 2002). In order to respond to a possible Hezbollah challenge, Israel's Prime Minister, Ehud Barak, decided to rely on deterrence. A crucial aspect of deterrence according to Barak was international legitimacy for the use of force against targets in Lebanon (Barak, 2015; Grossman, 2007; Kfir & Dor, 2015, p. 235). To this end, he insisted that Israel withdraw to the internationally recognized line, leaving no room for claims that Israel was occupying any part of Lebanon. To secure international legitimacy Israel framed its redeployment as an implementation of UNSCR 425 and 426 from 1978. It further engaged the United Nations and set a joint Israeli–United Nations team to mark the border.

Israel notified the United Nations in mid-April 2000 that it intended to comply with UNSCR 425 and 426. United Nations Secretary General Kofi Anan dispatched a team headed by his special representative for the peace process, Ambassador Terje Rod Larsen, to demark the exact border between Lebanon and Israel. For Israel, the UN seal was crucial in order to show that it had indeed completed its withdrawal. However, eighteen years of Israeli control on both sides of the border had led to dozens of minor changes of the border, favourable to Israel, which the UN could rectify. Relying on the UN and not the Israeli military's maps unit might have also allowed Prime Minister Barak to counter possible foot dragging by the military, which opposed complete withdrawal (Kfir & Dor, 2015, pp. 231–32). UN and IDF teams demarcated the border together, relying on maps the UN prepared. On June 22, 2000, the Secretary General of the United Nations notified the Security Council that 'Israel has met the requirements for the implementation of Security Council Resolutions 425 (1978) . . . namely Israel has completed its withdrawal in conformity with the line identified by the United Nations' (United Nations Security Council, 2000). Lebanon insisted, however, that the withdrawal was incomplete, as Israeli forces remained in the Shebaa Farms, which, Beirut argued, are Lebanese territory. Israel's position was that these areas belonged to Syria (and not to Lebanon) before 1967, and should therefore not be returned to Lebanon (BBC, 2000). A new conflict was born.

METHODOLOGY

In order to measure the intensity of the land and sea conflicts the paper borrows from, and adapts, the protracted conflict-crisis model proposed by Brecher and Wilkenfeld (*Crisis, Conflict, and War*, 1989). The model offers an effective set of variables that allow us to measure cases when a crisis erupts, in the framework of a protracted conflict. The model was selected because the territorial conflicts on land and at sea represent an escalation of the long protracted conflict between Israel and Lebanon that began in 1948. The model includes the following variables: trigger, value under threat, accumulated costs, crisis management, super power activity, global organization involvement, and outcome.

Trigger refers to the 'act, event or situation, or situational change that catalyses the basic conditions of an international and foreign policy crisis' (Brecher & Wilkenfeld, 1989, p. 129).

Value under threat refers to the most serious threat the conflict poses, as perceived by either party.

Accumulated costs is a variable added to the original model. It measures the actual human, monetary, and military costs that have been incurred by the parties since the territorial dispute discussed here erupted.

Crisis management refers to the 'primary method used by states to protect threatened values' (Brecher & Wilkenfeld, 1989, p. 129).

Superpower activity refers to the type and intensity of involvement by a superpower. In the context of the 2000s and onwards, the superpower is the United States. Superpower involvement serves as an indicator of conflict severity because it is a proxy to the weight allotted to the conflict by the international system.

Global organization involvement refers to the type and intensity of involvement by a global organization. In the context of the 2000s and onwards, the global organization is the United Nations. Global organization involvement serves as an indicator of conflict severity because it is a proxy to the weight allotted to the conflict by the international system.

Outcome refers to both the form and the substance in which the conflict ended, if it has.

COMPARISON OF THE TWO BORDER DISPUTES

Trigger

Land: The contemporary land-based dispute over border demarcation between Israel and Lebanon was retriggered following Israel's withdrawal from its self-declared security zone in Southern

Lebanon in May 2000. Therefore, the trigger of the land- based conflict can be defined as one of a political and non-violent military nature. While Israel's redeployment represented an overall de-escalation in the conflict between the two countries, at the same time it triggered the current territorial conflict, with Hezbollah opposing the exact line of the international border. Specifically, as Israel was preparing to withdraw, Hezbollah reiterated earlier claims that the Jewish state should also withdraw from two regions that Israel did not plan to leave: the Shebaa farms, and the 'seven villages'. Lebanon, the nominal sovereign, followed suit and adopted Hezbollah's claims, and both were heavily influenced by Syrian encouragement (Times of Israel, 2014). The Shebaa Farms is a small piece of land that lies in the 'border triangle' amid Israel, Syria and Lebanon (Al Jazeera, 2015).

Israel occupied the Shebaa Farms from Syria in 1967, but by the 1990s, both Syria and Lebanon claimed that the region was in fact Lebanese and should therefore be handed back to Lebanon. The claim had its sources in colonial times when France ruled both sides of the border and did not accurately demark the boundary between its two protectorates. Specific realities on the ground helped in creating the ambiguity regarding the specific location of the border, as farmers who resided in what is now the Syrian side had farmed on the Lebanese side during part of the year. It seems that although they resided in the Syrian border, at least some of these farmers were indeed Lebanese citizens (Kaufman, 2006a). The question was raised between the two countries and discussed in their joint border committee between 1969 and 1979, but was not concluded. Upon Israel's withdrawal, the latter kept the Shebaa Farms under its control. Its official position was that the area was occupied from Syria and hence might be handed back to Damascus when both countries reach a peace agreement.

Another territorial disagreement evolved after the war between the parties in summer 2006, around the Alewite village of Ghajar that stretches on both sides of the international border. Despite Resolution 1701, which called upon Israeli troops to withdraw to the Blue Line, Israel maintained its control over the northern part of the village for what it regarded as security reasons (Ynet, 2009).

Sea: Until 2009, the border demarcation between Israel and Lebanon at sea had not been determined, nor was it a matter of Lebanese, Israeli, or international concern. The first and only official delineation of the maritime border between the two states appeared in the Armistice Agreement of 1949. Article III (2) of this agreement simply states that:

No element of the land, sea or air military or pare-military forces of either Party, including non-regular forces, shall commit any warlike or hostile act against the military or pare-military forces of the other Party, or against civilians in territory under the control of that Party; or shall advance beyond or pass over for any purpose whatsoever the Armistice Demarcation Line set forth in Article V of this Agreement; or enter into or pass through the air space of the other Party or through the waters within three miles of the coastline of the other Party.

Beyond this, the border demarcation at sea between Israel and Lebanon was not addressed before Israel's withdrawal from Southern Lebanon in 2000. Importantly, the various United Nation Security Council Resolutions on Israel and Lebanon, particularly resolutions 425 from 1978, resolution 520 from 1982, and resolution 1052 from 1996, did not refer to the border demarcation between the countries at sea. Moreover, the armistice water boundary of three nautical miles has not been amended since then, despite the approval of UNCLOS III in 1982, which underlines a twelve nautical-mile line as territorial waters. Israel's withdrawal on land from South Lebanon in May 2000 did not include a demarcation of a maritime boundary. The war between Israel and Lebanon in 2006 took place predominantly on land (except for a major Hezbollah hit on an Israeli Corvette ship, INS Hanit). Therefore, UNSC Resolution 1701, which ended the violent hostilities, did not deliberate any maritime issues, including that of a demarcation of an international border between the two states.

The above account demonstrates the relative lack of interest in, and treatment of, the maritime boundary issue between Israel and Lebanon since 1949. Further, the account illustrates how little consideration was given to the maritime domain, and the perception that the maritime domain lacked intrinsic value to any of the adversaries. This changed in 2009. The current conflict between the adversaries at sea was triggered by an economic change – the discovery of a considerable amount of natural gas in the Tamar field, some fifty nautical miles off the shore of Haifa, which was followed by an additional, bigger discovery, of the Leviathan gas field, some eighty nautical miles off the shore of Haifa (Torbey, 2015). Both discoveries lie within Israel's exclusive economic zone, and in close proximity to the Lebanese exclusive economic zone. The resource potential of this area generated contradicting claims by both Israel and Lebanon about the accurate borderline between their respective EEZs (Khadduri, 2015). This state of affairs is not unique to the Eastern Mediterranean arena. It took the unfolding of global warming, before the Canadian government clearly asserted claims in the arctic and began investing in securing the area. Like the Israeli-Lebanese case, Canada, too, was largely motived by the potential of future extraction of energy sources in the seas (Lajeunesse, 2008).

Value under threat

The value under threat in both domains (land and sea) is not of the highest gravity. Neither on land nor at sea does the border-demarcation conflict involve a threat to the existence of the polity, a threat to the survival of the regime, grave damage, or the territorial integrity of the political entity. Moreover, in both cases, the area under dispute is quite limited – 25 square kilometres of land, and approximately 850 square kilometres at sea, with most of the Israeli and Lebanese gas potential located in their respective EEZ areas outside of the disputed zone.

Hezbollah's rhetoric indicates that the organization places a greater significance on the value of the 'occupied land' as compared to the value of the maritime space. Moreover, the organization repeatedly promises to take harsher action when faced with lost land, as compared to action taken in response to lost space in the sea. For example, in a 2001 speech, Hezbollah's leader Hassan Nassralla stated that his organization will never give up 'a single centimetre of Lebanese soil' and promised to occupy by force the Shebaa Farms (Globs Service 2001). When talking about the maritime dispute, Hezbollah's focus is on the economic loss and unjust nature of the Israeli acquisition of resources. For example, in 2011, Deputy Head of Hezbollah Sheikh Naim Qassem stated that: 'It is unacceptable to us that oil, gas, water and areas that belong to Lebanon are being stolen', and that 'we will take the necessary steps to protect our rights' (Globs Service 2011). The Lebanese state takes a similar tone. In 2010, the speaker of Lebanon's Parliament said that 'we are concerned that they will steal Lebanon's natural resources' (Yeshaayahu, 2010).

Land: From the Israeli perspective, the most serious threat is that the continued dispute justifies aggression against Israeli troops and continued violence (Kaufman, 2006b). Hezbollah has an on-going excuse to resume violence by targeting Israeli civilians and their property. An additional threat is the ignition of small skirmishes near the borders in which soldiers may be attacked or abducted. On the Lebanese side, in terms of size and topography, the area of the Shebaa Farms does not carry a significant strategic value. However, as Sheikh Naim Qassem, Hezbollah's second in command stated: 'The Shebaa Farms area carries a special importance that is related neither to its geographical position nor to its size . . . but rather to what it represents' (Qassem, 2010, p. 239).

Sea: The border conflict at sea creates economic threats for both Lebanon and Israel, mostly threat of the lost opportunity to extract natural gas in the disputed area in the sea. Given the close proximity of the disputed area to the already discovered gas reserves of the Tamar and Leviathan fields, the prospects of finding gas in the disputed area are relatively high. For both countries, this is not a major threat. Even without developing gas reserves in the disputed area, the Tamar and Leviathan fields will provide Israel with energy security for the near future (Shaffer,

2011). Likewise, the border conflict does not impede Lebanon from promoting its gas discoveries in its EEZ. According to Bassil, Lebanon's minister of finance, the area of dispute with Israel is over only 5% of Lebanon's EEZ, and gas drilling is not delayed because of the dispute with Israel, but rather it is due to domestic politics (Aziz, 2015). The Moreover, unresolved, the Israel-Lebanon conflict might deter potential international oil and gas companies from investing in these countries. This threat provides a common incentive to both Israel and Lebanon to resolve the conflict.

Cumulative cost

Land: Between 2000 and 2005, mainly around the area of the Shebaa Farms and Har Dov, there were minor border scuffles and rocket firing on a monthly basis, some of which resulted in casualties (Sobelman, 2004). The most serious cases included the abduction of three Israeli soldiers in October 2000 (who, as was found out later, lost their lives in the attack); the targeting of Israeli troops that crossed the international border, resulting in casualties in October 2003 and May 2004 (Sobelman, 2004); and a failed abduction attempt of Israeli soldiers by Hezbollah in the Ghajar village in November 2005. Israel retaliated against these assaults with air and artillery attacks on Hezbollah posts in Southern Lebanon. Also serious, Israel violated the sovereignty of Lebanon in the air on a regular basis.

The most serious violent incident between the adversaries, however, was the 2006 war, which erupted following a Hezbollah raid on an Israeli patrol during which two Israeli soldiers were abducted. The fighting lasted for 34 days with major costs to both sides. According to a Reuters report, Lebanon suffered a death toll of almost 1,200 people, 4,400 wounded, an estimated economic damage of 5–7 billion dollars, and a wave of almost 1 million refugees from the warzone. In Israel, 160 people lost their lives, and almost 2,000 were injured. The direct cost of the war for Israel was estimated at 3.5 billion dollars, and approximately 300,000 people fled their homes (Reuters, 2007). In addition, the war inflicted major damage – to civilian property, national infrastructure, and the environment – on both sides. Since 2006, there have been sporadic rocket launches from Lebanon to Israel, Israeli air patrols over Lebanese sky, and 4 border clashes (February 2008, August 2010, December 2013, and January 2015), with resulting casualties (Security Council Report, 2015). Also noteworthy, in February 2008, top military commander of Hezbollah, Imad Mughniyeh, was assassinated in Damascus. Israel was blamed for this act (BBC, 2008; Goldman & Nakashima, 2015).

Sea: Since 2000, the cost of the maritime conflict, for both sides, has been minimal. The only violent clash in that domain took place before the discovery of gas in the Eastern Mediterranean, during the war between Israel and Lebanon in the summer of 2006.[1] In that incident a land-sea missile hit an Israeli Navy frigate, and four crewmembers were killed (Harel, 2006). The tactical hit was a surprise, and it damaged Israeli morale. Yet it should not be considered a consequence of conflict in the maritime domain, but rather seen as supplemental to the war on land.

The maritime conflict has taken place mainly in the diplomatic arena, with both parties negotiating the borderline between their EEZs through American mediation. Only two military consequences of the conflict may be considered as a cost: One is a mutual arms race: Israel's development of its surface fleet with a recent purchase of four frigates from Germany to protect the gas facilities (Ravid, 'Israel to Purchase Four German Missile Boats to Protect Offshore Gas Facilities', 2014), and Hezbollah's developing an advanced land-sea missile capacity, mainly in the form of long-range Yakhont missiles (Stuster, 2014). The second is a series of Israeli attacks on Lebanese soil, allegedly meant to impede the delivery of Yakhont Missiles from Syria to Hezbollah (Gordon, 2013; Lazareva, 2014).

Superpower activity

Land: The conflict over the Shebaa Farms was of concern to the United States, but unlike post-2000 Israeli-Lebanese maritime disputes, it did not intervene. Washington stated its (changing) positions on the issue, but did not actively mediate the conflict. American involvement included a 2006 assurance to Israel that Israel would not have to withdraw from the Shebaa farms, even if the UN determined that Lebanon was the lawful owner of this territory (Benn, Harel, Ashkenazi, & Stern, 2006). Two years later, however, this policy seemed to have changed, with the United States pressuring Israel to return the Shebaa Farms to Lebanon (Nahmias, 2008; Security Council Report, 2015). European powers, such as France, Spain, and the United Kingdom, in 2007 and 2008, also stated official support for Lebanese claims over the Shebaa Farms and called for Israeli withdrawal from the area (Security Council Report, 2015).

Sea: Since April 2011, the United States has been constantly involved in mediation efforts to demarcate the maritime border between Israel and Lebanon. The United States stepped into the role after the UN refusal to intervene because the maritime boundaries were not considered in Resolution 1701.

The first American mediator, Frederic Hof, worked with a team of specialist cartographers and, in December 2012, submitted a proposal to both sides to settle the maritime dispute between them. In 2013, both countries rejected the suggested settlement. In 2013, State Department diplomat Amos Hochstein replaced Hoff. Hochstein is the State Department's Special Envoy and Coordinator for International Energy Affairs, and he continues efforts to reach a settlement on this issue. The last round of visits in the region to promote settlement on the maritime issue took place in July 2015 (Aziz, 2015), but no solution has been reached thus far. There is no evidence of other superpower intervention than US mediation.

Global organization involvement

Land: The land dispute between Israel and Lebanon is characterized by an intensive and ongoing involvement by the United Nations, and especially by its Security Council, Secretary General, and special envoys to the Middle East. In June 2000, Secretary General Kofi Anan endorsed Israel's deployment as conforming to the line of the international border (Philps, 2000). In October 2000, shortly after Israel's withdrawal to the Blue Line, Anan visited the region and restated that Israel must retreat to the international border. In 2003, Anan produced another statement, according to which the withdrawal line of 2000 remained 'calm but tense' (United Nations News Centre, 2003). During the 2006 war, the Security Council was instrumental in negotiating an end to the violence and eventually approved Resolution 1701. The resolution called for a roll back of Hezbollah from South Lebanon and expanded UNIFIL's role and number of forces. The UN Secretary General and the organization's special envoys to Lebanon report each quarter on the enforcement of resolution 1701. In addition, the UN took responsibility for the delineation of the international borderline in the Shebaa farms, as well as advanced Israeli retreat from the northern part of Ghajar village that was kept under Israeli control following 2006 (Security Council Report, 2015). Both issues are still unresolved because of lack of cooperation by Lebanon and Syria in submitting to the UN the contour of an agreed international border between them, a consistent demand by Israel as precondition for withdrawal. The civil war in Syria further halted any desire on Israel's behalf to relinquish land on its northern border.

Sea: The involvement of international organizations in the maritime dispute has been minor. Lebanon and Israel submitted their official standpoint regarding the line of their EEZs to the UN. Yet, while Lebanon is a signatory of UNCLOS, Israel never signed the convention.[2] Israel therefore determined its EEZ demarcation in an internal governmental decision in July 2011. The UN does have a force on the ground (UNIFIL) which even offered to help. However, the force noted that this was only to alleviate immediate security threats, not to delineate the borderline, because it is no included in its mandate (Benhorin, 2011; The Daily Star, 2011). For this reason, the UN refused to respond to Lebanese complaints regarding Israeli violations of the international border at sea.

Outcome

Despite numerous efforts, as of yet the two conflicts have not been resolved. On land, the regional instability and especially the civil war in Syria complicate things even further in terms of settlement of the Shebaa Farms. Israel does not have any incentive to withdraw and surrender this piece of land to rivalling factions. Likewise, given Hezbollah's deep involvement in Syria and the high cost paid by the organization for this involvement, any settlement or compromise with Israel may be perceived to be a sign of weakness. At sea, despite active American mediation and the significant economic stakes involved, no resolution in in sight.

DISCUSSION, ALTERNATIVE EXPLANATION, AND CONCLUSION

The comparison between the variables indicate that the Israeli-Lebanese conflict over the Shebaa Farms is more intense than the conflict between the two states over the delineation of the exclusive economic zone in the sea. This is perhaps most notable in the category of accumulated costs. The land-based conflict led to dozens of attacks from Lebanon into Israeli territory. One of these attacks, the 2006 killing of three Israeli soldiers and the abduction of 2 others, led to a 34-day war in 2006 in which over 1,700 people were killed and both countries suffered significant economic losses.

Realists could offer a number of explanations for the limited intensity of the conflict on the seas. Perhaps the land contains greater material or strategic value? Yet, as the paper shows, this is not the case. The Shebaa Farms comprise a small area with no material significance for either party. In contrast, the area contested in the sea has potentially large deposits of natural gas that could have a significant impact on the economies of either side. Yet the land area with fewer resources – the Shebaa Farms and the seven villages – actually led to greater conflict.

Another material explanation could be that Israel and Hezbollah have less capacity to exert power over water than over land. Military maritime activity is more costly: power can only be exercised through the deployment of expensive platforms, whereas on land, it is much less expensive and easier to deploy force. The data, however, does not support this explanation. Israel has an advanced navy that has been operating near and in Lebanese territorial waters since the 1940s. Indeed, during larger clashes between Israel and Lebanon, such as the 1982 and 2006 wars, Israel's navy placed a naval blockade on Lebanon's shores and had complete dominance in the maritime domain (Almog, 2007; Israeli Navy, 2016). The ease of operating Israeli maritime forces near and in Lebanese waters is not limited to times of war. For decades, Israel operated regular patrols of Lebanese waters, and although Israeli forces formally withdrew from Lebanese land in May 2000, Israeli ships enter Lebanese waters whenever Israel deems it important (Israel Defence Force, 2013; Times of Israel, 2014). The material capabilities Israel has in the seas, and its decade-long dominance there, allows Israel therefore to deploy force easily on the seas. Although Hezbollah does not have maritime platforms, it did develop anti-ship capabilities that also allowed it to use force on the seas, though not to a degree that prevents Israel from using its navy. As noted, during the 2006 war, a Hezbollah anti-ship missile, fired from the Lebanese shore hit an Israeli military vessel. Overall, however, Hezbollah places a far greater effort in developing rocket capability aimed at Israeli populated centres on land than it does in developing anti-ship capability (Harel, 2016).

The limited intensity of the conflict over the seas could also be a result of another material reality, the distance that the parties in conflict need to travel in order to engage each other. Scholars have shown that in some cases, such as Britain in nineteenth-century Africa, states did not take actions to defend, or even define, clear borders of their vast territories. This was due to the lack of capabilities because of the large size of the territory in question, as well as the lack of any external pressure to do so (Herbst, 1989). This is not the case here. The area of the sea that is under dispute is close to Israeli and Lebanese shores, and at least Israel has, as noted, great capacity and incentive to demonstrate its control over the area.

Constructivist arguments that focus on the religious significance of territory similarly do not help explain the intensity of the land dispute. All indications suggest that the 25–50 square-kilometre area of the farms holds no religious importance to either side.

So what does explain the intensity of the land dispute when compared to the sea dispute? Hezbollah, the main driver of the conflict, has military, political, and ideological reasons for maintaining an active conflict with Israel over sovereignty. The 1989 Taif accords allowed the organization to keep Hezbollah's security apparatus, operating parallel to the state. The justification for this unique status was Hezbollah's role in defending Lebanon's sovereignty. Back in 1989 Israel was still controlling South Lebanon, and Hezbollah was engaged in active resistance against Israel. However, when Israel withdrew from South Lebanon in May 2000, Hezbollah needed to show that it is still defending Lebanon's sovereignty from an Israeli infringement. It was imperative that such an infringement of a sovereign right be clear, comprehensive, and complete – one that conforms to traditional notions of sovereignty in which the right to the land is binary, not partial. The Shebaa dispute provides this. In contrast, sovereignty over the exclusive economic zone of the sea is only a partial right, limited to extracting the resources in the area. These differences are evident from the approach taken by all parties. While Hezbollah describes the Shebaa Farms as an 'occupied' Lebanese territory, it only complains about the alleged 'theft' of resources in the sea (Globs Service 2011). Similarly, Israel focuses on the economic aspects of the conflict in the seas, with only a limited discussion of strategic considerations, and no mention of historical rights that are central in all of its other territorial claims. Even the United Sates appointed as mediator an official whose portfolio centres on energy affairs rather than regional expertise, signalling its view of the focus of the conflict.

The finding that limited sovereignty at sea diminishes the severity of conflicts offers at least two of possible paths for future research. One that takes a pessimistic view would be to investigate whether the converse of the argument made in this paper is true: Does a growing degree of sovereignty in a specific space lead to more conflict? For example, global warming is leading more states to make claims of sovereignty in the arctic waters; should we expect more intense conflicts there? A more optimistic path would explore the conflict amelioration properties of limited sovereignty. If limited sovereignty diminishes conflicts, might it be possible to borrow notions of limited sovereignty at sea and re-classify land areas as having only a partial sovereignty?

ACKNOWLEDGEMENTS

The author wishes to thank Dr. Aviad Rubin, Professor Boaz Azili, Professor Burak Kadercan, the editors of TPG, and the reviewers.

NOTES

1. In another attack aimed at an Israeli Navy patrol boat a few rockets were shot from a Palestinian refugee camp. No damage was caused and Hezbollah was quick to criticize and oppose this action, as unauthorized and not in line with the organization's line of action (Sobelman, 2004).

2. There could be two reasons for Israel's refusal to join UNCLOS; One, Israel often conforms with the American position on matters of International law, and America refrains from signing the Convention. Two, Israel maintains a traditional reluctant position to participation in international treaties that might be perceived as adherence to international law.

REFERENCES

Agnew, J. (2005). Sovereignty regimes: Territoriality and state authority in contemporary world politics. *Annals of the Association of American Geographers, 95*(2), 437–461.

Al Jazeera. (2015, January 28). *Two Israeli soldiers killed in Hezbollah missile attack.* Retrieved November 14, 2015, from http://www.aljazeera.com/news/2015/01/israeli-soldiers-injured-shebaa-farms-missile-attack-150128 100642659.html

Almog, Z. (2007). The navy during the war for the peace of the Galilee. *Ma'arachot, 413*, 11–19.

Aziz, J. (2015, July 15). What's delaying gas exploration in Lebanon? *Al Monitor, 2*. Retrieved December 17, 2016, from http://theliberal.co.il/author/ehudbarak/.

Barak, E. (2015, June 14). 15 years to the withdrawal from Lebanon. *Liberal.*

Barak, O. (2001). Commemorating Malikiyya: Political myth, multiethnic identity and the making of the Lebanese army. *History and Memory, 13*(1), 60–84.

BBC. (2000, May 25). *In focus: The Sheba Farm.* Retrieved September 22, 2015, from http://news.bbc.co.uk/2/hi/middle_east/763504.stm

BBC. (2008, February 13). *Bomb kills top Hezbollah leader.* Retrieved September 23, 2015, from http://news.bbc.co.uk: http://news.bbc.co.uk/2/hi/7242383.stm

BBC. (2016, August 10). *Lebanon profile - Timeline.* Retrieved December 12, 2016, from http://www.bbc.com/news/world-middle-east-14649284

Benhorin, Y. (2011, January 6). UNIFIL refuses to define maritime borders. *YNET.* Retrieved September 23, 2015, from http://www.ynetnews.com/articles/0,7340,L-4009705,00.html

Benn, A., Harel, A., Ashkenazi, A., & Stern, Y. (2006, August 11). U.S. assures Israel it will not be forced to withdraw from Shaba. *Haaretz.* Retrieved September 23, 2015, from http://www.haaretz.com/news/u-s-assures-israel-it-will-not-be-forced-to-withdraw-from-shaba-1.194909

Brecher, M., & Wilkenfeld, J. (1989). *Crisis, conflict, and war.* Oxford: Pergamon Press.

Brus, M. (2002). Bridging the gap between state sovereignty and international governance: The authority of law. In G. Kreijen (Eds.), *State, sovereignty, and international governance* (pp. 3–24). New York: Oxford University Press.

Campbell, C. (1982, September 15). Gemayel of Lebanon is killed in bomb blast at party offices. *New-York Times.* Retrieved December 13, 2016, from http://www.nytimes.com/1982/09/15/world/gemayel-of-lebanon-is-killed-in-bomb-blast-at-party-offices.html

CNN (2006, July 14), *Timeline: Decades of conflict in Lebanon, Israel,* Retrieved December 13, 2016, from http://edition.cnn.com/2006/WORLD/meast/07/14/israel.lebanon.timeline/index.html?_s=PM:WORLD

The Daily Star. (2011, August 18). Lebanon, Israel, UNIFIL discuss disputed maritime borders. *The Daily Star.* Retrieved September 23, 2015, from http://www.dailystar.com.lb//News/Lebanon-News/2011/Aug-18/146566-lebanon-israel-unifil-discuss-disputed-maritime-borders.ashx

Diehl, P. (1996). Territorial dimensions of international interaction: An introduction. *Conflict Management and Peace Science, 15*(1), 1–5.

Erlich, R. (2000). *The Lebanon tangle: The policy of the Zionist movement and the State of Israel towards Lebanon – 1918–1958.* Tel-Aviv: Ma'archot.

Ertman, T. (2005). Building states—Inherently a long-term process? An argument from comparative history. In M. Lange and D. Rueschemeyer (Eds.), *States and development: Historical antecedents of stagnation and advance* (pp. 165–182). New York: Palgrave-Macmillan.

Globes Service. (1998, March 2). *Netanyahu and Mordehai: Israel is willing to withdraw from Lebanon bowing down to USCR 42.* Retrieved September 21, 2015, from http://www.globes.co.il/news/article.aspx?did=138319

Globes Service. (2001, June 10). *Nassaralla: Hezbollah will occupy the Shebba Farms*. Retrieved October 8, 2016, from http://www.globes.co.il/news/article.aspx?did=496679

Globes Service. (2011, July 14). *Hezbollah: We will not tolerate theft of our gas and oil*. Retrieved October 8, 2016 from http://www.globes.co.il/news/article.aspx?did=1000664206

Goldman, A., & Nakashima, E. (2015, January 30). CIA and Mossad killed senior Hezbollah figure in car bombing. *Washington Post*. Retrieved from https://www.washingtonpost.com/world/national-security/cia-and-mossad-killed-senior-hezbollah-figure-in-car-bombing/2015/01/30/ebb88682-968a-11e4-8005-1924ede3e54a_story.html

Gordon, M. R. (2013, July 13). Israel airstrike targeted advanced missiles that Russia sold to Syria, U.S. says. *New York Times*. Retrieved September 23, 2015, from http://www.nytimes.com/2013/07/14/world/middleeast/israel-airstrike-targeted-advanced-missiles-that-russia-sold-to-syria-us-says.html

Gros, J.-G. (1996). Towards a taxonomy of failed states in the new world order: Decaying Somalia, Liberia, Rwanda and Haiti. *Third World Quarterly, 17*(3), 455–72.

Grossman, G. (2007, August 6). Ehud Barak explains: Why did I decide to withdraw from Lebanon. *NRG*. Retrieved September 2, 2015, from http://www.nrg.co.il/online/1/ART1/618/129.html

Harel, A. (2006, July 15). Soldier killed, 3 missing after navy vessel hit off Beirut coast. *Haaretz*. Retrieved September 23, 2015, from http://www.haaretz.com/news/soldier-killed-3-missing-after-navy-vessel-hit-off-beirut-coast-1.193112

Harel, A. (2016, March 4). Israel's military now sees Hezbollah as an army in every sense. *Haaretz*. Retrieved October 11, 2016 from http://www.haaretz.com/israel-news/1.706956

Hashmi, S. H. (Ed.). (1997). *State sovereignty*. University Park: Pennsylvania State University Press.

Hassner, R. (2010). *War on sacred ground*. Ithaca: Cornell University Press.

Herbst, J. (1989). The creation and maintenance of national boundaries in Africa. *International Organization, 43*(4), 673–92.

Israel Defense Force. (2013). *Watchman of the sea*. Retrieved October 8, 2016 from http://www.idf.il/1283-18961-en/Dover.aspx

Israeli Navy. (2016). *The second Lebanon war*. Retrieved October 7, 2016 from http://www.navy.idf.il/1277-he/Navy.aspx

Jackson, R. H., & Rosberg, C. G. (1982). Why Africa's weak states persist: The empirical and the juridical in statehood. *World Politics, 35*(1), 1–24.

Jacobsen, T., Sampford, C., & Thakur, R. (Eds.). (2008). *Re-envisioning sovereignty: The end of Westphalia?* Aldershot: Ashgate.

Kadercan, B. (2014). Strong armies, slow adaptation: Civil-military relations and the diffusion of military power. *International Security, 38*(3), 117–52.

Kaufman, A. (2006a). *Contested frontiers in the Syria–Lebanon–Israel region: Cartography, sovereignty, and conflict*. Washington: Woodrow Wilson Center Press and John Hopkins University Press.

Kaufman, A. (2006b). *The Israel–Hezbollah conflict and the Sheba Farms*. The Joan Kroc Institute for International Peace Studies. Retrieved 9 23, 2015, from http://kroc.nd.edu/: http://kroc.nd.edu/sites/default/files/israel_hezbollah.pdf

Kfir, I., & Dor, D. (2015). *Barak: Wars of my life*. Tel-Aviv: Kinnert Zmora Bitan. 235.

Khadduri, W. (2015). East Mediterranean gas: Opportunities and challenges. *Mediterranean Politics, 17*(1), 111–17.

Krasner, S. (1999). *Sovereignty: Organized hypocrisy*. Princeton: Princeton University Press.

Kreijen, G. (Ed.). (2002). *State sovereignty and international governance*. New York: Oxford University Press.

Lajeunesse, A. (2008). Lock, stock, and icebergs? Defining Canadian sovereignty from Macke King to Stephen Harper. *The Calgary Papers in Military and Strategic Studies, 1*.

Lazareva, I. (2014, January 27). Israeli jets suspected of attacking Syrian missile store. *The Telegraph*. Retrieved September 23, 2015, from http://www.telegraph.co.uk/news/worldnews/middleeast/syria/10599987/Israeli-jets-suspected-of-attacking-Syrian-missile-store.html

Ma'ayan, G., & Erlich, R. (2000). An integrative method for researching the 1948 war: The case of the Malikiyya battles (May–June 1948). *History*, *6*, 97–138.

Morris, B. (2003). *Righteous victims: A history of the Zionist–Arab conflict*. Tel-Aviv: Am Oved.

Nahmias, R. (2008, June 16). Report: US backs Israeli withdrawal from Shebaa farms. *YNET*. Retrieved September 23, 2015, from http://www.ynetnews.com/articles/0,7340,L-3556190,00.html

Orme Jr, W. A. (2000, May 24). *Retreat from Lebanon; The Israelis; Barak Declares End to 'Tragedy' as Last Troops Leave Lebanon*. Retrieved December 13, 2016, from http://www.nytimes.com/2000/05/24/world/retreat-lebanon-israelis-barak-declares-end-tragedy-last-troops-leave-lebanon.html

Philpott, D. (2001). *Revolutions in sovereignty: How ideas shaped modern international relations*. Princeton, NJ: Princeton University Press.

Philps, A. (2000, June 19). Israel's withdrawal from Lebanon given UN's endorsement. *The Telegraph*. Retrieved September 23, 2015, from http://www.telegraph.co.uk/news/worldnews/middleeast/lebanon/1343868/Israels-withdrawal-from-Lebanon-given-UNs-endorsement.html

Qassem, N. (2010). *Hizbullah: The story from within*. London: Saqi.

Rasler, K., & Thompson, W. (2006). Contested territory, strategic rivalries, and conflict escalation. *International Studies Quarterly*, *50*(1), 145–67.

Ravid, B. (2014, December 25). Israel to purchase four German missile boats to protect offshore gas facilities. *Haaretz*. Retrieved from http://www.haaretz.com/news/diplomacy-defense/.premium-1.633814

Reuters. (2007, July 9). FACTBOX: Costs of war and recovery in Lebanon and Israel. *Reuters*. Retrieved September 22, 2015, from http://www.reuters.com/article/2007/07/09/us-lebanon-war-cost-idUSL0822571220070709

Ruggie, J. G. (1986). Continuity and transformation in the world polity: Towards a neorealist synthesis. In R. Keohane (Eds.), *Neorealism and its critics* (pp. 131–57). New York: Columbia University Press.

S/1264/Corr.1, U. D. (1949, February 23). Armistice agreement between Lebanon and Israel. *UN Doc S/1264/Corr*. Retrieved from http://unispal.un.org/UNISPAL.NSF/0/9EC4A332E2FF9A128525643D007702E6

Sassen, S. (2015). *Losing control? Sovereignty in the age of globalization*. New York: Columbia University Press.

Sebag, R. (2002). Lebanon: The Intifada's false premise. *The Middle East Quarterly*, *9*(2), 13–21.

Security Council Report. (2015). *Lebanon: Chronology of events*. Security Council Report. Retrieved September 23, 2015, from http://www.securitycouncilreport.org: http://www.securitycouncilreport.org/chronology/lebanon.php

Sela, A. (2007). Civil society, the military, and national security: The case of Israel's security zone in South Lebanon. *Israel Studies*, *12*(1), 53–78.

Shaffer, B. (2011). Israel – New natural gas producer in the Mediterranean. *Energy Policy*, *39*(9), 5379–5387.

Sobelman, D. (2004). Four years to the retreat from Lebanon: The struggle to shape the rules of the game in the north. *Adkan Estrategi*, *7*(2), 25–32.

S/RES/72. (1949, March 23). *Lebanese-Israeli general armistice agreement*. Retrieved from http://unispal.un.org/UNISPAL.NSF/0/71260B776D62FA6E852564420059C4FE

Stuster, D. (2014, January 3). Why Hezbollah's new missiles are a problem for Israel? *Foreign Policy*. Retrieved September 21, 2015, from http://foreignpolicy.com/2014/01/03/torches-lit-ukrainian-nationalists-celebrate-an-inconvenient-hero/

Times of Israel. (2014, February 25). *IDF sees steep rise in submarine operations*. Retrieved October 8, 2016, from http://www.timesofisrael.com/idf-sees-steep-rise-in-submarine-operations/

Torbey, C. (2015). Political impasse stops Lebanon exploiting oil resources. *BBC*. Retrieved December 14, 2016, http://www.bbc.com/news/world-middle-east-31604143

United Nations News Centre. (2003, July 24). Withdrawal line between Israel and Lebanon remains calm but tense – Annan. *United Nations News Centre*. Retrieved September 23, 2015, from http://www.un.org/apps/news/story.asp?NewsID=7819&Cr=lebanon&Cr1

United Nations Security Council. (2000, June 16). Report to the secretary general on the implementation of security council resolutions 425 (1978) and 426 (1978), 16 June 2000. Retrieved September 22, 2015, from http://www.un.org/en/ga/search/view_doc.asp?symbol=S/2000/590

UNSCR 425, 426. (1978, March 19). Retrieved from http://unscol.unmissions.org/portals/unscol/SC20 Resolutions2042520and2042620(1978)20on%20Lebanon-Israel.pdf

Vasuqez, J., & Valeriano, B. (2010). Classification of interstate wars. *Journal of Politics, 72*(2), 292–309.

Witte Jr, J. (2006). Facts and fictions about the history of separation of church and state. *Journal of Church and State*, 15–45.

Yeshaayahu, K. (2010). Lebanon acts. *Globs*. Retrieved October 8, 2016, from http://www.globes.co.il/news/article.aspx?did=1000582507

Ynet. (2009, May 13). *Ghajar discussions to wait until after elections*. Retrieved November 14, 2015, from http://www.ynetnews.com/articles/0,7340,L-3715439,00.html

Index

Page numbers in *italics* refer to figures. Page numbers in **bold** refer to tables. Page numbers with 'n' refer to notes.

Printed in the United States
by Baker & Taylor Publisher Services